The Effectiveness of
UN Human Rights Institutions

The Effectiveness of
UN Human Rights Institutions

Patrick James Flood

Westport, Connecticut
London

Library of Congress Cataloging-in-Publication Data

Flood, Patrick James, 1939–
    The effectiveness of UN human rights institutions / Patrick James
Flood.
       p. cm.
    Includes bibliographical references and index.
    ISBN 0–275–96052–8 (alk. paper)
    1. Human rights.   2. United Nations.   I. Title.
    K3240.4.F547   1998
    341.4'81—DC21   97–17516

British Library Cataloguing in Publication Data is available.

Library of Congress Catalog Card Number: 97–17516
ISBN: 0–275–96052–8

First published in 1998

Praeger Publishers, 88 Post Road West, Westport, CT 06881
An imprint of Greenwood Publishing Group, Inc.

Printed in the United States of America

The paper used in this book complies with the
Permanent Paper Standard issued by the National
Information Standards Organization (Z39.48–1984).

10 9 8 7 6 5 4 3 2 1

For my wife, Anita,
whose inspiration and encouragement
helped so profoundly to bring this book to life.

Contents

Contents

Preface

UN human rights institutions are an integral part of the late-twentieth-century effort to safeguard human dignity through promoting greater practical observance of human rights by states. Acting through the United Nations, the community of states seeks to influence individual states to observe internationally established human rights standards.

The community of states has created several kinds of UN mechanisms to act as community agents for specified human rights purposes; this study claims that some of these UN agents have had a positive impact on the situations they were created to address, and it explores the reasons for this result—especially the factors that make a positive outcome more or less likely.

The possibility of UN effectiveness is rooted in the fact that, as members of a community, states pursue goals whose achievement depends significantly on avoiding political isolation. Most states seek to avoid isolation because it impedes efforts to achieve national policy goals. It also entails the discomfort and cultural pressure that accompany severe ethical disapproval by peers. The need to avoid political isolation has permitted the gradual development of community mechanisms that can bring steady, year-round pressure on a state to reduce human rights abuses.

A state has several incentives for cooperating with a UN human rights institution. Most states want to be thought well of by their peers—to be seen by other states and publics as civilized and humane polities and as cooperative and responsible members of the community of states. While some revolutionary regimes reject these values during their early years, most return to them because prolonged disregard for the good opinion of other states and publics usually leads to political isolation.

UN human rights institutions rely primarily on private or public diplomacy, usually on a combination of these, to persuade states to halt or reduce violations and to restore respect for rights. There are many different ways to structure these diplomatic efforts. One distinction is between mechanisms based on the UN Charter and those based on special multilateral treaties. I argue that the former are more effective primarily because they have an immediate relationship to intergovernmental political bodies and, through them, to the authority of the Charter—the highest political and legal embodiment of the will of the community of states. A second distinction, among Charter-based agents, is between thematic and country-specific institutions. A thematic institution addresses a single type of human rights violation on a worldwide basis; a country-specific institution deals with a wide range of abuses in a single country.

After appraising the relative strengths and weaknesses of the main structural types, I assess the thematic and country-based institutions through four case studies. While domestic economic and political developments, bilateral pressures, and international economic factors normally weigh more heavily than United Nations–related concerns in states' policy deliberations, UN human rights mechanisms have become an enduring part of the external political environment within which states make choices. Their existence and activity have influenced some of these choices in ways that contribute to improved human rights practices.

In 1993 the achievements of Charter-based mechanisms encouraged the international community to move to the next level of institution-building through creation of the office of UN High Commissioner for Human Rights, which coordinates and complements, but does not replace, the older mechanisms and incorporates many of their more successful functional and structural approaches.

OUTLINE OF CHAPTERS

Chapter 1 poses basic questions, defines key terms, mentions the statutory sources of authority for UN involvement in human rights, very briefly sketches the main types of UN human rights institutions, and introduces the broad arguments of the book.

Chapter 2 explores in greater depth the meaning of the term ''human rights,'' traces its historical development, and examines selected theoretical issues, including the question whether any human rights are universal. It discusses how human rights came to acquire the status of international prescriptive and behavioral norms and how these relate to the norm of sovereignty. It also addresses the question whether or not states have an international legal obligation to respect human rights and explores the notion of an international community of states that has certain responsibilities and functions related to rights implementation.

Chapter 3 examines the system of UN human rights institutions in more detail, presenting the main categories and their respective structures and roles. After analyzing the advantages and disadvantages of Charter-based and treaty-based mechanisms, it moves to a closer examination of the structural and operational strengths and weaknesses of the two principal types of Charter-based agents: thematic (universal) and country-specific. It concludes with a discussion of the role of the professional staff of the Center for Human Rights of the UN Secretariat.

Chapters 4 and 5 present case studies of two thematic institutions: the Working Group on Enforced Disappearances and the Special Rapporteur on the Elimination of Religious Discrimination and Intolerance. Each is analyzed in terms of the reasons for its successes and shortcomings.

Chapters 6 and 7 assess the work of the UN Special Rapporteurs on Chile and Iran, as examples of country-specific mechanisms, in terms of the reasons for their successes and/or failures.

Chapter 8 examines, in the light of the foregoing analyses, ways in which Charter-based UN mechanisms have been effective in implementing internationally recognized human rights. It weighs the relative effectiveness of the various types of UN human rights mechanisms and the reasons for such effectiveness or lack thereof, including specific features of these institutions that have contributed to their success or failure. It also traces the background of the establishment of the post of UN High Commissioner for Human Rights, relating this story and the mandate of the new office to the experience of earlier Charter-based mechanisms.

AUTOBIOGRAPHICAL NOTE

Before beginning to study UN human rights institutions and activities from an academic perspective, I had the opportunity to work directly on human rights issues in several multilateral contexts during a career with the U.S. Department of State.

For instance, I was officer in charge of OAS (Organization of American States), South American and Caribbean affairs in the Bureau of Human Rights and Humanitarian Affairs from 1978 to 1980, when bilateral and multilateral efforts to deal with the issue of enforced disappearances were high on the international agenda. In addition, I served as the bureau's acting UN human rights policy officer during the 1979 and 1980 sessions of the UN Commission on Human Rights (a term interchangeable with the more common "Human Rights Commission").

From 1980 to 1984 I was officer in charge of human rights affairs at the U.S. Mission to the United Nations in Geneva, where UN human rights activities are centered. My personal priority was to improve and strengthen UN human rights structures and procedures; I worked directly with most of the mechanisms discussed in this study, serving as a U.S. delegate to the many conferences and specialized meetings held annually in Geneva and as principal U.S. liaison with the UN Secretariat's Human Rights Center. I also developed a series of initiatives aiming at establishment of the post of High Commissioner for Human

Rights. Some of these Geneva-based activities are described in this study, with citations from telegrams and other official documents I authored at the time.

Although not covered in this book, my human rights experience also included work on Eastern European and Soviet human rights issues in connection with CSCE (the Conference on Security and Cooperation in Europe) in the early 1970s and later, from 1984 to 1986, as counselor for political affairs at the American Embassy in Warsaw, where I also addressed human rights issues in a bilateral context.

From 1986 to 1989 my work in the State Department's Bureau for Refugee Programs focused on human rights aspects of refugee issues, some of which, of course, concerned international organizations, albeit not UN human rights mechanisms per se.

My State Department career is an important source of the information, judgments, and ideas found in this study. In addition to my personal recollections, I have drawn upon a selection of declassified Department documents covering the years when I was most directly involved with the subject. I thank my many U.S. Foreign Service and Civil Service colleagues, officials of the UN Center for Human Rights, fellow delegates to the Human Rights Commission from many countries, independent experts of the UN Subcommission on Prevention of Discrimination and Protection of Minorities, and leaders of nongovernmental organizations who shared their knowledge and insights with me over the years. The list is far too long to risk mentioning anyone by name without missing someone equally important. I am grateful to them all.

Acknowledgments

I am grateful to many people for helping me bring this project to completion. Thanks to Eric Einhorn, Chair of the Political Science Department at the University of Massachusetts Amherst, for many policy and scholarly insights, much sincere encouragement, and for helping me keep a proper balance among empirical, legal, theoretical, and historical aspects of the project; to James Der Derian of the Political Science Department for valuable perspectives on international relations theory and for helping me shape this work in many other perceptive ways; to Stephen Pelz of the Department of History for expert counsel on balancing diplomatic history with policy analysis and many other constructive comments on both substance and presentation; and to David Forsythe of the University of Nebraska–Lincoln for probing questions, insightful comments, helpful suggestions as to additional good recent scholarship, and encouragement to be bold in dropping less essential material. All this in addition to positive reinforcement about the value of the project.

Special thanks go to Donna Dove for preparing successive drafts of this manuscript in professional form, expertly, expeditiously, and with patience and good humor.

Deepest thanks of all go to my wife, Anita, for believing in the worth of this project, for uncounted ideas, suggestions, and constructive criticisms, and for encouraging me to persevere when I needed encouragement. My parents and children also deserve sincere gratitude for their ideas and encouragement; they understood, they participated, and they helped make it work. Extra thanks to our son, John, for the computer on which this was written, and without which it would not have been written for a much longer time indeed.

Any shortcomings or mistakes are of course my responsibility.

1

Introduction

OVERVIEW

The totalitarian systems of our century have demonstrated, in their concentration camps and in the daily lives of the people they rule, the ultimate consequence of abandoning the concept of human dignity as a normative political and legal value. This is why people have sought ways to make human dignity more visible and more secure in the contemporary world. The first important postwar achievement of this effort was to identify and define human rights as the modern means of expressing the requirements of human dignity in a social context. The Universal Declaration of Human Rights, adopted in 1948, explicitly recognizes the link between rights and dignity. Human rights, then, are titles, rooted in the intrinsic value—the dignity—of every human being, to live and to have or to do things that are essential to lead a life in keeping with this dignity.

Since World War II, the promotion and protection of human rights have become a leading theme of international political life. While some scholars and policymakers debate whether to expand the list of internationally recognized rights, the primary focus since the mid-1970s has shifted to the question, How can a state be influenced to observe human rights in practice? This study looks at how the process of getting states to do this has been pursued through UN human rights institutions. It seeks to analyze the effectiveness (or ineffectiveness) of the different structures and procedural approaches taken by UN human rights institutions, to evaluate the reasons for these results, and to explore the conditions in which one type of structure or procedure is more likely than another to have positive impact.

In other words, it seeks answers to these questions: How does the international community, through UN human rights institutions, influence states to observe human rights standards? Which types of UN human rights institutions have worked well, and which have not, and why? What factors contribute to, or impede, their effectiveness?

I should make clear that my focus is squarely on UN *human rights institutions*, that is, those structures and mechanisms established by member states, acting in community, for the specific purpose of promoting and/or protecting internationally recognized human rights. It does not encompass human rights activities undertaken by other UN institutions, such as the Security Council, although these have assumed new importance since the end of the Cold War.

A great many of the Security Council's new activities under Chapters VI and VII of the Charter have involved what may properly be called human rights activities, and they have added a new dimension to the United Nations' involvement in human rights protection. Since about 1990 the Council has begun to act as a sort of international legislature, laying down rules for specific polities in connection with peacekeeping and peacemaking actions, on such matters as democratic elections, respect for human rights, and police and judicial activity. It has backed up this rule making with military forces, international police contingents, and economic measures profoundly affecting the status of human rights observance in such countries as Cambodia, El Salvador, Haiti, Iraqi Kurdistan, Somalia, Mozambique, Angola, and Namibia.[1]

Whether intentionally or not, the framers of the Charter gave the Council enough de facto power to interpret its own mandate and to carry out its decisions, and for the last several years this is exactly what the Council has done without serious challenge. As David Forsythe notes, for instance, in 1992 the Council expanded its working conception of international peace and security to encompass almost any major international problem.[2]

My purpose here, however, is to trace the evolution of what might be called diplomatic methods of protection, looking for the factors that contribute to, or detract from, their effectiveness and the conditions in which one approach rather than another is likely to have more impact. I outline the ways in which the international community of states has conferred specific authority on designated UN human rights institutions to hold states accountable for their conduct regarding internationally accepted human rights standards and has authorized these institutions to act on the community's behalf as agents for the implementation of these standards. I show, through case studies, how this system has contributed to influencing some states to reduce human rights abuses under certain circumstances. The account concludes, except for a few updated facts, with the establishment in December 1993 of the office of UN High Commissioner for Human Rights, whose mandate includes all of the kinds of powers and techniques used by previous UN human rights agents—who continue to carry out their tasks as before, under the general guidance of the High Commissioner and the Commission on Human Rights and other UN political bodies. (I use the terms ''Commission on Human Rights'' and ''Human Rights Commission'' interchangeably.)

In discussing the two main types of diplomatic UN human rights mecha-nisms—those based on the Charter and those based on separate multilateral treaties—I argue that the former are more effective because they act as the agent of a *political* body of the community of states. Their impact is further strength-ened if states of importance to a target state actively support action by UN human rights agencies and in addition take bilateral policy initiatives to support the same human rights goals.

Within Charter-based mechanisms, the major division is between thematic institutions—those authorized to apply to any state or individual anywhere in the world the *international* obligation of each state to respect the human right(s) specified in its mandate—and country-specific mechanisms—those established to apply international human rights obligations with regard to all issues in a single country. I argue that the two types have distinct advantages and disad-vantages but are in general equally effective. Much depends on the specific circumstances they seek to address.

I also provide evidence that a state's readiness to cooperate with a UN human rights institution is greater when the state faces pressure from more than one UN agent, for instance, by a thematic as well as a country-specific mechanism. Effectiveness is further enhanced by the sustained commitment of the commu-nity of states to a particular mechanism, as expressed in periodic reaffirmation of its mandate.

I attach importance to on-site visits by UN human rights agents as an effective tool for fact-finding and for diplomatic efforts to promote improvement in hu-man rights practices. In exploring this aspect, I also examine the need to balance public criticism or praise with confidential diplomatic activity and offer com-ments on the extent to which the personality and energy of the individual chosen to carry out a UN human rights mission contribute to success or failure.

A FEW DEFINITIONS

I use key terms in the following ways:

By *international community*, I mean the community of states, including the governments that represent them. I thus distinguish the community from the institutions and agencies it creates to carry out joint policy decisions, although I recognize that the ''line'' between policy and implementation is actually a broad and porous band. Likewise, although nongovernmental organizations and the media participate in the ongoing dialogue on human rights issues, I do *not* include them here in the term ''international community,'' because they have only a voice, not a vote, in multilateral policy decision making and implemen-tation.[3]

A *Charter-based mechanism* finds its authority in the human rights and gen-eral provisions of the UN Charter, which binds all member states of the United Nations.

A *treaty-based mechanism* finds its authority in a specific intergovernmental agreement covering a specific subject and binds only those states that have become parties to the agreement.

Following John Gerard Ruggie, I see a *multilateral institution* as a type of institution that incorporates "multilateralism," defined by Ruggie as "an institutional form which coordinates relations among three or more states on the basis of generalized principles of conduct—that is, principles which specify appropriate conduct for a class of actions, without regard to the particularistic interests of the parties or the strategic exigencies that may exist in any specific occurrence."[4]

For Ruggie, a multilateral institution can be an international *order* (such as an open international economic order), an international *regime* (using Stephen Krasner's definition of "principles, norms, rules, and decision-making procedures around which actor expectations converge in a given issue-area"),[5] or an international *organization* ("a separate and distinct type of institutionalized behavior, defined by such generalized decision-making rules as voting or consensus procedures").[6] Before proceeding to this technical definition, Ruggie says that "formal international organizations are palpable entities with headquarters and letterheads, voting procedures and generous pension plans."[7]

In this study I use "multilateral institution" in a sense that encompasses the second and third categories listed by Ruggie; the first is too broad for my purposes, and I do not think it is useful to distinguish here sharply between "multilateral regime" and "multilateral organization." To understand the actual and potential effectiveness of UN human rights institutions, it is important to think of them as encompassing both *standards* (principles, norms, etc.) and *organizations* ("palpable entit[ies] with headquarters and letterheads . . . etc." Otherwise the discussion will fail to connect with the historical context in which the United Nations' human rights role is developing. A discussion confined exclusively to principles, norms, and the like is likely to fail to answer the questions posed at the beginning of this inquiry: How do UN human rights institutions influence states to observe human rights standards? Which types of UN human rights institutions have worked well, and which have not, and why? What factors contribute to, or impede, their effectiveness? For actor expectations really to converge in terms of action to protect and promote human rights, the notion of a palpable organization is essential. Such a notion recognizes the importance of real people acting within, and in the name of, organized structures, with budgets and other physical resources at their disposal.

I use the terms *multilateral institution* and *international institution* interchangeably. I also use the terms *institution, mechanism*, and *agent* interchangeably.

A BRIEF NOTE ON ASSESSING CAUSES AND EFFECTS

During a career in policy making and diplomacy, I saw empirical evidence almost daily of the difficulty in inferring direct causal connection between an act by a multilateral institution and a subsequent event in a particular country. Too many other causes are operating to enable the simple judgment that "effect B results directly and exclusively from cause A."

Even within a single polity, every "output" (effect) has many "inputs" (causes), and it is not easy to disentangle them for purposes of study. Within the Department of State, for example, every policy decision (as output) results from several sources of initiative, energy, and power (inputs) that shape the content, thrust, and scope of that decision through a process of advocacy and bargaining, with most decisions reached by consensus. Even when a top official resolves a controversial issue on which consensus proved impossible, the decision usually tries to continue the multiple-actor bargaining process by giving something to each of the disputants. The same process is replicated within the Executive Branch as a whole, and this is also the way Congress typically adopts or does not adopt proposed legislation.

While the *implementation* of domestic laws and standards may seem to present a simpler cause-effect relationship, in fact, efforts to obtain compliance are uneven and seldom produce uniform results. Once we leave the area of domestic jurisdiction and enter a world of independent and legally equal political entities that interact with each other and with their own societies simultaneously in hundreds of ways, the task of trying to identify which external factor caused what internal behavior change on the part of the ruling structure in a given polity becomes extraordinarily difficult. Still, policymakers need to know what kinds of actions are *more* likely to produce a desired result, and scholars search for causes to explain what has happened and is likely to happen. I try to identify some key factors that have operated in UN efforts to address cases of human rights abuse in different political systems and cultures.

STATUTORY SOURCES OF AUTHORITY FOR UN INVOLVEMENT IN HUMAN RIGHTS

The range and character of international measures to promote the practical observance of human rights have evolved over time.

As noted, the authority for UN efforts to implement human rights standards is found either in the text of the Charter or in subsequent international agreements. These subsequent treaties, such as the Covenant on Civil and Political Rights and the Covenant on Economic, Social and Cultural Rights, and conventions on single issues, such as racial discrimination, torture, and the rights of the child, apply only to states that have acceded to them.

The Charter, on the other hand, creates both legal obligations for and among the parties—like any treaty—*and* a permanent, multipurpose organization. The founding member states, acting in community, created the organization and granted it broad authority in certain fields. Since 1945, newly independent or newly formed states have joined the United Nations as the first tangible sign of their full membership in the international community.

Member states are accountable to one another as members of a community on matters dealt with by the Charter, in the ways specified therein. In the case of human rights, the Charter says in Article 1 that a purpose of the United Nations is "to *achieve* international co-operation . . . in promoting and encouraging respect for human rights and for fundamental freedoms for all without distinction as to race, sex, language, or religion; and . . . to be a center for *harmonizing* the actions of nations in the attainment of these common ends" (emphasis added).

In Chapter IX of the Charter, Article 55 states clearly that "the United Nations [i.e., the Organization] *shall promote* . . . universal respect for, and observance of, human rights and fundamental freedoms for all." In Article 56: "All Members [i.e., states] pledge themselves to take *joint* and *separate action in cooperation with the Organization* for the achievement of [these] purposes" (emphasis added). Article 60 specifies that "responsibility for the discharge of the functions of the Organization set forth in this Chapter shall be vested in the General Assembly and, under the authority of the General Assembly, in the Economic and Social Council." Article 62 authorizes the Council to "make recommendations for the purpose of promoting respect for, and observance of, human rights and fundamental freedoms for all." Finally, Article 64 authorizes the Council to "obtain reports [from member states] on the steps taken to give effect to its own recommendations and to recommendations on matters falling within its competence made by the General Assembly. It may communicate its observations on these reports to the General Assembly."

These provisions are the basis of the authority of the UN Human Rights Commission, a functional commission of the Economic and Social Council. The Commission can make recommendations on human rights issues, and it can call countries to account for the way they have or have not acted on them. It can then evaluate state performance in public reports to the full community of states represented in the General Assembly.

TYPES OF UN HUMAN RIGHTS INSTITUTIONS

While the role of states is changing under the pressures of economic, environmental, communications, and other forms of interdependence—sovereignty cannot mean exactly what it meant two centuries ago, or even 30 years ago—states will continue to be the major political units of human society for the foreseeable future. To provide effective external incentives to protect human rights requires an institutional environment in which states will find it easier to carry out their human rights responsibilities, even when there may be strong domestic forces pushing in the opposite direction.

As noted, Charter-based implementation efforts have taken two principal institutional forms: thematic and country-specific. Both types have sometimes been accompanied by the inscription of a special item on the agenda of UN bodies, mentioning the topic or country by name. I chose to study the special rapporteurs on Chile and Iran because these countries concern different regions of the world and different cultures and political systems; the aim is to show how such institutions work in very different contexts and how these cases can illustrate the structural and procedural factors that facilitate or impede the work of the UN institution. The Chile and Iran cases also deal, in part, with the subjects of the thematic mechanisms; this partial overlap lends itself to a comparison of the relative effectiveness of the two types of Charter-based institutions.[8]

Treaty-based implementation efforts include the Human Rights Committee established under the Covenant on Civil and Political Rights, the Committee on Economic, Social and Cultural Rights, under the Covenant of that title, and several single-issue committees established under separate treaties dealing with such subjects as the rights of the child, torture, and racial discrimination. I do not look at single-issue regimes in this study.

At the 1993 intergovernmental World Conference on Human Rights in Vienna, the more than 170 states present made notable progress toward creating an environment in which states will find stronger incentives to carry out their human rights responsibilities. After reaffirming by consensus "the solemn commitment of all States to fulfill their obligations to promote universal respect for, and observance and protection of, all human rights and fundamental freedoms for all in accordance with the Charter," they called for establishment of an office of UN High Commissioner for Human Rights to strengthen and improve the international community's ability to implement established standards.[9] In December of that year, in a historic act following 40 years of discussion and struggle by proponents of a stronger UN human rights structure, the General Assembly accepted the World Conference's recommendation and established the new office.[10] (Chapter 8 discusses the Assembly decision and its antecedents in some detail.)

REVIEW

This chapter introduced basic questions and general propositions concerning the effectiveness of UN human rights institutions, defined key terms, and outlined the general statutory sources of authority and main types of UN human rights institutions.

The following chapter traces the history of the term "human rights," explores how human rights came to acquire the status of international norms, and examines how these norms relate to the norm of sovereignty. It also addresses the question whether or not states have an *international* legal obligation to respect human rights and how the community of states has developed certain methods to implement these norms.

NOTES

1. Two documents prepared for the 1993 World Conference on Human Rights deal in some detail with these developments and argue for closer integration of human rights

concerns in UN peacekeeping and peacemaking operations. See Ian Martin, ''The Pro-motion of Human Rights and Prevention of Human Rights Violations,'' in *Human Rights at the Dawn of the 21st Century* (hereafter *HR/COE*), report of an interregional meeting organized by the Council of Europe (A/CONF.157/PC/66/Add.1); and Amnesty Inter-national, ''Facing Up to the Failures: Proposals for Improving the Protection of Human Rights by the United Nations'' (A/CONF.157/PC/Add.1). See also David P. Forsythe, *Human Rights and Peace* (Lincoln: University of Nebraska Press, 1993), 8–9, 165–67.

2. For a good summary of these developments, see David P. Forsythe, ''The UN and Human Rights at Fifty: An Incremental but Incomplete Revolution,'' *Global Gov-ernance* 1 (1995), 297–318. One of the best sources for authoritative, concise, but amply documented information on UN decisions in this area is John Carey, ed., *Unofficial Reports concerning Legal Matters in the United Nations* (New York: Walker), monthly.

3. In saying this, I do not mean to imply that individuals or groups have no standing in international law; to the contrary, it is a fundamental premise of this study that indi-vidual human beings have rights under international law, that these are guaranteed by the international community, and that the latter has undertaken an obligation to promote and protect these rights.

4. John Gerard Ruggie, ''Multilateralism: The Anatomy of an Institution,'' *Inter-national Organization* 46 (Summer 1992), 571.

5. Stephen D. Krasner, ''Structural Causes and Regime Consequences: Regimes as Intervening Variables,'' in Stephen D. Krasner, ed., *International Regimes* (Ithaca, NY: Cornell University Press, 1983), 1.

6. Ruggie, ''Multilateralism,'' 574.

7. Ibid., 573.

8. As of March 1996, there were thematic mechanisms also on such topics as torture, summary or arbitrary execution, rights to own property, mercenaries, the sale of children, racism, and the right to development. In addition to Iran, there were country-specific mechanisms on Afghanistan, Burundi, Cuba, El Salvador, Equatorial Guinea, Guatemala, Haiti, Iraq, Myanmar, Rwanda, the Sudan, Yugoslavia, and Zaire. (The Chile mechanism had been discontinued in 1990.) These do not count the countries considered under the confidential procedures established by Economic and Social Council Resolution 1503. This procedure is described in Chapter 3.

9. Vienna Declaration and Programme of Action, adopted by consensus by the World Conference on Human Rights on June 25, 1993, contained in A/CONF.157/23.

10. UN General Assembly resolution 48/141, adopted by consensus on Dec. 20, 1993, reproduced as Appendix H.

2

Human Rights: What They Are, How They Acquired International Importance, and How They Relate to State Sovereignty

WHAT ARE HUMAN RIGHTS?

Of several good definitions of human rights in the contemporary literature, Louis Henkin's is among the clearest:

Human rights are rights of individuals in society . . . [e]very human being has . . . legitimate, valid, justified claims upon his or her society . . . to various 'goods' and benefits . . . they are defined, particular claims listed in international instruments . . . deemed essential for individual well-being, dignity, and fulfillment, and that reflect a common sense of justice, fairness, and decency.[1]

Alternatively, I offer a slightly different formulation; I suggest that human rights can be thought of as titles, rooted in the dignity (intrinsic value) of every human being, to live and to have or to do certain things that are essential to live a life in keeping with this dignity. Human rights are ways of expressing the requirements of human dignity in a social context and of safeguarding respect for that dignity.

"Human rights" entered the language of political discourse only three centuries ago. This does not mean, of course, that what we call human rights did not exist before then or that they were never respected. They were often respected in practice for a wide variety of religious, cultural, and social reasons only vaguely related to the reasons we usually cite for observing rights today. Throughout antiquity and the Middle Ages, the language of politics was cast in terms of obligation (duty) rather than rights.[2] One encountered the term "right," but not "rights," and by "right" was meant "morally correct," "just," or "law," not an attribute or claim of an individual human being.[3]

Not until the time of John Locke, in the late seventeenth century, do we find the term "human rights" used in anything like its contemporary meaning, although elements of this meaning were implicit in much of the natural law tradition of the Romans (Cicero, Epictetus) and the medieval Scholastics (especially Aquinas). Locke himself used the term "natural rights," signaling that the concept indeed grew out of the natural law tradition. Still earlier writers, including Plato and Aristotle, had well-developed notions of natural law that incorporated a conception of intrinsic human dignity, but without a sense that this dignity gives rise to individual rights as socially valid and legally protectible claims. After Locke, however, the idea of individual human rights took root in Europe and the Americas and became one of the chief subjects of political discourse during the eighteenth century.[4]

Agnes Heller sees rights as part of the unfinished "project of modernity," in which a previous "natural artifice" of asymmetric reciprocity is being replaced by a political and social arrangement based on symmetric reciprocity. "Asymmetric reciprocity" means a world hierarchically organized into clusters, within which members are equal to each other and unequal in relation to members of other clusters. One's role in life is determined by the cluster of birth. But in the modern world, "human existence is now to be renegotiated" by persons enjoying a relationship of "symmetric reciprocity"—people who have, before starting to negotiate, achieved sufficient power vis-à-vis the other that they can negotiate on a basis of rough parity.[5]

The concept of human rights enters this scenario in the eighteenth century as "natural rights," which Heller says were a tool to deconstruct the old "natural artifice." She sharply distinguishes natural *rights* from natural *law*, which she sees as having served as a legitimating tool for the natural artifice.[6] She uses "natural law" in a different sense from the way I have used the term previously to allude to that part of the work of classical and medieval political thinkers that foreshadows modern human rights concepts by insisting on an inherent human dignity; my usage approximates the sense in which Heller uses the term "natural rights." For her, these rights spring from a mutual recognition of the values of freedom and life. But she insists that "the claim that men ought to be what they are (namely free), is based . . . upon an arrangement of symmetric reciprocity."[7] In other words, one needs a degree of power to negotiate one's freedom in practice.

Practical equality—or symmetric reciprocity—opens the way to recognition of the values of freedom and life as *universal*. Natural rights helped to replace inequality with equality, and equality then opened the way to human rights as "institutionalized forms of the concretisation of universal values (of freedom and life)." Rights provide concrete frameworks for action and negotiation, for problem solving and crisis resolution.[8]

"Right-language" is a supplemental language to the many distinct "mother tongues" of the world. It is open and empty; different cultures fill it up with specific, concrete forms of the values of freedom and life. Right-language also provides the institutionalized procedures through which people have recourse to values; it is "the language of conflict-management within the socio-political arrangement of symmetric reciprocity." This language and this arrangement, says Heller, are both universalizable.[9]

Throughout, Heller emphasizes that the discussion of rights and speaking "right-language" take place within the realm of the practical rather than the theoretical. I would agree, adding that when Locke and Rousseau were writing their pioneering works on natural rights, they were not primarily interested in discovering new truths about human nature. They approached the study of politics as a practical matter, as something to be shaped and molded by human judgment and will. They wanted to ground politics on a better foundation than the situation they found. For Locke, the goal was a stable and peaceful political order free of sectarian violence; for Rousseau, it was institutionalized social recognition of equality.

In order to convince their contemporaries that action was necessary and appropriate to achieve these values in concrete social life, Locke and Rousseau constructed theoretical justifications. Their approach was not, Let us study the human being as an object of intellectual analysis and then see what the results of this analysis tell us about the best forms of political society. The starting point was, There is something wrong with sectarian civil war or a rigid class system. One way to solve the problem would be to provide a new theoretical foundation for organizing political society. For Locke, in particular, a philosophy of individual rights provided such a basis. Rousseau's overwhelming concern with equality led him to give priority to the general will rather than to individual rights as a guardian of freedom.[10] But both of them contributed in major ways to the intellectual "start-up capital" of contemporary human rights thinking.

Is Heller right that symmetric reciprocity, or practical equality based on some sort of parity of power, is a prerequisite for the concretization of values as "rights"? The historical record suggests that she is probably correct. While practical ideas themselves have some power because they provide stimuli to the human will, as goals to attract it and reasons to move from inaction to action, most social action is completed through the mediation of psychological or material power. Psychological power can take the form of public protests, petitions, an advertising barrage, editorials, books and magazines, letters, visits to officials, and street demonstrations. It combines the force of ideas with the power of their advocacy by actual persons. One thinks of mid-twentieth-century civil rights advocacy in the United States and other countries, which accomplished new "concretizations of the value of freedom." In this case those struggling for legal equality had to achieve a certain critical mass of public support in order to be able to act from a position of rough "symmetric reciprocity" from which legal changes could be negotiated. In the case of material power, the importance of prior symmetry needs no explanation.

The success of the American and French Revolutions, launched in the name of natural rights, had a powerful influence on political thought and history in the early nineteenth century, although that tide ebbed in the wake of the destruction and suffering caused by the Napoleonic Wars and had difficulty regaining momentum in the new era of industrialization, urbanization, the bureaucratic-technical militarized national state, and colonial expansion.

Even during this fallow period for the intellectual and political influence of the concept of human rights, the slave trade was eradicated throughout most of the world. Human beings finally abolished the slave trade because they eventually came to understand that human dignity means at least that one human being must not buy or sell another. This notion links the ideas of equality and dignity; more and more people came to think that if any human being has dignity as a human, then all of us have that dignity, and we have it equally.[11]

Ending the slave trade did not end social or political inequality, of course, but it ended one very specific form of that inequality. The struggle is a good example of the power of an idea when mediated through psychological and material means. Because the British people were among those who came to espouse the notion that the slave trade was wrong and must be halted, because they articulated this belief effectively through political channels, and because the British Navy controlled much of the world's ocean surface, the practice could, in fact, be stopped. The active support and cooperation of other Western European maritime nations made an important contribution to this result.[12]

THE SECOND WORLD WAR AND THE COLD WAR

Human rights returned to the main agenda of political discourse only during the Second World War, largely as a result of the massive assault on human dignity represented by Nazi policies. As the Dutch diplomat Jan Herman Burgers has recently shown, the impetus toward the postwar human rights effort in United Nations actually began early in the war, in connection with the articulation of war aims and planning for a postwar security organization. In the United Kingdom, H. G. Wells and other prominent British public figures issued a prototype of the Universal Declaration of Human Rights in 1940 in order to stimulate public discussion of war aims. In the United States, career State Department officials pushed throughout the war for inclusion in the postwar world security system of explicit commitments to promote and protect human rights.[13] While Burgers notes that Jacques Maritain, Rene Cassin, Emmanuel Mounier, and other French writers began to give the subject of human rights serious attention even before the war, he does not add that discussion of a human rights declaration continued during the war at the Free French Government in London. Simone Weil was inspired to write her brilliant work *The Need for Roots: Prelude to a Declaration of Duties toward Mankind* as a counterpoint to the developing drive among De Gaulle's team to compose a declaration of rights.[14] Weil's work actually restates the case for human rights from another vantage point.

The systematic abuses by Nazi Germany and Stalinist USSR, some of which were widely known,[15] inspired a reexamination of the Westphalia heritage of a state's exemption from external responsibility and accountability for the way it treats its citizens. This reexamination led to Western efforts to include broad human rights provisions in the UN Charter and to establish specific new standards and mechanisms for the treatment of certain classes of noncitizens (refugees, prisoners of war, etc.).

The Geneva Conventions and the Refugee Convention and Protocol, which concern the rights of noncitizens in specific kinds of situations, have been acceded to by almost every state. Both assign significant implementation responsibilities to international organizations—the International Committee of the Red Cross in the first case, the UN High Commissioner for Refugees in the second. Another virtually universal instrument, the Vienna Convention on Consular Relations (1963), and the hundreds of bilateral consular conventions in force between states impose certain obligations on governments toward nonnationals within their borders that may be more protective of certain individual rights than the obligations found in their domestic law toward their own citizens at home. For example, in case of arrest of a citizen of a party to the Vienna Convention within the territory of another party, there are provisions requiring prompt notification to the consular authorities of the arrestee's country, consular access, and other forms of consular assistance. In a strict sense, of course, the obligation runs from state to state, but the effect is to protect individuals.[16]

This situation is perhaps based on a presumption that one is more capable of defending one's rights against one's own state than is a foreigner; a citizen has therefore less need of international protection. This is no doubt generally true. Also a citizen even of a nondemocratic state can often look to domestic institutions—social, economic, familial, and religious—and personal contacts for advocacy and at least limited shelter in the event of becoming a target of governmental repression. (Totalitarian states are an exception.) A foreigner is much less likely to have the personal, familial, and other contacts to activate such a safety net.[17]

Another explanation, which probably better reflects the actual reasons for this differential level of protection, is that statesmen long ago accepted the legitimacy of the demand of important and influential groups of citizens—merchants, bankers, sailors, and so on—that *their* state protect *their* interests abroad. In order to accomplish this, there had to be a reciprocal recognition of the legitimacy of other states' intercession on behalf of their citizens in one's own territory. Thus arose the doctrine that to injure another state's citizens was to injure that state itself and to risk retaliation from the latter. Although an individual had no recognized rights or standing in international law, his or her state certainly did, and could, act on behalf of the individual's interests if it chose to do so.[18] This is the origin of the doctrine of consular representation.

The concept that a consul is entitled to protect fellow citizens abroad was later extended to permit designated international organizations to protect certain categories of persons who are beyond the effective protection of their states, even by consuls: wounded soldiers on the battlefield, prisoners of war, and, after the Second World War, refugees and residents of occupied territory.

But until the adoption of the UN Charter, for a state to accept that international law reached its *own* citizens at home seemed to most governments to threaten the foundations of their internal power. Until 1945, this factor forestalled creation of international human rights institutions that could address the rights of citizens within their own countries.[19]

The Charter provisions were also the first time the community of states had agreed that there exist human rights standards for *everyone* and that the community had some responsibility for their promotion; the Universal Declaration, adopted pursuant to the Charter in 1948, gave specific content to the broad concept of "human rights." In the same year, through adoption of the Genocide Convention, the community sought to act against the most grievous violation of these standards.[20] The Nuremberg trials also represented a form of international acceptance of an obligation to forestall repetition of such abuses.

But with the onset of the Cold War, a realization grew among statesmen, scholars, and the public that ideological incompatibility among the Great Powers was going to impede efforts to build effective international institutions to implement human rights standards. The sunny hopes of the immediate postwar era disappeared in the dark shadows of the struggle with Soviet expansionism and the threat of universal nuclear destruction.

Most scholars of human rights at the time tended to focus on bilateral policy initiatives, arguing that this is the only way states can have impact on substantive issues. In 1970, Ernst Haas reflected the still-prevailing gloom in his *Human Rights and International Action*[21] on the International Labor Organization (ILO), in which he concluded that prospects for truly effective multilateral human rights institutions were frankly dismal. In his perspective, even the most sophisticated machinery developed to that point—that of the ILO—had little more effect than the tide crashing against rocks—the rocks of state sovereignty. (Fortunately, during the intervening decades the ILO has significantly strengthened its mechanisms and procedures.)

RESURGENCE OF HUMAN RIGHTS ON POLICY AND SCHOLARLY AGENDAS

In Western countries, academic and public attention to human rights began to revive in the 1970s, with growing awareness of significant and systematic abuses by a wide range of governments, including those not on the front line of the East-West struggle. In the United States, another impetus came from the increased consciousness of human rights issues that had spurred the domestic civil rights movement of the 1960s. In newly independent countries, the experiences of the anticolonial struggle and awareness of the growing harshness of the apartheid regime in South Africa contributed to greater concern with human rights issues. The vastly heightened capacity of modern mass communications awakened strong emotional and intellectual responses and commitments among a much wider public.

In the United States in the mid-1970s, Congress and a few American scholars began to call for closer links between human rights concerns and policy decisions and sometimes for stronger action by intergovernmental organizations.

The 1970s also saw a quickening of international human rights activity: the two International Human Rights Covenants—the binding agreements intended to implement the Universal Declaration—entered into force in 1976. Successful completion of the Conference on Security and Cooperation in Europe (CSCE) in Helsinki in 1975 broadened acceptance of the view that human rights practices are subject to multilateral evaluation. In the Western Hemisphere, the American Convention on Human Rights entered into force in 1978, adding strength to the ongoing human rights work of the Organization of American States.

In 1977, the Carter administration brought human rights concerns into the mainstream of American foreign policy, and for four years human rights policy officers had an opportunity to ensure that human rights factors were weighed in every important U.S. policy decision. Of course, this was not the first time an American president had invoked human rights in a foreign policy context. From Franklin D. Roosevelt on, presidents had paid public homage to human rights at critical moments. During World War II and the Cold War they articulated policy in terms of freedom and sometimes even used the term "human rights." These utterances were intimately bound up with the global struggles then under way, which were, at bottom, about human rights. But Carter is the first president to insist on the full integration of human rights in U.S. foreign policy, bilateral and multilateral, in all substantive fields—political, economic, and security—vis-à-vis all countries, not only those on the other side in the global contest. This does not mean that human rights considerations always proved controlling in the policy-making process; it would be naive to expect, then or ever, that human rights advocates need do no more than state their views for the rest of the Executive Branch to fall into line, even when the sitting president is the person responsible for bringing the issue to policy councils and has declared it to be one of his most important priorities. National security and national and international economic interests and their advocates did not suddenly absent themselves from the policy process. What was different from 1977 on was that human rights concern was now *also* part of the process along with economic and security concerns. It is not remarkable that human rights did not always win out in battles over specific issues; what is remarkable is that for the first time human rights *did win* some of the time—indeed, much of the time.[22]

Although the Carter administration also worked hard to strengthen multilateral human rights institutions—an effort in which this writer was a direct participant—most of the administration's energies were absorbed by struggles along the bilateral front (in which I was also engaged). Whatever an individual state—even a superpower—might be able to accomplish through bilateral action could prove ephemeral. This was vividly illustrated when the Reagan administration took office in January 1981, after having vilified the Carter human rights policy as inimical to U.S. national interests. Although this antipolicy spent itself after about a year, the year of negativity dissipated previous momentum. Because the Carter administration had given insufficient priority to long-term multilateral institution-building, there was a vacuum in the multilateral area that other pro-human rights states were only partially able to fill.

Scholarly attention to human rights continued to be strong in the 1980s and early 1990s. The following sections briefly describe debates, both of which began much earlier, on two fundamental aspects of human rights as an international issue: first, among realist and other schools of international relations and second, between universalists and relativists.

REALIST, IDEALIST, AND OTHER THEORETICAL PERSPECTIVES

The realist tradition of scholars and practitioners—Morgenthau, Kennan, Kissinger, and Kirkpatrick,[23] for example—has seen the effort to construct strong human rights institutions as, at best, a poor tool to achieve really important goals, namely, national power interests. During the Cold War, these thinkers saw human rights promotion as a hopeless utopian crusade that undercut serious, responsible Western foreign policy and actually hampered the rational pursuit of U.S. national interests. The additional thought that international institutions, including the United Nations, should be asked to take on a major role in this crusade struck them as the height of quixotic absurdity.

Dependency and global systems theorists, such as Galtung and Wallerstein,[24] have seen Western initiatives to strengthen multilateral human rights institutions as cats' paws of neocolonialism, part of the West's strategy to further enhance their prosperity at the expense of poor countries. Western appeals for civil and political rights, they believe, are intended to rob governments of weak countries of the necessary power to mobilize the energies of their people to overcome poverty. Such appeals also deflect attention from the structural human rights exploitation resulting from the alliance between international capitalist power centers and local elites. Even the bloodiest excesses of non-Western governments, while sometimes regretted by these theorists, were nevertheless typically justified by them as part of the struggle against exploitation. That most theorists of these schools are Marxists has made it easier for them to devalue civil and political rights, since these rights relate primarily to the individual. For these thinkers, only collectivities really matter; only class-based parties and states are authentic bearers of value in the international system, and they are the logical allies of ex-colonies—the exploited—against the exploiting West. The strongest possible doctrine of sovereignty, for these writers, is needed to guard against neocolonialism.

Another theoretical school, broadly in the idealist tradition, sees the world as ready for the creation of a new and more just order on the basis of certain norms or ideals (including human rights), espoused by small groups of advocates and growing into large popular movements to create a global consciousness and will to change. Richard Falk, Saul Mendlovitz, and participants in the World Order Models Project exemplify this approach.[25] For them, ideas alone, or almost alone, can change the world, if fortified with imagination and enthusiasm. States are, at best, passive impediments and, at worst, formidable (but declining) opponents of this process. Change, they say, will come about in spite of states, not through them or because of them. But they do not make clear how such change will occur in a world still comprising states as the fundamental operating political units.

A fourth approach, which we might call the "institutional-legal" school, includes such contemporary international relations scholars and human rights specialists as David Forsythe, Jack Donnelly, and the late R. J. Vincent and legal scholars Louis Henkin, Theodor Meron, Antonio Cassese, and Hurst Hannum. This school sees the effort to protect human rights internationally as the expression of a growing consensus on what is to be included in the list of rights and on the legitimacy of international community action in this area. Such an approach obviously challenges traditional conceptions of state sovereignty and argues for an innovative approach to the topic of international intercession. This school tries to get beyond debates about whether international actions on behalf of human rights are really only subtexts of the old battles over neocolonialism or the East–West or North–South contest for global preeminence. They want to lead the discussion into questions of whether or not the organized international community of states has a right to intercede on behalf of human rights, of how that intercession should be conducted, and of how to enhance the effectiveness of this type of activity.[26] Theo van Boven and B. G. Ramcharan, legal scholars who have also served as high-ranking UN human rights officials, join those just mentioned in arguing that states have placed some rights in the international domain as subjects of legitimate concern to other states and that states have consciously built structures and mechanisms in order to express this concern and try to make it effective.[27]

Forsythe and Vincent, among others, have also called attention to the significance of judicial developments that tend to strengthen international recourse against violations—such as the *Filartiga-Pena* case, in which a U.S. court asserted jurisdiction over a Paraguayan torturer for torture inflicted in Paraguay on another Paraguayan—thus treating torture as a crime similar to piracy, the slave trade, and aircraft hijacking as an offense subject to universal jurisdiction.[28] They point out, in agreement with Henkin, Meron, and Hannum, that such developments contribute to a growing body of customary human rights norms legally binding on all states.

While Falk and Mendlovitz are probably right that ideas, expressed as values, have a certain power of their own to motivate human conduct, it seems improbable that such power directly *causes* events. With Vincent, Forsythe, Cassese, and Henkin, I hold that an idea can provide an important impulse, but that it must be mediated through institutions that represent the will of the community of states in order to affect state practice. States still possess most power in the world, including the power to respect or violate human rights. John Gerard Ruggie has accurately summarized this perspective: "Human rights are more than a mere rationalization of structures of power, yet their international normative status remains closely dependent upon the projection of power, the defense of interests, and the nature of political community existing among states."[29]

HUMAN RIGHTS—HOW UNIVERSAL ARE THEY?

The Universal Declaration of Human Rights, the two International Covenants on Human Rights, and other widely accepted postwar international instruments begin by affirming that concern with human rights is rooted in recognition of the inherent and equal dignity of all human beings.[30] *"Dignity," therefore, is the underlying* concept. The drafters of the Charter and the Declaration did not try to define "dignity," but it is probably not stretching the term to say that it conveys a sense of internal value found in every human being; that is, dignity is not something conferred on some or all humans by an external power. It simply goes with being human.

Some writers, usually called "relativists," hold that concepts such as equal dignity and rights based thereon, derive their meaning as values *entirely* from the concrete historical contexts and specific cultures in which they operate.[31] As Jack Donnelly points out, such a view, which he calls "radical relativism," denies the very idea of human rights, for it holds that there are no rights that everyone is equally entitled to, simply as a human being.[32] A less radical form of relativism is found in views such as that expressed in 1988 by Adam Roberts and Benedict Kingsbury:

It remains the case that, despite the existence of many purportedly definitive agreements on the subject, different societies have very different conceptions of the content and importance of human rights. These different conceptions, reflecting different national experiences, are not likely to change quickly.[33]

Roberts and Kingsbury did not include human rights among the "obvious possibilities for [the United Nations] to expand its involvement in various activities to which a multilateral approach is especially suitable."[34]

Jack Donnelly contrasts "radical relativism" with "radical universalism," a view that

human rights are . . . in no way subject to modification in light of cultural or historical differences. In its pure form, radical universalism holds that there is only one set of human rights, which applies at all times and in all places.

Between these two poles, which he rejects, Donnelly identifies two intermediate positions: "strong relativism," which holds that "human rights . . . are principally, but not entirely, determined by culture or other circumstances," that is, rather like the view of Roberts and Kingsbury just quoted, and "weak relativism," in which "human rights are held to be largely universal, subject only to secondary cultural modifications."[35] This is Donnelly's own view.

It seems to me that Donnelly's "weak relativism" could also be called "weak universalism," since it accords first place to the concept of universality. Universalists and "weak relativists" alike hold that there exists something common to all members of the human species, a fundamental intrinsic reality—an inherent value—that is the source of our dignity and the basis of our rights.[36] As for cultural variations, I would explain change in the ways different epochs have thought about human rights by pointing to the fact that people learn by stages and build on what has been learned before. Human rights are products of history in the sense that humans have gradually become *aware* of this or that right. Sometimes it takes the application of power, or a great struggle, for the truth to come home to enough people to effect change; the American Civil War is an example. But I would insist that the rights themselves are attributes that are closely tied to what constitutes us members of the human species and that attach to every actual human solely and simply as a member of the species. This means that wherever we find human beings, there also will we find human rights, whether or not they are recognized in law and practice. It does not mean that all concrete manifestations of these rights will be identical. Developing countries, for instance, may be right that the Universal Declaration reflects a Western conception of human rights because it was drafted by Westerners and therefore includes Western *specifications* of human rights—the Declaration was written to try to make clear what "human rights" meant, and no doubt the drafters adopted some historically shaped formulations to accomplish this. But these specific formulations can be distinguished from the underlying concepts they seek to convey.

The Universal Declaration and other human rights documents refer to "every human being," "everyone," "all members of the human family," and "all individuals" as subjects of human rights. Article 6 of the Universal Declaration, for example, states, "Everyone has the right to recognition everywhere as a person before the law." Article 16 of the International Covenant on Civil and Political Rights repeats this in terms of state obligation: "Everyone shall have the right everywhere to recognition as a person before the law." Just as these documents do not seek to define "dignity," they do not define "person." The drafters decided it was not necessry to settle these philosophical debates definitively; it was more important to accept a broad, rough-edged "working understanding" of these key terms and to move on to more practical dimensions on which a fuller degree of agreement seemed possible.[37]

I would add that, as only individual human beings exist (a "generic human" is not to be found), this means human rights are existentially rooted in individuals. However, if the individual's humanity—the human essence—is the same in all persons, then it is not an individual's unique or distinguishing features that make a person the bearer of *human* rights; it is instead that common substrate, the human essence. This is also the basis for the doctrine that all rights properly called *human* are held *equally* by all members of the species, even though the particular ways they are manifested vary from culture to culture.

It is not my intention here to do much more than recognize the existence of the universalist-relativist debate and state my position in it. It is not necessary to resolve this issue in order to achieve my initial purpose, which is to show that the community of states has authorized certain UN bodies to act on its behalf to protect human rights vis-à-vis individual member states and to hold states accountable for their conduct. I argue that the political decision to establish an implementation mechanism affirms the will of the international community to implement the rights mentioned in the document creating it and that it therefore implies recognition of these rights as prescriptive normative standards of international conduct.

NORMS AND RIGHTS

This raises another line of inquiry: how does an idea, for example, an idea of a right to life or to some freedom, become first a prescriptive norm (an idea of something that is good) and then a behavioral norm (a complex prevailing practice), and how do norms change? If we assume that material interests alone cannot account for what happens in the world, we need to try to explain the other factors at work. Neta Crawford has addressed these issues in considerable depth.[38] She notes that prescriptive norms—beliefs about what it is good and right to do—are embedded in larger ethical systems. Behavioral norms—complex, prevailing international practices—are based on both prescriptive norms and material interests. All norms, however, are functional in the sense that they make certain actions appear to be "normal" and others "abnormal" and because as shared expectations about behavior they decrease uncertainty about what actors are likely to do and thereby also facilitate coordination. They can also shape interests (or conceptions of interest) and limit or expand the range of options that an actor will consider. Finally, prescriptive norms can also legitimate certain actions and delegitmate others.

Crawford points out that actors in fact *use* both prescriptive and behavioral norms in arguments to do just these things ("normalize," decrease uncertainty, promote coordination, and legitimate or delegitimate). She illustrates her treatment of norm change with a brief study of how the norms of sovereignty and nonintervention that accompanied the decolonization process have gradually been eroded by a shift to a norm of humanitarian intervention. While understanding the process of norm change is valuable in itself, for my purpose Crawford's discussion has special salience because she attributes much of the shift concerning humanitarian intervention to the spreading acceptance of human rights as prescriptive norms.[39]

Crawford says that while norm *maintenance* is dependent on traditional practices, behavioral norm *change* occurs through a process of political argument in which prescriptive norms have an important part. Arguments about prescriptive norms refer to larger ethical systems. When two prescriptive norms conflict, the argument turns to the larger ethical system or systems in which they are embedded. But as a new prescriptive norm gains support among decision-making elites, it tends to defamiliarize and thereby delegitimate dominant practices and helps change actors' conceptions of their interests. In other words, the process of norm change begins with beliefs that change prescriptive norms, which, in turn, change behavioral norms—and sometimes they also change actors' conceptions of their own interests.[40]

This has led to a new universalization of human rights norms, as Crawford has shown:

Arguably, the impulse behind humanitarian intervention is part of a long-term trend toward the humanization and awareness of the ''other'' and an enlargement of international ''community.'' . . . The people of the colonies became human and thus, at least theoretically, capable of governing themselves. International law should protect them. . . . Exclusions and differential treatment are impossible to sustain with any sense of legitimacy once separate identities and differentiations have broken down or been declared irrelevant. Now, in the late twentieth century, the people of Asia, Africa and Latin America are further humanized: there is no logical limit to their human rights once their humanity is granted. It is also no longer acceptable to let those ''others'' die of hunger and maltreatment if something can be done about it. Two identities have thus been reconceptualized: the ''other'' is more human and ''we'' are more responsible for them.[41]

RIGHTS AND COMMUNITY INSTITUTIONS

We can use Crawford's framework to analyze the process of norm change in considering how the international community of states came to the view that it has a legitimate role in (1) articulating human rights standards (prescriptive norms) and (2) trying to influence states to uphold human rights standards in practice, including holding them accountable to the community when they fail to do so (behavioral norms). She points out that ''in international politics, states must provide legitimate arguments for their actions'' and that international organizations provide many locations where states have to justify their behavior. Even if a practice is not universally observed, it can still be a behavioral norm ''if the behavior is commonly expected and if when actors do not follow the expected behavior, sanctions are considered and/or applied against those who violate the norm.''[42] This fits the human rights case well.

Crawford's conclusion leads directly to the topic of the role of international institutions in influencing states to observe international human rights standards (norms) of behavior toward their inhabitants:

The fact that people even talk of humanitarian intervention and abandoning strict notions of sovereignty in favor of human rights indicates that we are in the midst of a redefinition of international norms similar to the long arguments over slavery and colonialism. . . .

The normative consensus that emerged through the abolition and decolonization arguments will influence the normative consensus that emerges around the problem of humanitarian intervention.[43]

Of course, as humanitarian intervention involves the use of force, it is already at a more distant remove from the doctrine of sovereignty than the methods normally used by UN agencies to implement international human rights standards. If Crawford is right about the shifting relationship between intervention and human rights, then the less intrusive human rights implementation methods used by the United Nations may already be part of a new behavioral normative consensus.[44]

COMMUNITY INSTITUTIONS: INTRODUCTORY REMARKS

Human rights have a social as well as an individual existence. For possession of a right to be meaningful, there must be mutual recognition of an obligation to respect that right in all possessors within a society. This obligation is typically discharged on an individual basis—one person respecting the right of another in one-on-one contacts—but it also implies an obligation to see that the rights of all are respected by all. The latter obligation arises from the fact that humans need society to survive and to develop our multidimensional capacities; community is a necessary condition of human existence. We must share space, resources, goods and services, and information; our intercommunication and interaction occur within this communal context, where it becomes impossible to ensure that the rights of all are respected except through community institutions. They play a role in keeping symmetric reciprocity a daily reality; without them, the continuous interaction of individuals is wholly subject to factors of power in which the stronger may choose to dominate the weaker.

Even if most individuals live up to their obligations to respect others' rights, in the absence of community institutions charged with ensuring rights observance, rights-respecting individuals have no real security for their own rights other than that deriving from the reciprocity they extend to, and receive from, other specific individuals. Since we live our lives through countless daily interactions with a multitude of other persons, absent community institutions we would have to conclude scores or hundreds of such reciprocal agreements in order to secure our fundamental rights. But as these would rest entirely on one-on-one agreement and practice, they would be highly perishable, subject to all human frailties. We would need to spend all of our time looking to our individual defenses, thus defeating the purposes of life in community. We would have no way to assure protection for any members of society besides those with whom we had concluded individual agreements. The weaker members of such a community would probably soon be enslaved or eliminated. The people living in a community thus have a right and an obligation to see to it that their community has structures endowed with sufficient resources and power to carry out the task of protecting the rights of all and of enabling their exercise.

In domestic society, these institutions guarantee that the obligation to respect rights is fulfilled by all members vis-à-vis all other individuals, and they ensure the existence of opportunities for the exercise of those rights that require some object or instrument or service for their realization, such as the right to education or employment.[45]

By analogy, the community of states also needs institutions to act as agents to promote the practical observance of human rights. I hold that governments that respect human rights as a behavioral norm do so for one or more of several reasons: they think it is the right thing to do on the merits (they accept it as a prescriptive norm); they think it promotes domestic stability and prosperity; their people demand it; their allies and major trading and aiding partners ask them to do it; they want to travel in respected international company; it is firmly grounded in their own national tradition; it is clearly accepted international law; or the material or political costs of nonrespect are too high.

Even if some governments do not accept human rights as good in themselves, most governments want to be seen as civilized and humane by their peers and by the publics of countries whose cooperation is important to them. If they abuse their citizens, most of them try to hide their abusive practices, not to justify them. Moreover, questions of material interest interact with prescriptive norm considerations: most governments are aware that economic and other forms of international cooperation are vital to their prosperity and perhaps even to their survival.

Violation of a behavioral norm has costs. A government may decide to ignore the international community and violate fundamental rights even at a price in its external relationships, but there is a price. Sometimes it is political-psychological, sometimes it directly affects material interest, and sometimes it is all of these costs. A contemporary state must weigh them in the balance when deciding on internal policies; the UN human rights system now constitutes an external factor that any government must take into account in determining policies that affect practical observance of human rights.

The international community usually begins to create a new norm by tackling the prescriptive element, defining it as a standard of conduct against which performance can be measured. In the event of a breach there can thus be official recognition by the international community of that fact, *if a suitable community institution exists for that purpose.*[46] An individual state can publicly recognize breaches by another, but unless its own interests are involved, it cannot invoke a *bilateral* obligation by the offending state to *it*. The obligation runs toward the community of states and through the community to each state as a member thereof. Thus, there must be a community institution formally to determine when breaches occur.

This is quite apart from the question of what the community does about such breaches, in other words, how the international community seeks to induce states to comply with a new norm. UN institutions that do these things in the human rights field are described in the next chapter. While the existence and functioning of these institutions are not themselves direct material deterrents to breach of human rights obligations, they often act effectively as political deterrents. When the community of states acts through agencies with reference to jointly accepted standards, individual states find it useful to be able to say to other states: It isn't just we who want you to do this or that about a situation— it's the international community, of which you and we are fully and equally part, speaking through our jointly designated agent on this issue.

HUMAN RIGHTS AND STATE SOVEREIGNTY

After the Peace of Westphalia (1648), Europeans reacted to perceived threats of imperial absorption by throwing up walls of sovereignty, fortifying them, and forging alliances to defend them. Instead of the medieval lord's stone castle, surrounded by a moat and defended by his knights, modern Europe opted for the feudal castle-writ-large of the sovereign state. Europe imposed this model on the rest of the world. This heritage is still powerful and constitutes a counterforce to the trend toward greater institutional coordination flowing from the gradually intensifying realities of interdependence.

After Westphalia, the doctrine of state sovereignty came to mean that, while a state had to account to another state for the treatment of the latter's nationals, it did not have to account to any external power for its conduct toward its own citizens. According to the International Court of Justice, this traditional doctrine of state sovereignty has meant that the state "is subject to no other state, and has full and exclusive powers within its jurisdiction."[47]

From the seventeenth to the mid-twentieth century, the retreat behind the walls of sovereignty largely excluded international action to ameliorate abuses of a people by their own government. Moreover, the institutional framework that would be needed for such a task did not exist. The loose, pluralistic system of the High Middle Ages, with multiple countervailing centers of power within and among polities and even, very loosely, above them in the form of emperor and pope, might have provided the political precondition for such a framework, but that system was gone.[48]

Affirming that human rights are *international* obligations of a state to its citizens—indeed, to *all* persons who are lawfully present within its territory[49]— *and* to the international community as a whole raises core issues concerning state sovereignty.

It is one thing for states to agree upon standards of conduct toward their citizens and other legal residents that bind only those states that formally accept these standards. That is simply an act of contract among sovereigns, to be implemented by each sovereign vis-à-vis the other contracting parties according to whatever methods are specified in the contract, that is, the treaty. If they agree on exclusively unilateral implementation, then each relies on the good faith of the other to carry out its obligations, although any party can at least remind the other that it has such obligations. If they agree on multilateral methods, then these can be invoked by any of the parties in accordance with whatever terms are in the treaty.

It is something else to say that the community of states as a whole has a "corporate right" to establish binding standards (prescriptive and behavioral norms) for *all*. But this is essentially what the International Court of Justice has said (in, for instance, the *Barcelona Traction* case, described in Chapter 3), and one can also argue that the UN Charter specifically establishes such a corporate right. That it exists is a conviction held by such leading theorists of international law as Louis Henkin[50] and Theodor Meron[51] and by international relations scholars such as R. J. Vincent and David Forsythe.[52]

Multilateral standard-setting itself—apart from implementation—implies that states are accountable to the community of which they are a part for their actions toward their own people and that the community has a right and responsibility to create and operate a system of accountability.[53]

States have primary capacity to protect rights, and the organized international *community of states* has a responsibility to help see that states do this—to develop structures that can assist states or, in cases where states fail to protect the rights of their inhabitants, to bring to bear the influence of the community on behalf of restoring respect for rights.

We should consider briefly the question of the nature and origin of the "corporate right" to establish and implement binding international standards. If the world is made up of *absolutely* sovereign states, then no such right exists. Nor can it. In such a world, a state that has accepted a standard of conduct (toward its inhabitants) as binding can renounce it as freely as it accepted it in the first place. Otherwise, what would sovereignty mean? How could choices about internal policies be limited by the need to obtain the consent, albeit tacit, of external sources?

But *is* the world made up of absolutely sovereign state actors? States still have exclusive power to raise armies and police forces directly, to operate judicial systems and prisons, to tax their citizens and residents; thereby they have direct control over the liberty and economic resources of individuals and direct access to the basic tools of physical power. No one else does. But this is not the whole story, because states exist within a larger universe, in which they interact with other states and nonstate actors.

As Neta Crawford points out, "Beyond international law, international practice, despite persistent hypocrisy and inconsistency, has tended in recent years more toward the affirmation and protection of human rights than it has the affirmation and protection of sovereignty."[54]

In a recent essay, Kathryn Sikkink has developed this theme persuasively:

Human rights policies and practices are contributing to a gradual, significant, and probably irreversible transformation of sovereignty in the modern world. . . . Any international activities to protect human rights . . . challenge the premise of the traditional doctrine of sovereignty. . . . claims about sovereignty are forceful because they represent shared understandings and expectations that are constantly reinforced both through the practices of states and the practices of nonstate actors. . . . when a state recognizes the legitimacy of international interventions on the topic of human rights and changes its domestic human rights practices in response to these international pressures, it reconstitutes the relationship between the state, its citizens, and international actors.

Sikkink concludes that

The human rights issue . . . suggests a future model in which understandings of sovereignty are modified in relation to specific issues that are deemed of sufficient importance to the international community . . . such as the environment, the delivery of emergency food supplies, and the protection of minorities. . . . Human rights is . . . part of a significant though circumscribed subset of international issues for which modified understandings of sovereignty are increasingly accepted and practiced.[55]

R. J. Vincent wrote eloquently about "the opening, or reopening, of the frontiers of the sovereign state into a global society of the existence of which the universal culture of human rights is one indicator."[56] "[I]n the contest between the principle of state sovereignty and the doctrine of universal human rights, neither side has scored a famous victory, but each sets limits to the domain of the other."[57]

The following chapter continues to explore some of the shifting limits of these respective domains.

REVIEW

This chapter examined the concept of human rights, how the idea entered history in the late seventeenth and eighteenth centuries, and how it gradually became an international prescriptive and behavioral norm. After touching on the question of the universality of rights, I discussed the social dimension of rights and the need for authoritative community institutions to implement them on both domestic and international levels. Noticing that the degree of international protection for the rights of foreigners still exceeds that available to citizens, I searched for an explanation in the history and contemporary dimensions of sovereignty. Although sovereignty remains powerful, contemporary conditions are tending to favor the growth of multilateral responsibility for important areas of life, including human rights. International politics, diplomacy, and law have contributed to the formulation of rights as prescriptive and behavioral norms and to the establishment of institutions to promote their practical observance.

As I noted in Chapter 1, in the UN Charter, member states invested the organization with broad authority to implement human rights standards. The next chapter explains how the organization has used this authority to develop specific implementation machinery. It surveys and analyzes the existing system of UN human rights institutions and assesses general characteristics that contribute to their strengths and weaknesses.

NOTES

1. Louis Henkin, *The Age of Rights* (New York: Columbia University Press, 1990), 2. Jack Donnelly's definition is also good, although it is limited mainly to functional aspects—what rights *do*:

Rights are titles that ground claims of a special force. To have a right to *x* is to be specially entitled to have and enjoy *x*. The right thus governs the relationship between right-holder and duty-bearer, insofar as that relationship rests on the right. In addition . . . to have a right is to be empowered to press rights *claims*, which ordinarily "trump" . . . other grounds for action . . . the duties correlative to rights "belong to" the right-holder, who is largely free to dispose of those duties as he sees fit.

Jack Donnelly, *Universal Human Rights in Theory and Practice* (Ithaca, NY: Cornell University Press, 1989), 9–10. Ronald Dworkin was the first to use the term "trumps" in connection with rights: "Individual rights are political trumps held by individuals." Ronald Dworkin, *Taking Rights Seriously* (Cambridge: Harvard University Press, 1977), ix. R. J. Vincent (crediting Alan Gewirth) also uses the language of "claims": "a right-holder . . . has a claim to some substance . . . which he or she might assert, or demand, or enjoy, or enforce . . . against some individual or group . . . citing in support of his or her claim some particular ground." R. J. Vincent, *Human Rights and International Relations* (Cambridge: Cambridge University Press, 1986), 8.

2. Vincent, *Human Rights*, 7.

3. Ibid, 20–23. For very similar treatments, see Donnelly, *Universal Human Rights*, 9–10, and Henkin, *The Age of Rights*, 1–3.

4. Vincent, *Human Rights*, 19–25.

5. Agnes Heller, *Can Modernity Survive?* (Berkeley: University of California Press, 1990), 145–48.

6. She writes,

If all customs as well as social or political institutions that happen to be shared by all integrations, exist "by nature," one can easily draw the conclusion that the common aspect of socio-political arrangements is that they are what they are by the "law of nature." (Heller, *Can Modernity Survive?* 149)

7. Ibid., 150.

8. Ibid., 151–52.

9. Ibid., 154, 156.

10. As J. L. Talmon has pointed out incisively, Rousseau's general will also served as a gateway to terror during the French Revolution and contributed to twentieth-century totalitarianism (J. L. Talmon, *The Origins of Totalitarian Democracy* (New York: Praeger, 1960).

11. Heller puts this development in the context of freedom: "Once it has become a self-evident truth that all men are born free, everything that is due to free persons is due to all persons" (Heller, *Can Modernity Survive?* 153).

12. A good summary account of the successful international campaign to abolish the slave trade and slavery can be found in A. H. Robertson and J. G. Merrills, *Human Rights in the World* (Manchester: Manchester University Press, 1989), 14–16.

13. Jan Herman Burgers, "The Road to San Francisco: The Revival of the Human Rights Idea in the 20th Century," *Human Rights Quarterly* 14(4) (1992), 447–77.

14. Simone Weil, *The Need for Roots: Prelude to a Declaration of Duties toward Mankind* (New York: G. P. Putnam's Sons, 1952). Weil, for philosophical reasons based in the Platonic tradition, held that duties have priority over rights and that a focus on obligations related to human needs discloses what justice demands in a given situation (*The Need for Roots*, 91).

15. Before the war there was some knowledge of serious and extensive abuses in the Third Reich and the USSR. How much had been confirmed and was certain at the time is debated, as is the question of what Western states could have done and why they did not do more. In the 1930s, the recent memory of World War I and the then-current nightmare of the depression strongly influenced Western leaders and publics against any action that might lead to war. The depression probably accounted for the failure of the multilateral Evian Conference in 1938 to save Germany's Jewish population through extra immigration quotas. The fury of *Kristallnacht* exploded only a few months later, yet the West, seemingly hypnotized by the "spirit of Munich," remained aloof.

16. This is not new; in ancient Rome, the evolution of the concept and practice of *jus gentium* derived from the perceived need to formally recognize legal rights of non-Romans.

17. On the other hand, a citizen who is a member of a religious or racial or ethnic minority (or even, in some cases, of a majority) may have available and accessible none of the domestic protections presumably available to all citizens.

18. Henkin, *The Age of Rights*, 13–14. See also Antonio Cassese, *Human Rights in a Changing World* (Philadelphia: Temple University Press, 1990), 162–63.

19. There were limited exceptions. The International Labor Organization already functioned on behalf of workers' rights from 1919, although it became much stronger after World War II, especially from the 1970s. The minorities regime administered by the League of Nations also dealt with rights of citizens vis-à-vis their own government. See Robertson and Merrills, *Human Rights in the World*, 19–21.

20. Cathal J. Nolan, *Principled Diplomacy* (Westport, CT: Greenwood Press, 1993), Ch. 7. See also Burgers, "The Road to San Francisco," 447–77.

21. Ernst Haas, *Human Rights and International Action* (Stanford, CA: Stanford University Press, 1970).

22. There are several excellent studies of the Carter administration's human rights policy. Among the better are David Newsom, ed., *The Diplomacy of Human Rights* (Lanham, MD: University Press of America, 1986) and Gaddis Smith, *Morality, Reason, and Power: American Diplomacy in the Carter Years* (New York: Hill and Wang, 1988). David Forsythe, *Human Rights and World Politics*, 2d ed. (Lincoln: University of Nebraska Press, 1989) also provides extensive, well-documented coverage of the Carter administration.

23. Even though Kirkpatrick's concern with domestic regime type differentiates her from other realists, her emphasis on the importance of national interest and of power places her broadly in the realist tradition. Even her concern with regime type can be seen in power-politics terms: from her standpoint, any regime that was not totalitarian was a candidate for the Western side in the Cold War; authoritarians were welcome, and only totalitarians need not apply (they were already on the other side anyway).

24. See, for instance, Johann Galtung, *The True Worlds: A Transnational Perspective*

(New York: Free Press, 1980) and his earlier "A Structural Theory of Imperialism," *Journal of Peace Research* 2 (1971), 81–98. For Immanuel Wallerstein, the principal standard work is *The Modern World System* (New York: Academic Press, 1974).

25. Two good recent examples are Richard Falk, Samuel Kim, and Saul Mendlovitz, eds., *The United Nations and a Just World Order* (Boulder, CO: Westview Press, 1991) and Richard Falk, *The Promise of World Order: Essays in Normative International Relations* (Philadelphia: Temple University Press, 1987).

26. David P. Forsythe, *The Internationalization of Human Rights* (Lexington, MA: Lexington Books, 1991); Donnelly, *Universal Human Rights*; Jack Donnelly, *International Human Rights* (Boulder, CO: Westview Press, 1993); Vincent, *Human Rights*; Henkin, *The Age of Rights*; Theodor Meron, *Human Rights and Humanitarian Norms as Customary Law* (New York: Oxford University Press, 1989); Hurst Hannum, "Human Rights," in Oscar Schachter and Christopher Joyner, eds., *United Nations Legal Order*, Vol. 1 (Cambridge: Cambridge University Press, 1995), 319–48; Antonio Cassese, *Human Rights in a Changing World* (Philadelphia: Temple University Press, 1990).

27. Theo van Boven, *People Matter* (Amsterdam: Meulenhoff, 1982); B. G. Ramcharan, *The Concept and Present Status of the International Protection of Human Rights: Forty Years after the Declaration* (Dordrecht, Netherlands: Nijhoff, 1989).

28. Forsythe, *The Internationalization*, 78, 80, 132; Vincent, *Human Rights*, 104, 108.

29. John Gerard Ruggie, "Human Rights and the Future International Community," *Daedalus* 112(4) (1983), 98–99.

30. Especially the Universal Declaration of Human Rights, Preamble and Articles 1 and 6; International Covenant on Civil and Political Rights, Preamble and Article 16; International Covenant on Economic, Social and Cultural Rights, Preamble; Declaration on the Right to Development (UNGA Res 41/128), Preamble and Articles 1 and 2.

31. See, for instance, Richard Bernstein, *New Constellation: The Ethical/Postethical Horizons of Modernity/Postmodernity* (Cambridge: MIT Press, 1992).

32. Donnelly, *International Human Rights*, 36.

33. Adam Roberts and Benedict Kingsbury, "The UN's Roles in a Divided World," in Adam Roberts and Benedict Kingsbury, eds., *United Nations, Divided World* (New York: Oxford University Press, 1988), 16.

34. Roberts and Kingsbury, *United Nations*, 27.

35. Donnelly, *International Human Rights*, 36. The explanation of weak relativism continues on 37–38. The author discusses these distinctions at greater length in his *Universal Human Rights*, Chs. 1–3.

36. An illustrative list of authors who share the view that human rights are universal would include, in addition to Donnelly, Maurice Cranston, David Forsythe, R. J. Vincent, Louis Henkin, Theo van Boven, Theodor Meron, Antonio Cassese, Asbjørn Eide, Henry Shue, B. G. Ramcharan, and the present writer.

37. There is a vigorous contemporary theoretical debate about the nature of personhood, which I do not enter here.

38. Neta C. Crawford, "Changing International Norms: An Argument about Arguments," paper prepared for the Thomas J. Watson, Jr., Institute for International Studies, Brown University, Providence, RI, 1994.

39. Ibid., 2–7.

40. Ibid., 15–19, 23–24.

41. Ibid., 34.

42. Ibid., 4, 19.

43. Ibid., 39–40.

44. For an excellent brief summary of the institutionalization of international human rights norms, see David P. Forsythe, "The UN and Human Rights at Fifty: An Incremental but Incomplete Revolution," *Global Governance* 1 (1995), 297–318, esp. 297–303. For book-length exposition of this topic, see Forsythe, *The Internationalization*, particularly Chs. 1–3. See also Donnelly, *International Human Rights*, Chs. 1, 2, 4. For a law-oriented account of the development of international norms and their implementation, see Hannum, "Human Rights."

45. See also Donnelly, *Universal Human Rights*, 147–50.

46. Most states, in fact, observe most norms of international law most of the time, even in the absence of any formal implementation regime, let alone any enforcement machinery. They do so not as a result of a daily cost-benefit recalculation of self-interest but because of an ingrained acceptance of a common interest in which universal observance of the norm benefits all over time.

47. International Court of Justice decision in the Wimbledon case, cited in Richard Falk and Saul Mendlovitz, eds., *The Strategy of World Order*, Vol. 2 (New York: World Law Fund, 1966), 164.

48. Until the late eighteenth century, the collapse of the medieval system of pluralistic, multilevel polities had little impact one way or the other on the practical observance by states of most civil, political, and economic rights, as the concept of rights was simply not part of the consciousness of most Europeans. But the rise of sovereign militarized unitary states, with power increasingly concentrated in the executive, created conditions in which atrocities could take place on a wide scale with impunity.

49. I use the terms "citizens," "residents, and "inhabitants" to refer to persons to whom states have human rights obligations because they are lawfully present on the territory of a state. Even temporary visitors are the object of fundamental human rights obligations if they are legally present. I leave aside the question of a state's obligations toward persons illegally on its territory, since this would raise another set of issues not directly relevant to my purpose.

50. Henkin, *The Age of Rights*, 18–21, 55–59.

51. Theodor Meron, *Human Rights*, 1, 93–96, 195.

52. Vincent, *Human Rights*, 44–47; Forsythe, *The Internationalization*, 36–37, 57–58, 77–87, 184.

53. Vincent, *Human Rights*, 130; Meron, *Human Rights*, 208, 239ff.

54. Crawford, *Changing International Norms*, 37.

55. Kathryn Sikkink, "Human Rights, Principled Issue-Networks, and Sovereignty in Latin America," *International Organization* 47 (Summer 1993), 413–41. The citations are from 413–15. Although the body of the essay focuses on two Latin American case studies, the passages quoted are clearly intended to have general applicability.

56. Vincent, *Human Rights*, 3.

57. Ibid., 131.

3

The UN Human Rights System

This chapter surveys the system of UN human rights institutions, assessing the structural and operational advantages and disadvantages of treaty-based and Charter-based mechanisms, with particular attention among the latter to universal "thematic" institutions vis-à-vis country-specific mechanisms. The comparative analysis of the Charter-based types is developed in depth in the next four chapters.

During World War II, Western leaders sought to lay an institutional groundwork for a world in which the horrors of general war and massive human rights violations could not happen again—or at least would be much less likely to occur. Early in the war Franklin D. Roosevelt articulated a profound Western concern with human rights in his Four Freedoms speech (freedom from fear and from want, freedom of speech and of religion).[1] Truman, Churchill, Attlee, and DeGaulle also lent their names to the human rights cause. Chapter 2 noted recent scholarship outlining the role of career U.S. Department of State officials during the war in pushing first the U.S. government and then other Allied governments to demand inclusion of human rights provisions in the UN Charter.

Eleanor Roosevelt became one of the foremost advocates for a vigorous multilateral effort to place human rights principles among the foundation stones of the postwar order. As chairman of the UN Human Rights Commission when it drafted the Universal Declaration of Human Rights, she told the General Assembly that the Declaration was "first and foremost a declaration of the basic principles to serve as a common standard for all nations. It might well become the Magna Carta of all mankind."[2]

Western leaders recognized that a world in which mass atrocities would be less likely would have to rest on two pillars: safeguards against war and safeguards against abuse of individual human beings. The difficulty, of course, was that these two needs were not easy to satisfy simultaneously. War and its attendant horrors had come because the territorial integrity of states had been violated. Armed force had been used across borders to impose the will of one ruler on the people of another state. Anything that weakened the concept that borders must not be crossed without permission would tend to increase the likelihood of such crossings; hence, conflict would become more frequent, not less, and the savagery of war—which had fallen increasingly upon civilians—would become more and more a part of the existence of ordinary people everywhere.

On the other hand, to shore up the walls of state sovereignty in order to make borders become the highest values—even absolute values—would be to abandon any possibility that the community of humankind could do anything to assist its individual members, no matter how horribly they might be treated in the political unit of which they happened to be citizens. Moreover, as Secretary of State George Marshall said, ''Governments which systematically disregard the rights of their own people are not likely to respect the rights of other nations and other people and are likely to seek their objectives by coercion and force in the international field.''[3]

Could the world liberate itself simultaneously from international war and from massive slaughter, torture, enslavement and persecution of citizens by their own government?

The international community recognized that neither goal could simply be sacrificed to the other. But perhaps because those who made the decisions in the late 1940s were themselves representatives of governments, they established the postwar world on a basis that gave priority to strengthening the rights of states and their borders.[4] Cathal Nolan provides a good account of wartime efforts by State Department officials to include provisions for a human rights declaration and covenant in the postwar security organization then being sketched out. These efforts met with some opposition within the administration, but the United States eventually pushed hard for inclusion of human rights provisions at the 1944 Dumbarton Oaks preparatory conference for the United Nations. Because of British (!) and Soviet opposition, the results were meager. The United States did much better at the San Francisco Conference next year.[5] Jan Herman Burgers credits support by Latin American delegations and by American nongovernmental organizations at San Francisco for encouraging the United States to try again, this time successfully, to win a place for human rights in the Charter.[6]

The strongest powers granted to the United Nations were vested in the Security Council, expressly for the purpose of preventing or halting wars.[7] Atrocities against civilians and other noncombatants (such as prisoners of war) during wartime were to be controlled outside the UN framework through the new Geneva Conventions, then being prepared.

The powerful example of the Nuremberg trials, with their forthright insistence on individual accountability for acts performed under color of state authority, could have served as a precedent deterrent to later crimes against humanity. But for a precedent to have deterrent force, indeed, for it even to be considered a true precedent, it must be invoked and acted upon in a later case or cases. As this was not done, the effect of the trials was short-lived. Moreover, the Nuremberg Principles governing the tribunal were limited to crimes against peace (planning or waging war) and war crimes; crimes against humanity were covered only in connection with one of the first two categories.[8] Not until 1993 was a similar official tribunal established, this time to deal with crimes in the former Yugoslavia, and only in late 1994 did it begin to return indictments. The first trial opened in May 1996. A similar court was established in 1995 to deal with crimes during the Rwanda genocide. The first trial was held in late 1996.[9]

The decision to give legal, political, and institutional priority to avoiding war could have left human rights during peacetime to the mercy of governments acting behind sacrosanct borders. But having made the choice in favor of "order by borders," states also recognized that something had to be done internationally for human rights. There was general agreement on the need for some kind of institutional capacity—some legal and institutional framework and procedures—to respond on behalf of the international community to massive violations of human rights.

The effort proceeded on both global and regional levels. Within the former, it led first to the creation of the UN Commission on Human Rights, of which governments, rather than individual experts, are the members. As noted, the Commission drafted the Universal Declaration of Human Rights as one of its first acts. The Commission is still the principal human rights policy-making body within the UN system; its functions are described and assessed later and in the following chapters. Also, in 1966 the General Assembly approved the texts of binding Covenants on Civil and Political Rights and on Economic, Social and Cultural Rights (both entered into force in 1976) and later adopted other legal instruments, each of which established separate implementation mechanisms comprising experts serving in their individual capacity. Most recently, the long-term effort to strengthen UN human rights machinery led to creation of the office of High Commissioner for Human Rights (December 1993), a major innovation discussed in Chapter 8. Two of the UN specialized agencies—the International Labor Organization (ILO) and the UN Educational, Scientific, and Cultural Organization (UNESCO)—have also instituted human rights procedures, but these will not concern us here.

On the regional level, the early postwar period saw the establishment of an Inter-American Commission on Human Rights, under the auspices of the Organization of American States (OAS) but comprising individual experts serving in their personal capacity, and a similarly constituted European Commission set up within the framework of the Council of Europe. Each is linked with a regional Human Rights Court, for which there is no counterpart in the United Nations. In the 1980s an African Commission on Human and People's Rights was formed, and somewhat less systematized arrangements have come into existence in Asia and among Arab countries.[10] These regional institutions and arrangements are mentioned here only for the purpose of illustrating the range of intergovernmental organizations active in the field. They will not be discussed in depth, although the OAS will be mentioned briefly in the case studies on disappearances and on Chile.

TREATY-BASED INSTITUTIONS

While I do not regard treaty-based UN human rights institutions as effective as Charter-based mechanisms, it is important to discuss them because they are relatively recent, and the treaties have attracted a fairly large number of states parties. Also, the contrast with Charter-based institutions in composition, methods, and authority will help to clarify the issue of effectiveness. This section focuses on the implementation structures of the two International Covenants.

The Covenants were intended to spell out in legally binding terms the obligations of states to respect and observe the human rights articulated in the 1948 Universal Declaration. In this sense, their drafters regarded them as unfinished business from the early days of UN human rights standard-setting. A declaration, of course, is not a legally binding document, at least at the time of its adoption. It is not signed, and it is not submitted to states for accession or ratification; therefore it cannot by itself become part of conventional international law. While many legal scholars argue that the Universal Declaration has become part of *customary* international law,[11] in the late 1940s pro-human rights states could not foresee this development and were concerned primarily with ensuring that the shining values and principles set forth in the Declaration would not remain mere aspirations.

That it took 18 years to craft the Covenants, as compared with 2 years for the Declaration, illustrates how difficult it had become to reach agreement in a world sharply divided by the Cold War and rapidly changing under the impact of decolonization.[12]

For implementation machinery, the text of the Covenant on Economic, Social and Cultural Rights set up none at all; states parties are merely required to submit to the Secretary-General "reports on the measures which they have adopted and the progress made in achieving the observance of the rights recognized [in the Covenant]."[13] The Secretary-General is to transmit them to the UN Economic and Social Council (ECOSOC) and to the specialized agencies, and ECOSOC *"may"* transmit them to the Human Rights Commission "for study and general recommendation," after which states parties and specialized agencies *"may* submit comments to ECOSOC on any general recommendation" and ECOSOC then *"may* submit . . . to the General Assembly reports with recommendations of a general nature" and *"may* bring to the attention of other organs . . . and specialized agencies . . . matters arising out of the reports"[14] (emphasis added).

In other words, a vast and largely optional paper shuffle is supposed to somehow provide enough impetus to states and other actors, for example specialized agencies, to carry out the commitments in the Covenant. This is better than nothing, although not a great deal better; until 1987, ECOSOC held only per-functory discussions of state reports, and these took place in a working group that met during one of the regular semiannual sessions of the Council, when Member States' attention is dispersed across a lengthy agenda. ECOSOC essentially did little more than receive the state reports and make them available to those member states of the Council that might want to see them; very few states requested copies. The flow of UN paper is so vast that few, if any, governments can read and absorb the documents that reach them through normal distribution; there is little incentive to ask for more paper, especially when it merely transmits an unexamined, self-serving state report.

In 1987, the Council established a Committee on Economic, Social and Cultural Rights to give more systematic attention to the reports and to explore ways to make meaningful use of them. But as its chair, Philip Alston, lamented in a paper prepared for the 1993 World Conference on Human Rights, the Committee has suffered from lack of trained staff, the absence of books and other materials, lack of interest by nongovernmental organizations, neglect by states, and low priority in the allocation of Secretariat resources. He wrote:

Functions are expected to be carried out by a Committee whose members meet for a single annual session, who receive no honorarium, who are provided with no facilities whatsoever in Geneva (beyond limited access, without borrowing privileges, to the over-all UN library) and who receive virtually no substantive documentation or information of specific relevance to the Committee's work from the Secretariat between sessions.

In the absence of access to adequate alternative sources of information, and as long as no analysis of issues and materials is undertaken in advance by the Secretariat, the quality of the supervisory work performed by the Committee can never meet even the minimum standards which should be expected, indeed demanded, of any serious international human rights monitoring procedure.[15]

The situation is better with the Covenant on Civil and Political Rights, which establishes an 18-member Human Rights Committee of

persons of high moral character and recognized competence in the field of human rights, consideration being given to the usefulness of the participation of some persons having legal experience. The members of the Committee shall be elected [by the states parties] and shall serve in their personal capacity.[16]

The Committee's powers are not terribly impressive, however:

The Committee shall study the reports submitted by States Parties. . . . [and] transmit [them] and such general comments as it may consider appropriate, to the States Parties. The Committee may also transmit to the Economic and Social Council these comments along with the copies of the reports. . . . States Parties . . . may submit to the Committee observations on any comments that may be made [by the Committee].[17]

While this looks like just another international paper shuffle, there is a difference in practice that makes this Committee a more effective body than its counterpart under the Covenant on Economic, Social and Cultural Rights. This is the fact that when it considers the report of a state party, the Human Rights Committee invites representatives of that state to appear before it to answer questions. A state may choose not to appear, but then its written report is left to speak for itself, and the state is, in a sense, at the mercy of critics on the Committee. The state may also have friends and defenders on the Committee, but it is rare nowadays that a government passes up the opportunity to state its own case in person and to answer criticisms directly. Although sessions of the Committee are little noticed by the press, governments are aware of the possibility that something said there might find its way into the broader public discourse. Thus, a government whose report is on the agenda normally takes the trouble to send a well-prepared representative to testify.

A decade before the United States ratified the Covenant on Civil and Political Rights, I attended several sessions of the Committee as an observer for the U.S. Government. The proceedings are rather like a Congressional hearing, with the experts taking turns quizzing the state's representative with regard to assertions made by the state in its written submission. Often the questions are merely requests for elaboration, but sometimes members probe more sharply, asking the representatives to explain how their statements square with credible reports from the press and other sources concerning human rights violations said to be taking place within their country. While the state representative can decline to answer a particular question, the very fact of the process is a form of accountability to the international community—although a mild one, to be sure, because it is so indirect. Still, over the years the Committee has grown bolder in its questioning.

While it is not clear whether or not this process has had any direct impact on specific human rights conditions, I think it has probably increased the sensitivity of many governments to the need to weigh their present conduct in light of the prospect that they will need to answer for it in this particular forum in addition to other UN forums. Governments now expect criticism here and come prepared to respond to it. In the early years of the Committee, they usually did not come at all, and when they did, it was only to explain the meaning of this or that constitutional or statutory provision.

Once the "hearing" is over, though, nothing much happens. The Committee makes its required public reports, but these have not been in the form of judgments of state practice or specific recommendations for improvement therein. Even the "general comments" that the Committee is invited to make have, on the whole, been politically safe. The state need do nothing, really, until the next report is due, usually in two or three years. The knowledge that there will be a next report and a next hearing probably has a slight moderating effect on some aspects of state conduct, but the nonstate nature of this forum and its very limited powers suggest that such influence is indeed slight.

The Civil and Political Rights Covenant also contains a provision allowing one state party to bring a complaint against another state party for failure to observe the Covenant and for resolution of the complaint by the Committee either directly or through an ad hoc Conciliation Commission.[18] For this provision to be invoked, both states must have made a separate declaration accepting it. That only a third of the states parties have made the declaration and that none has invoked the provision is probably due to the fact that states already have ample opportunity in other UN forums to complain about each other's shortcomings. States do not eagerly or gratuitously invite criticism.[19]

The Convention on the Elimination of All Forms of Racial Discrimination, which was adopted by the General Assembly in 1965 and entered into force in 1969, contains implementation machinery almost identical to that of the Civil and Political Rights Covenant. So do the Convention on the Elimination of Discrimination against Women (entered into force in 1981) and, more recently, the Convention against Torture (entered into force in 1987) and the Convention on the Rights of the Child (entered into force in 1989). By and large, these committees have been able to meet regularly—usually two or three times a year—and, unlike the Committee on Economic, Social and Cultural Rights, they have made only minor complaints about the level of Secretariat support.

But there are important questions about the value of this treaty-based machinery. First and most obviously, the machinery applies only to states parties. For nonparties, these structures may as well not exist.

But could we not say almost the same thing about states parties? After all, they have been willing only to allow a committee of experts, nominated and elected by states parties but thereafter in principle independent of state control, to review and comment publicly on self-serving reports submitted by the states parties themselves on their own laws and practices.

Members of these committees serve in their personal capacity, that is, not as representatives of their states. They are not subject to instruction by their governments or, indeed, by anyone else, including the Secretary-General or their own chair. This is at once a strength and a weakness. The strength is that they are free to be objective and impartial in examining reports and questioning state witnesses. This freedom is qualified somewhat by the fact that they will need their government's support if they wish to be renominated and the support of a majority of states parties to be reelected, but with occasional exceptions the system produces the expected advantages in terms of impartiality.

However, it does so at a price. The treaty committees' mandates are quite limited; for instance, they have no authority to *initiate* investigation of reported violations. They also cannot act in urgent situations, even when emergencies occur while the committee is in session. They have no writ to *solve* problems, except in the narrowly restricted ways described earlier; they cannot perform a ''good offices'' role, nor are they authorized to conduct on-site visits. Their agenda and their reports are linked to the states' own reports, and there is little scope for making specific recommendations to improve state practices. They have direct opportunity to influence state practice only when they are actually examining a state report. Their indirect influence is even less, as their reports are soon lost in the vast ocean of UN documentation, largely unnoticed by press, media, governments, or nongovernmental organizations.

While the effort to depoliticize treatment of human rights issues in these treaties and their implementation machinery has allowed for the consideration of some human rights matters in calm forums in accordance with technical criteria, the structure within which the experts must operate is inherently stifling. Serving in their personal capacity, they have no organizational power behind them—not of any of the United Nations' political bodies and not of the Secretary-General; they speak only in their own name.

They have little ability to follow through on their work; although they can submit written follow-up questions related to the instrument whose implementation they seek to monitor, they have little ability to press governments to reply. Often several months pass before the committee even takes official notice of the fact that no reply has been received. In short, the composition of the committees, the narrow, technical nature of their mandates, their lack of capacity for initiative, and the absence of a meaningful link with a political body deprive them of serious impact.

THE COMMISSION ON HUMAN RIGHTS

The UN Commission on Human Rights comprises states, not individual experts. It is formally subordinate to the Economic and Social Council (ECOSOC) and through it to the General Assembly, but in practice ECOSOC typically transmits Commission reports and recommendations to the Assembly verbatim after formal, but routine, discussion. (This is probably because ECOSOC meets shortly after the annual Commission session, at which member states—many of them also ECOSOC members—have just spent a month and a half thrashing out the issues.) Despite the large, proactive role envisaged for ECOSOC in the Charter, the Commission takes the lead in addressing issues and shaping the substance of UN policy in human rights affairs. The Assembly's Third Committee, on which all UN member states are represented, occasionally initiates action; however, the Assembly usually prefers to have the views of the Commission before proceeding.

Commission member states are elected by ECOSOC for three-year terms on the basis of geographic apportionment, and they may be reelected. ECOSOC members are chosen by the General Assembly according to the same rules. Under the informal "Permanent Members Convention," any of the five permanent members of the Security Council is customarily elected to any UN body on which it wishes to participate, and the United States, U.K., France, and Russia have been members of the Commission and of ECOSOC since the beginning. Mainland China has been an intermittent member since its admission to the United Nations in 1971.[20]

The UN Charter provided for establishment of the Commission[21] and set forth its primary responsibility in broad terms: "[to] make recommendations for the purpose of promoting respect for, and observance of, human rights and fundamental freedoms for all."[22] Given that a fundamental purpose of the United Nations is "to achieve international cooperation in . . . promoting and encouraging respect for human rights and fundamental freedoms for all,"[23] it can be said that the Commission carries out its task in the name of the entire community of member states. In this it differs from treaty-based organs, which do not speak on behalf of the community of states or even of states parties to the particular agreement.[24]

Making recommendations is clearly not the same thing as making decisions, but since the framers had given the General Assembly only recommendatory authority, they obviously could not give more than this to a subordinate body. Does this mean that the Commission is merely a place for government representatives to gather and discuss ideas and suggestions that they might pass along to their superior organizations and then close the conference room doors and turn off the lights until next year's meeting and then repeat the process? To be quite honest, there is a fair amount of this at the annual six-week sessions of the Commission, in which I participated as a delegate for four years (1981–84). But there is a great deal else, much of it considerably more useful.

The Commission's work divides about equally among three categories: (1) political warfare—bilateral conflicts replayed in a multilateral setting; (2) standard-setting—that is, formulating new international declarations and conventions; and (3) efforts to improve and strengthen implementation procedures and institutions. I argue that the Commission has done effective work in the second and third categories. It has also reacted to crises that have arisen just before or during one of its annual sessions, usually by adopting a resolution or sending a telegram.

In the first category, it is important to bear in mind that a Commission session is an annual meeting of representatives of sovereign states whose first duty, as they see it, is to protect their own government from censure by fellow sovereigns. Each state delegate[25] enters the hall wearing a figurative suit of armor, knowing that a time of peril and challenge lies ahead. For delegates, the psychological atmosphere is one of being on guard, of being ready for defense against criticism from any quarter, of building alliances or at least temporary coalitions for mutual defense, and of readying counteroffensive measures. The nightly cocktail receptions, hosted, in turn, by different delegations, take some of the edge off this warlike atmosphere, but they do not change the conflictive character of this part of the Commission's work.

Whenever one member of a pair of currently contending states criticizes human rights abuse by another, the reaction is almost invariably along these lines: "The charge just made is unfounded, worse, it is made not for the sake of human rights but in order to defame and undermine my government; it amounts to an unwarranted interference in our internal affairs and thus threatens our independence; the attacking government merely wishes to further its own selfish interests at the expense of my country and my people; and besides, the attacker's hypocrisy is unmasked by its own execrable behavior, which I will now recount.''

In the next scene, the attacker, having become the attacked, assumes a defensive posture and launches a counterattack. Verbal arrows and spears fly through the room, bouncing off the delegates' armor and into the summary records. Delegations demand and receive ample time to reply, filling the air with more arrows, more spears. Each acts as if its statehood is at stake.

I do not think one can expect states to behave otherwise in the face of public attack by a peer. To be an independent polity in an anarchic world of polities is to be in a competitive and therefore vulnerable situation. In a world of shifting power distribution, a state that is attacked publicly by another tends to think and react in a highly defensive mode.

Paradoxically, the public that is thought to be watching this political warfare is often bored with it, insofar as it amounts to an annual reenactment of well-known rivalries—rivalries that are played out in other UN forums as well. For example, for decades the first week of each annual session of the Commission was devoted to condemning Israel and the second week to condemning South Africa, through speeches and resolutions that varied by, at most, a few words from year to year. Most delegations used these first two weeks for corridor lobbying to promote what they regarded as more important goals under agenda items that would be dealt with later in the session. Given the Israel–Palestine Liberation Organization (PLO) accords and the successful transition to multiracial, multiparty democracy in South Africa, delegates have an opportunity to make more productive use of these early weeks. The reenactment of other long-running disputes and debating the usual resolutions on them typically occupy the stage for another week.

There is also about a week of confidential sessions, from which the press and public, including nongovernmental organizations, are barred.[26] Here also, governments are "charged" with various offenses against human rights and given an opportunity to defend themselves; in this case the charges have a certain weight and credibility because they reach the Commission through a careful screening process by a subcommission of independent human rights experts.[27] Governments charged with abuse defend themselves vigorously, although the tone is less histrionic and more businesslike. For those in the dock, the aim is to have one's country's case dropped or, at worst, merely "kept under review" and not made the subject of an in-depth investigation by a special rapporteur[28] or similar mechanism, even under these closed-door rules.

In the second area, standard-setting, the Commission has managed to produce an impressive number of international human rights instruments. Since the early 1980s, these include the Convention against Torture, the Convention on the Rights of the Child, the Declaration on the Right to Development, and the Declaration on the Rights of Minorities.

A *declaration* is a statement of the considered position of the international community on a subject; it represents a political commitment to respect the principles enshrined in the document and to live up to the general norms of conduct spelled out therein. It is an agreement on what is right and a general commitment to do one's best to do what is right.[29] A *convention* is a legally binding document spelling out precise legal rights and obligations and rules and procedures for implementing them. As pointed out earlier, conventions bind only states that become parties to them through formal accession procedures.

While the standard-setting aspect of the Commission's work has drawn little criticism on substantive grounds from scholars, governments, nongovernmental organizations, or the general public, there is a widely supported view, with which I concur, that sufficient standards now exist in either declaratory (political) or binding (legal) form. The real issue is whether or not time and energy spent on elaborating new documents could be better spent on implementation of already agreed upon standards, on improving methods of implementation, and on dealing with actual violations.[30]

THEMATIC AND COUNTRY-SPECIFIC IMPLEMENTATION MECHANISMS

In the third area of the Commission's work, the search for better tools and methods of implementation, the Commission has ventured cautiously into new experiments since the mid-1970s. Two of these—thematic and country-specific rapporteurs, representatives, and working groups—are discussed later and in the case studies in the following chapters. Both differ in fundamental respects from the treaty-based expert committees.[31]

The Commission has moved rather cautiously in strengthening implementation mechanisms because, as a body of governmental representatives concerned, first of all, to get through each session unscathed and, second, to scathe bilateral opponents if at all possible, it is naturally reluctant to give responsibility to a third party to do some of the scathing in the future. A government can feel it is in control of the situation to some extent if implementation means only a shouting match between peers; one can always shout back. There is a kind of "mutual assured damage." But setting up a new authority, even one limited to a specific theme or geographic area, means new risks, since it is never clear at the outset how and to what extent one's own state will be able to control the new entity or to deal with its impact. Learning how to cope with the new agency will require time, energy, and trial and error. It is safer and easier to go on with old ways, unproductive as they may be.

Still, the Commission concluded that limited mandates can be written for particular implementation mechanisms without jeopardizing the bases of state sovereignty. It was easiest to do this regarding states that had become pariahs for geopolitical and human rights reasons. Thus, the earliest special procedures concerned South Africa, Israel, and Pinochet's Chile. As the goal of the chief sponsors of the resolutions was to discredit and weaken the governments concerned, the new mechanisms were created for the purpose of serving as political hammers.

Because the earliest country-specific procedures were so clearly political, it was almost inevitable that subsequent efforts to create such mechanisms would be viewed as attempts to dump additional states into the pariah category so as to produce or intensify their political isolation.

A "thematic" mechanism, on the other hand, is based on a very different premise, despite the fact that the two procedures have some similarities in their modes of operation; for example, in both cases the rapporteur, special representative, working group, or other agent makes a formal oral and written report to the Commission. The premise of a thematic institution is that the international community of states, acting in a legislative capacity through the Commission establishes a mechanism to oversee, on behalf of the whole community, the observance by all states of a single right. The mechanism is intended to promote such observance by all states equally, in view of their universal obligation, and by measures employed impartially. It is, in short, an agent of the community to act on behalf of the whole community for a specified purpose on a global basis.

A thematic rapporteur is typically authorized to act on his or her own initiative to address individual complaints, to investigate situations of widespread abuse, to undertake confidential contacts with the government concerned both to acquire information and to try to ameliorate abuses, and to exercise judgment about how to deal with specific countries by name in his or her annual public report to the Commission (and through the Commission to ECOSOC and the General Assembly). No country finds itself *singled out* for criticism in a thematic procedure. Government efforts to cooperate with the rapporteur and to improve respect for human rights can be noted in the public report, along with the lack thereof where this is the case. Recommendations for remedial action are usually included, as are recommendations for positive UN assistance measures, for example advisory services, training, and technical assistance. The public report of a thematic mechanism identifies specific violations, but the transgressions of any single government do not stand out so egregiously. A government that cooperates and takes steps to investigate and correct abuses can expect to find these positive measures fully recognized in the report. The rapporteur has discretion as to whether to report violations in detail, even lurid detail, or to describe them in more general terms. When a rapporteur is convinced that something may be gained for the sake of the rights of the people concerned by employing a restrained vocabulary, he or she may well choose that course. When convinced of the opposite, more vivid imagery and the naming of names may be the preferred option. This applies to both types—country-specific and thematic— but it is obviously easier to convey subtle, but important, distinctions among violations of a particular right when a wide range of countries is being written about.

A thematic or country-specific rapporteur knows that his or her task will not be accomplished simply by the publication of a single report. Follow-up action is needed, including attention to recommendations. An extension of the mandate will be sought, at least for a second year. Some cooperation by governments subject to inquiry is important; for instance, a rapporteur who wants to visit a country for fact-finding and to play a good-offices role must have a visa. All of these factors argue for caution in the first public report. An overly cautious or general report, on the other hand, will be widely denounced as dishonest and less than useful.[32]

Perhaps the principal structural advantage of the thematic approach is that it combines the objectivity of focusing on a single type of violation on a global basis with the capability of addressing actual, concrete violations, experienced by real people. At the same time, it appears to avoid many of the disadvantages of the highly politicized country-specific approach. We would therefore expect to find that it contributes more to actual improvements in human rights practice and, at the same time, to the enhanced credibility and acceptance of UN human rights institutions. As we shall see in the following chapters, some of these expectations are fulfilled, and others are not. Sometimes country-specific procedures seem to have more impact. The case studies and concluding analysis seek to identify more precisely the factors and circumstances that contribute to the effectiveness of the two types of Charter-based implementation mechanisms.[33]

THE ROLE OF THE UN CENTER FOR HUMAN RIGHTS

A great deal of information comes to the UN Center for Human Rights—the branch of the Secretariat that supports all UN human rights activities—from nongovernmental organizations, individuals, the press, other intergovernmental organizations, and states. While Commission rapporteurs/representatives/working groups are authorized actively *to seek* information, not merely to react to reports that reach them, they have other jobs and do not work full-time on UN projects; as a rule, the United Nations budgets for one to three fact-finding trips a year for each rapporteur and two short visits to Geneva to review and approve preliminary and final versions of the report. Some rapporteurs carry out their mandates with great vigor—examples include Reinaldo Galindo Pohl (El Salvador), the second rapporteur on Iran, and Rajsoomar Lallah, the second rapporteur on Chile. Viscount Colville (U.K.) was an active and effective chairman of the Working Group on Disappeared Persons, whose charter membership included such outstanding figures as Jonas Foli (Ghana). Some other rapporteurs, however, do little except put their names to what the Center has written.

A great deal of the work of a rapporteur actually falls on the Center—mainly on the particular staff member assigned to the project. The professional staff of the Center in Geneva consists of about 70 international civil servants, career members of the UN Secretariat, drawn from all regions of the world. (Since the opening of field missions in 1994, the number of temporary staff stationed in various countries has risen into the hundreds.) Although the hiring principle of equitable geographic distribution applies to the Secretariat as a whole and not to each of its units separately, as a matter of administrative policy an effort is made to achieve balance among the nationalities of permanent members of the staff. Until 1994 the Directors of the Center were Westerners (though never an American), with the Deputy Director usually an African, and other senior posts distributed among other regions. Since 1994 the High Commissioner for Human Rights, has been in charge of the center. His deputy has the rank of Assistant Secretary-General. The professional staff is well educated; most hold advanced degrees, including some doctorates, and several are lawyers.

Many preliminary decisions are made by the professional staff—concerning, for instance, what information is to be accepted as credible and what is to be disregarded, what requires corroboration and what does not, how and from whom to seek such corroboration, which governments and other actors should be contacted and by what means (telephone, cable, fax, conversation with resident diplomatic representative, etc.), which countries should be visited, and the actual content of the report—including how much detail to include and how much to leave in the filing cabinet. The staff also plans the rapporteur's travel and sends one or more people to accompany and assist him or her. All of this is subject to review and approval by the rapporteur, but, as I have noted, some of these are more industrious than others.

The Center for Human Rights, then, has scope to shape the way Commission decisions are implemented. Because the Center is part of the Secretariat and under the authority of the High Commissioner, it is generally regarded as impartial in its operating methods. The fact that professional staff are, at least in theory, appointed on the basis of merit as well as with due regard to geographic distribution [34] strengthens the appearance of impartiality, but it is unrealistic to expect perfect objectivity in a human being, who is, after all, shaped in important ways by the particular culture in which he or she grew to adulthood. On the whole, however, I found over the years that the prevailing practice is faithful to the idea, expressed in Article 100 of the Charter, that in the performance of their duties the staff are "international officials responsible only to the Organization."[35]

The following paragraph of Article 100, however, is observed less strictly: "Each Member of the United Nations undertakes to respect the exclusively international character of the responsibilities of the Secretary-General and the staff and not to seek to influence them in the discharge of their responsibilities."[36] In fact, governments lobby the Secretariat every day. When a government is concerned about whether and how it might appear in a public report, it will seek opportunities to tell its side of the story to the Secretariat. Whether one calls this cooperating with the Commission by providing information and documentation and facilitating contacts between the government and the rapporteur, or "seek[ing] to influence" the Center is difficult to determine—probably it is both—but this nevertheless draws states into the implementation process; it thereby upholds the Commission's authority and can contribute to improved human rights observance.

REVIEW

I conclude that treaty-based committees are, on the whole, ineffective in bringing about actual improvements in human rights practices because of their compostition, the narrowness of their mandates, their lack of capacity for initiative, and the absence of a meaningful link with a political body. They are simply not in a position to bring steady pressure to bear on governments. Charter-based institutions—specifically, the Human Rights Commission and its designated thematic and country-specific agents—represent the community of states in politically meaningful ways and are closely linked with intergovernmental bodies in which significant political influence can be brought to bear.

In Argentina, Chile, and Iran (Chapters 4, 6, and 7, respectively), a government has engaged in a policy of systematic human rights abuse over a period of several years. The severity and extent of these abuses aroused sharp criticism within international forums and led to organized efforts by the United Nations and other international organizations to press these governments to halt violations. The abuses also stimulated bilateral criticism and pressure, as well as various patterns of domestic unrest in the three countries.

As will be seen, at first each government firmly rejected external criticism and appeals and maintained its repressive policies. Later, for at least a time, the government reduced the number of violations and cooperated with UN human rights agents. UN action played a role in influencing this changed pattern of governmental behavior. Together with other internal and external factors it contributed to raising the cost to the government of *not* reducing human rights abuses and *not* cooperating with international human rights machinery. The following chapters seek to identify specific factors in country-specific and thematic mechanisms that contribute to, or detract from, their effectiveness.

NOTES

1. Message to Congress of January 6, 1941.

2. Quoted in A. H. Robertson and J. G. Merrills, *Human Rights in the World* (Manchester: Manchester University Press, 1989), 26.

3. Quoted in David Forsythe, *Human Rights and World Politics*, 2d ed. (Lincoln: University of Nebraska Press, 1989), 30. The same author's *Human Rights and Peace* (Lincoln: University of Nebraska Press, 1993) is a detailed analysis of recent developments in the complex relationships between the promotion of rights and peace.

4. For a brief review of this process, see, for instance, Tom J. Farer, "The UN and Human Rights: More than a Whimper, Less than a Roar," in A. Roberts and B. Kingsbury, eds., *United Nations, Divided World* (New York: Oxford University Press, 1988), 99–102.

5. Cathal J. Nolan, *Principled Diplomacy* (Westport, CT: Greenwood Press, 1993), Ch. 7.

6. Jan Herman Burgers, "The Road to San Francisco: The Revival of the Human Rights Idea in the 20th Century," *Human Rights Quarterly* 14(4) (1992), 447–77.

7. Before 1991, the Security Council did use its authority under the Charter to impose mandatory economic sanctions and arms embargoes on two countries—Rhodesia and South Africa—whose domestic human rights practices (official racial discrimination) amounted, in the Council's view, to a threat to international peace and security. The choice of these two cases, among so many situations of severe and massive official abuse in the world, is attributable, in part, to the perceived link between them and the powerful movement toward self-determination. For many newly independent member states of the United Nations, the efforts by ruling elites to preserve white minority rule in these countries may have seemed to threaten international peace. Whether such a threat existed or not, the Council chose to interpret the cases that way. In 1991, the Council broke new ground by establishing a safe zone within the territory of Iraq to protect Kurds fleeing the wrath of Saddam Hussein; for the first time, the Council authorized military forces to take control of part of the territory of a member state, specifically for human rights reasons.

8. The text of the Nuremberg Principles can be found in Richard Falk, Samuel Kim, and Saul Mendlovitz, eds., *The United Nations and a Just World Order* (Boulder, CO: Westview Press, 1991), 220–21.

9. The International Tribunal for the Prosecution of Persons Responsible for Serious Violations of International Humanitarian Law Committed in the Territory of the Former Yugoslavia was established by the Security Council in Resolution 827, acting under Chapter VII of the Charter. The Tribunal met for the first time in November 1993 to elect its officers (Antonio Cassese of Italy, president) and to begin work on its rules of procedure and evidence. A chief prosecutor, Richard Goldstone of South Africa, was named in July 1994. The first indictments were returned later that year. Fifty-three indictments had been issued by April 1996. The first trial, of Bosnian Serb Dusan Tadic, began in May 1996 at The Hague.

10. A small human rights unit, the Office of Democratic Institutions and Human Rights, functions within the framework of the Organization (formerly, Conference) on Security and Cooperation in Europe. The Organization also has a High Commissioner for Minorities. Jack Donnelly, *International Human Rights* (Boulder, CO: Westview Press, 1993) has a good, brief summary of regional human rights organizations at 82–98. For a more in-depth look at the inter-American system, see David P. Forsythe, *The Internationalization of Human Rights* (Lexington, MA: Lexington Books, 1991), Ch. 4.

11. Many respected international legal scholars, including Louis Henkin, Theodor Meron, Louis Sohn, and Tom Farer, have argued persuasively that the Universal Declaration has acquired the status of customary law through its incorporation by reference in international conventions, national statutes, and other instruments and through state practice. See, for instance, Louis Henkin, *The Age of Rights* (New York: Columbia University Press, 1990), esp. 18–21, and Theodor Meron (also citing Sohn), *Human Rights and Humanitarian Norms as Customary Law* (New York: Oxford University Press, 1989), 82–84.

12. As of March 1996 the Covenant on Civil and Political Rights had 132 parties, and the Covenant on Economic, Social and Cultural Rights had 132. The Optional Pro-

tocol to the Civil and Political Covenant had 87. (UN Document E/CN.4/1996/103.) There were over 185 member states of the United Nations.

13. Article 16, para. 1, Covenant on Economic, Social and Cultural Rights.

14. Covenant on Economic, Social and Cultural Rights, Articles 16 through 22.

15. Philip Alston, "The Importance of the Interplay between Economic, Social and Cultural Rights and Civil and Political Rights," in *Human Rights at the Dawn of the 21st Century* (hereafter *HR/COE*), report of an interregional meeting organized by the Council of Europe (A/CONF.157/PC/66/Add. 1), 34.

16. Covenant on Civil and Political Rights, Articles 28 and 31.

17. Ibid., Article 40.

18. Ibid., Articles 41 and 42.

19. The Covenant on Civil and Poliltical Rights also has two optional protocols. The first establishes a procedure for handling individual complaints. Under this procedure, complainants must first exhaust all available domestic remedies. Then the Committee must determine whether or not the complaint meets its criteria for admissibility. After that, the state accused of the violation has six months in which to provide the Committee "written explanations or statements clarifying the matter and the remedy, if any, that may have been taken by that state." This is hardly an urgent-action mechanism, which is probably why few victims seek relief through it. The second protocol abolishes the death penalty in states that accede to it, and it gives individuals the right to bring their cases to the attention of the Human Rights Committee if their states have also acceded to the first protocol.

20. The Permanent Members Convention also provides that the other four permanent members will vote for the candidacy of any of the five seeking election.

21. UN Charter, Article 68: "The Economic and Social Council shall set up commissions in economic and social fields and for the promotion of human rights."

22. UN Charter, Article 62, para. 2.

23. UN Charter, Article 1, para. 3.

24. In a weak sense, a treaty body does represent states parties, since it can be said to represent the agreement itself and thus the will of states parties that the agreement be carried out through the action of the treaty body. However, the fact that members of treaty-based organs serve in their personal capacity means that they cannot in any direct sense represent anyone but themselves.

25. This includes observer states as well as Commission members. The former have the right to speak and to cosponsor resolutions (if at least one member state is a sponsor), but they cannot vote. Nongovernmental organizations in consultative status with ECOSOC are entitled to attend all public meetings and to speak, but not to vote or cosponsor resolutions.

26. These are the "1503 Procedures," so named because they are spelled out in ECOSOC Resolution 1503 (of 1970), which set up a two-tier system to screen and evaluate the thousands of human rights complaints submitted to the United Nations annually. The resolution directs the Commission and its Subcommission to focus on abuses that constitute "a consistent pattern of gross violations of internationally-recognized human rights." In a sense, we can speak of a four-tier system, since both the Subcommission and the Commission have working groups that screen the documentation for them.

27. The Subcommission on Prevention of Discrimination and Protection of Minorities consists of 26 experts on human rights from all regions of the world. Historically, most

of these have been genuinely independent—as their charter provides—while some have been de facto representatives of their governments.

28. The functions of Commission special rapporteurs, special representatives, and working groups are described later in this chapter.

29. As noted earlier in connection with the Universal Declaration, some authorities hold that declarations can mature into customary law. See, for instance, Louis Henkin, "Introduction," *The International Bill of Rights* (New York: Columbia University Press, 1981), 8.

30. There is, however, a movement in favor of devoting effort to preparing declarations and, subsequently, conventions on such rights as a right to peace, a right to a clean environment, and certain other desirable international goals. Critics usually say that the main difficulty with such exercises is that it is next to impossible to identify the subject of the legal obligations to be imposed by such agreements.

31. Also, the good offices role of the secretary-general, about which I have said little because little is known publicly about it, qualifies as a multilateral human rights "procedure." B. G. Ramcharan, *Humanitarian Good Offices in International Law* (Boston: Nijhoff, 1983) is the best-informed treatment of the subject.

32. I use the term "public report" to refer to the written and oral accounts presented by the rapporteur in public session of the Commission, including any responses made to questions or comments. As reports submitted to the Commission under the 1503 procedures are confidential, the issue of specificity is not as significant.

33. For a thoughtful summary treatment of the meaning of "effectiveness" as applied to UN institutions, see Forsythe, *The Internationalization*, 76–78. Forsythe emphasizes the long-term nature of UN efforts to promote and implement human rights standards:

The sum total of UN activity is supposed to socialize or educate actors into changing their views over time toward a . . . universal human rights standard. . . . Or, the sum total of UN activity is to dispose or withhold a stamp of legitimacy on member states according to their human rights record. (77)

He cites several examples in which a ruling regime "lost its legitimacy in the eyes of important actors to considerable degree because of human rights violations" (78), a theme he reiterates in *Human Rights and Peace*, 72–73. I think this is correct as far as it goes, although I believe Forsythe undervalues the impact of UN human rights institutions in the shorter run. The case studies in the present book offer evidence in support of a view that some UN agents have had greater short-term impact. Jack Donnelly, in his *International Human Rights*, also takes a long and decidedly modest view:

The pattern is one of modest incremental change. . . . Lives are being saved in ways that just a few years ago would not have seemed possible. . . . [but] I see no evidence to suggest that the international community is willing to undertake major new initiatives to deal with direct violations . . . by governments. (141, 145)

I find this overly cautious; I address these points more directly in Chapter 8.

34. UN Charter, Article 101, para. 3.

35. UN Charter, Article 100, para. 1.

36. Charter, Article 100, para. 2.

4

The Working Group on Enforced
Disappearances

INTRODUCTION

This and the following chapter explore how an international institution can contribute to the protection of the right to life and the right to religious liberty,
respectively, when these rights are violated by a state through enforced disappearance and religious discrimination. The international community has created
a thematic mechanism to address each of these problems.[1] How well have they
functioned? What about them contributes to, or weakens, their impact?

As the problem of disappearances affected Argentina more than other countries in the late 1970s and early 1980s, the present chapter devotes particular
attention to the ways in which the United Nations sought to deal with the issue
in that country.

It first provides background for the discussion by surveying internal political
developments in Argentina, including the role of political parties, churches, and
the press, with some attention also to domestic economic developments that
might have had a bearing on government policy making. I also examine in some
depth the impact of external factors—bilateral and multilateral, intergovernmental and nongovernmental—on the evolving situation in Argentina.

Direct evidence of UN influence on government policy making is difficult to
obtain, for the same reason that applies to all external factors, namely, that
governments do not customarily acknowledge that a change in policy is due to
external pressure, especially not to a specific source of that pressure. It is rare
to find an admission by an official that foreign pressure from a particular source
was a driving force in a particular decision. Moreover, policymakers try to weigh
the total policy environment in making decisions, and usually multiple forms of
internal and external pressure are operating simultaneously. An observer can

look for signs that one factor probably played a greater role than another, but the empirical evidence for such a conclusion is not extensive. In addition, the Argentine press and media were subject to significant governmental intimidation and control, and there was no parliament, thereby limiting the amount of information in the public domain. However, I argue that one can reasonably conclude from the available evidence that sustained pressure exercised through institutions of the organized international community, including UN institutions, loomed sufficiently large in the policy environment with which the government was concerned that it was accorded weight in policy making. I find the same result in the cases dealing with the country-specific mechanisms established for Chile and Iran.

DISAPPEARANCES: EARLY BACKGROUND

Enforced disappearance as a tool of state policy, of course, existed well before the United Nations took official cognizance of the problem in 1978.[2] The Soviet state caused the disappearance of millions of people, particularly under Stalin, and its satellite regimes also engaged in the nighttime knock on the door to send their opponents to oblivion. But the geopolitical realities of the Cold War prevented UN action on Soviet or satellite conduct. Although the Geneva Conventions of 1949 prohibited clandestine detention, mistreatment, and killing during wartime, they did not cover such abuses during peacetime, nor did they address violations of human rights by a state against its own citizens and residents.

In the 1970s in certain Western countries there was growing awareness among governments, parliaments, the press, nongovernmental organizations, and the general public of horrifying human rights abuses by governments of countries counted as members of the Free World. These abuses included enforced disappearance, which is, in fact, a multiple human rights violation: abduction and clandestine detention by official forces mean not only arbitrary deprivation of liberty but also denial of judicial due process and of access to family and counsel; in Argentina, Chile, and some other countries, it usually also meant torture and arbitrary and summary execution.

DISAPPEARANCES, ARGENTINA, AND THE UNITED NATIONS: EARLY STAGES

In an earlier contribution to the literature on human rights, I assessed the effectiveness of the U.S. Government response to the issue of disappearances and other grievous abuses in Argentina. In that essay I emphasized that a combined bilateral-multilateral effort made more sense from many standpoints and in the end was more effective than bilateral efforts alone. I will return to this point, which I continue to believe is valid.[3]

In their excellent essay on the development of the UN role concerning disappearances, Daniel Livermore and B. G. (Bertram) Ramcharan pointed out that the Argentine junta in the mid-1970s expanded and systematized the practice of enforced disappearance that had been employed by the Pinochet regime in Chile a few years earlier following his seizure of power in 1973.[4] Pinochet's excesses, which included from 600 to 1,000 well-documented cases of enforced disappearance during the period 1973–78, brought condemnation by the General Assembly in 1974 and the subsequent establishment by the Human Rights Commission of a country-specific working group to investigate this and other abuses.[5] (Chapter 6 considers the ad hoc Working Group on Chile and its successor, the Special Rapporteur on Chile.)

The Argentine military regime committed about 9,000 confirmed disappearances between 1976 and 1980.[6] Thanks to work by Argentine human rights activists—especially the Permanent Assembly for Human Rights and the Mothers of the Plaza de Mayo[7]—by Amnesty International and other international nongovernmental organizations, and by some governments—notably the United Kingdom, Canada, the United States, and France—the story reached the UN General Assembly in 1978. By this time there were also credible reports of disappearances in countries other than Argentina and Chile.

By adopting Resolution 33/173 (1978), formally identifying the practice of enforced disappearance as a major human rights violation and calling for states and intergovernmental organizations to take measures to halt the practice, the General Assembly set the stage for the implementation machinery established in 1980 that has functioned ever since. But the 1978 resolution itself set up no machinery, and this omission led to a protracted battle by the Argentine Government to fend off any meaningful UN intercession.[8]

Joseph Tulchin argues that Argentine foreign policy must be understood as being driven fundamentally by a century-long drive for prestige and a major voice in world and hemispheric affairs. For most of this period, Argentina's ambitions have been frustrated by internal political and economic turmoil and by incoherence and instability in its approach to the international scene. Still, Tulchin says, each Argentine government pursues the vision with renewed vigor. When the outside world fails to take Argentina seriously or criticizes its conduct and urges a change therein, Argentina's leaders of the day become frustrated, angry, and resentful. When they are in this frame of mind, they firmly resist all criticism and refuse to change their behavior. This explains, he says, why the military junta reacted so angrily to the Carter administration pressure on human rights abuses, which he compares with the campaign by Secretary of State Hull and Ambassador Spruille Braden to get Argentina to join World War II against the Axis. (Argentina ultimately declared war two months before Germany surrendered.)[9]

The wartime episode left a sour aftertaste.[10] Peron won the first postwar election, but Tulchin says that ''the persecution of Argentina by the United States'' left a ''bitter legacy'' in bilateral relations.[11]

Tulchin writes of the junta that seized power in 1976, ''Like so many of its predecessors, civilian and military, [it] was obsessed with international prestige.''[12] The new military government also pursued economic policies designed to build up hard-currency reserves and reinsert the economy into the international market. At the same time, it was dedicated to a doctrine of the national security state that led it to wage a campaign of "total extirpation of subversive elements from the body politic by whatever means necessary."[13]

Tulchin is probably right that a desire for international acceptance and respect underlay many Argentine foreign policy attitudes and actions during the period of military rule from 1976 to 1982. This desire also helps to explain Argentina's sustained efforts to escape UN scrutiny for its human rights abuses.

Between autumn 1978 and February 1980, the Argentine Government fought to ensure that any UN activity concerning disappearances would take place under the existing confidential procedure, known as "1503" from the number of the Economic and Social Council (ECOSOC) resolution that established it in 1970.[14] ECOSOC resolution 1503 provided a method within the United Nations for examining reports of "consistent patterns of reliably attested gross violations of human rights"; before then, the United Nations had no procedure for handling such material. Under 1503, a five-member working group of the expert-level Subcommission, then the full Subcommission, then a working group of the Human Rights Commission, and finally the full Commission examine reports of violations. But a case may be dropped at any stage by the body reviewing it.

The strength of the 1503 procedure is that it at least provides a forum in which states can be held to a limited sort of accountability by and to their peers. Its principal weakness is that this calling to account and, indeed, all of the steps that lead to this stage have to take place under conditions of strict confidentiality. States members of the Commission learn of complaints against themselves and have a chance to respond, but the complainants—usually the victims of alleged abuse or nongovernmental human rights organizations—never see the government response, nor do they know the ultimate disposition of the complaint. Only the other member states of the Commission learn of a complaint if and when the Subcommission decides to forward it to the Commission.[15]

Moreover, as noted, there are ample possibilities along this four-stage gauntlet for a case to be dropped. Such a gauntlet means that few complaints have much chance of being considered by the full membership of the Commission. Even if they reach this stage, nothing happens beyond a decision to conduct a "thorough study" or "investigation" of the situation or merely to keep the matter "under review," that is, on the agenda for discussion next year—again, with no public knowledge of what is going on or of the results of such study, and so on. The original idea behind this confidentiality was that governments could be expected to cooperate with the Commission only if their dignity as sovereign states was never in the slightest questioned in public. Sins were not to be subject to public scrutiny.

As a matter of fact, extensive documentation on disappearances in Argentina was submitted to the Subcommission under the 1503 rules, and in 1979 that body forwarded this material to the Commission for consideration at its 1980 session. The Argentine military regime had submitted confidential replies to the accusations against it in an effort to ensure that its case would remain under the cloak of confidentiality. Argentine representatives argued that a case could be considered by UN institutions under only one procedure and that Argentina's cooperation under the 1503 system exempted it from being considered in any other UN forum.[16] Chile had earlier attempted to "forum-shop" on human rights issues by claiming that its submission of a report to the expert-level Human Rights Committee of the Covenant on Civil and Political Rights exempted it from having to answer to any other UN body.[17] Chile's claim was rejected by the Commission; so, eventually, was Argentina's.

ARGENTINA'S INTERNATIONAL IMAGE

As I have noted, Argentina was deeply concerned about its international image. The junta said it had undertaken its war against subversion in order to save Western civilization from the international Communist conspiracy. It did not want to be seen as undermining such important foundations of Western civilization as justice and respect for human dignity or to be thought of as a barbaric band of inhumane gangsters. Indeed, a panel of senior Navy officers emphasized precisely that sentiment to me during my visit to Buenos Aires in April 1979.

Joseph Tulchin says:

[B]y 1979 the refutation and rejection of the international "campaign" against Argentina had become an obsessive issue in foreign policy and had spilled over into areas of economic and political policy. The issue of human rights had assumed significant proportions by 1978. The accusation touched the very heart of the military's sense of its mission *and threatened its long-term objectives* (emphasis added).[18]

Tulchin outlines the junta's public relations efforts to protect their image. In 1978, the government-controlled press ran a postcard campaign in an Argentine magazine designed to influence U.S., UN, and Amnesty International officials, and the following year the junta hired a U.S. public relations firm, launched a monthly bulletin from their embassy, and established strong ties to certain influential conservatives in Washington. The next year they hired a private publishing firm to distribute printed materials and to conduct American–Argentine seminars on public policy.[19]

The junta wanted very much to gain international support or at least sympathy for their struggle against Montonero and Trotskyite (People's Revolutionary Army) guerrilla terrorists. They portrayed the country as having been on the verge of political and economic chaos when they seized power in March 1976, and they offered abundant evidence for this contention. Along with most other observers, I agree that the terrorist problem was of massive proportions and that the government of Isabel de Peron seemed unable to deal effectively with it.[20]

But the regime erred in assuming that there was a consensus within Western

civilization that terrorism had to be fought by any means whatsoever; Jacobo
Timerman has tried to understand the junta's worldview on this matter as comprising, first, a conviction that Argentina was on the front line of a third world
war already under way in which the contest was not between Communism and
democracy but between left-wing terrorism and the entire world. Second, says
Timerman, this meant that Argentina could maintain good diplomatic and trade
relations with the USSR. But, third, "Argentina is alone and misunderstood by
those who ought to be her natural allies, the Western democracies. Hence [in-
ferred the regime], the unleashing of the anti-Argentine campaign" by certain
democracies and the Vatican.[21] Timerman is, of course, a prominent victim of
the junta's antisubversion campaign. His analysis here, however, is not at all
distorted by his personal experiences; indeed, it conforms with the public record
and with my own observations during the time I shared responsibility for U.S.
human rights policy toward South America.

Once the junta had decided they were at war, but a war without the usual
features of uniformed combatants and defined battlefields, they decided that the
agreed-upon ethical rules governing armed conflict—the Geneva Conventions—
did not apply. The cleansing of society and the security of the state were the
only goals, and the methods could therefore be as ruthless as those used by the
terrorists. Indeed, they had to be, in the junta's view, because otherwise the war
could not be won. The end justified the means. As Tulchin, Alison Brysk, and
others point out, the regime found it hard to understand why Western countries
did not appreciate this line of thought. In a comment related to the decision to
invade the Falklands/Malvinas Islands but applicable more generally, Tulchin
wrote that "the Argentine leaders lived in a world of dreams created in the
course of a century of distorted perceptions of the world and of a tradition of
acting without taking account of the possible consequences of their actions."[22]

DISAPPEARANCES, ARGENTINA, AND THE UNITED
NATIONS: PHASE TWO

By 1979, the phenomenon of enforced disappearances, involving as it did the
presumption that lives were being destroyed arbitrarily on a large scale by the
Argentine authorities, had become so widely known that a strong feeling began
to develop among member states of the Human Rights Commission that the
junta must no longer be allowed to hide behind the cloak of confidential procedures. Moreover, the remoteness of Argentina from the U.S.–Soviet front line
created favorable conditions for activist pro-human rights states on the Commission—the Western group plus important African states, such as Senegal and
Ghana, and traditional Latin American leaders such as Costa Rica—to break
new ground in shaping human rights machinery. Although it proved impossible
to establish a mechanism on disappearances at the 1979 session, later that year
the Economic and Social Council and the General Assembly urged the Com-

mission to take definitive action at its next annual meeting in February–March 1980.

Argentina was at the time a member of the Commission. In order to achieve consensus adoption of a resolution at the 1980 session, the group of human rights activist states first introduced a separate resolution specifically on disappearances in Argentina and Chile, mentioning both countries by name. By no means was Argentina willing to be lumped together with Chile. The two countries had nearly gone to war over the Beagle Channel a little over a year earlier. Chile had long since acquired pariah status at the United Nations and could not have successfully resisted the new draft resolution. Argentina, on the other hand, although actually a worse human rights offender, had thus far escaped any special public attention from UN human rights organs. This was due, in part, to the greater skill of its diplomats[23] (Pinochet had heavily militarized Chile's diplomatic service) and because the Soviet Union and its allies had not targeted Argentina as they had Chile. (The Soviet angle is discussed later.)

The United States and several other influential countries indicated that we would support the country-specific resolution, even though we preferred a universal, thematic approach. At the time I was in temporary charge of Commission matters in the Department of State's Bureau of Human Rights and Humanitarian Affairs and led a successful fight within the Department rapidly to clear an instruction to support the draft resolution, in order to arm our Geneva delegation with a valuable negotiating tool. When it became clear that such a resolution would pass if put to a vote, Argentina agreed to consensus adoption of a universal mechanism—the Working Group on Enforced Disappearances—in return for withdrawal of the other proposal.

DISAPPEARANCES, ARGENTINA, AND THE UNITED NATIONS: PHASE THREE

Argentina thought it might be able in 1981 to reverse the 1980 decision to set up the new working group, because of the change in U.S. presidential administrations. Ronald Reagan had criticized Jimmy Carter's human rights policies during the campaign, and one of his first acts was to appoint Jeane Kirkpatrick Ambassador to the United Nations. Ambassador Kirkpatrick had made no secret of her belief that the Carter administration had been too hard on Argentina, Chile, and other authoritarian states.[24]

At the 1981 session of the Human Rights Commission, Argentine Ambassador Gabriel Martinez took the floor for an hour and a half in an attempt to deny that his government practiced enforced disappearance. Instead, he asserted, many reported disappearances were actually cases of death in armed combat with security forces, execution by fellow terrorists, desertion, travel abroad, or simply a "descent into clandestinity." While he nevertheless acknowledged during his remarks that some disappearances were caused by "official excesses," he emphasized repeatedly that Argentina would provide individual case information to the Commission only under the 1503 rules concerning admissibility and confidentiality.[25] Lord Colville, the working group chairman, told the Western delegation caucus that adoption of 1503 rules would completely change the character of the working group and its operations.[26] In the end, the Commission upheld the integrity of the working group's procedures and rejected the renewed Argentine bid to hide its activities under the 1503 rules.

The fact that Argentina had supplied information to the Commission under the confidential procedures does not mean that it actually accounted in this manner for disappeared persons. As noted earlier, Resolution 1503 was designed to provide a way for the Commission to evaluate *situations* amounting to "consistent patterns of gross violations," not as a way to resolve individual cases of abuse. A state responding to complaints under the 1503 procedure customarily focuses its reply on this situational aspect, citing laws and procedures that protect rights, in an attempt to weaken the credibility of the charges made against it and to avoid becoming the target of continuing attention by the Commission. Often, a state that makes a show of cooperating under the confidential procedures finds that it can thereby escape being singled out for treatment in public proceedings—that is, the Commission will be unlikely to appoint a public country-specific rapporteur, working group, or similar mechanism. It did not do so in the Argentine case, despite the fact that the Commission rejected Argentina's formal request to limit scrutiny to the confidential forum.

In a November 1980 memo to the Department of State, this writer commented from the U.S. Mission at Geneva:

The Human Rights Commission will presumably review the Working Group's terms of reference next February when it considers the Group's future. The Working Group and the UN Human Rights Division are still feeling their way in developing procedures to deal with the complex issue of disappearances.[27]

A few months later, a new U.S. administration had taken office, with, as noted, an initial determination to ease bilateral and multilateral pressure on certain authoritarian governments that had drawn fire for human rights abuses. At the 1981 Human Rights Commission session, this new policy made us an ally of the Argentine junta's efforts to weaken the working group. As Argentina was still a member of the Commission, consensus renewal of the working group's mandate required Argentine acquiescence. The U.S. delegation, led by Reagan administration appointees, sent many signals of support to the Argentines, thereby causing strains within the Western caucus. The delegation reported to the State Department at the close of the annual session:

Our position favoring a consensus decision [on renewing the mandate] . . . was obviously a factor in the willingness of France and Lord Colville to go almost the last mile to achieve consensus. The issue at stake was the extent to which the Working Group would be obligated to keep its proceedings confidential. The compromise language is subject to varying interpretations. . . . The shift in the U.S. position on this issue [from that of the Carter administration] caused strain with our Western allies, who favored the original French proposal and opposed the effort to impose rules which could provide a basis for claiming confidentiality.[28]

But the group itself subsequently chose to interpret the resolution as not imposing confidentiality and, indeed, as not changing its mandate in any respect. The United States decided not to further irritate our Western allies by challenging the working group's interpretation; instead, we let the matter drop. I should add that from the outset the working group took to heart the need to balance carefully the value of public disclosure with the value of discretion.[29]

THE ROLE OF THE SOVIET UNION

In December 1981, the U.S. Mission in Geneva was able to report:

The WG [working group] has continued to operate effectively and discreetly during 1981. Lord Colville . . . has told us that Argentina—which formerly declined to cooperate with the WG—has begun to change its attitude and is unlikely to oppose extension of the mandate. However, he expects the Soviets to make trouble, as they did last year.[30]

Lord Colville's reference to the Soviet Union requires a brief explanation. The anticommunist Argentine junta did not single out the Moscow-backed Argentine Communist Party as a particular target in its war against domestic opposition groups (see later). The Soviet Union obtained a measure of protection for its client party in Argentina by refusing to join in international condemnation of the junta's practices and by giving the junta quiet support at UN Human Rights Commission sessions. This is not to say that no Argentine Communist Party members were victims of disappearance. But more often they were left alone, and they were not very active in the opposition to the junta. After the Soviet invasion of Afghanistan in December 1979, the USSR relied on Argentina for grain imports far more than it had previously. The junta did not join the United States-led grain embargo imposed against the USSR, and Argentina made a great deal of money from sales to the Soviet Union during this period.[31]

WHO WERE THE DISAPPEARED?

Joseph Tulchin says that "the decline in disappearances after 1979 was more likely the result of the fact that the military felt they had won the war on terrorism and that there were few subversives left, if any."[32] As far as hardcore terrorists and guerrillas are concerned, probably few were still alive and at large in Argentina by 1980 or, indeed, even by 1978. However, the military regime's definition of "terrorist" went well beyond the bomb-throwing, machine-gunning Montonero and Revolutionary People's Army guerrillas.

President Videla said that "a terrorist is not only one who carries a bomb or a pistol, but also one who spreads ideas contrary to Western Christian civilization."[33] Admiral Ruben Chamorro, Director of the Naval Mechanics School in Buenos Aires (the Argentine Navy's principal torture and killing center), said that "an infinite minority cannot be allowed to continue upsetting the minds of our youths, teaching them foreign ideas and converting them into social critics, with an interpretation cunningly distorted of what Christian doctrine is. All this is subversion."[34]

Besides the actual Montonero terrorist guerrillas (a splinter Peronist group of vaguely leftist ideology) and the (Trotskyite) People's Revolutionary Army, most disappearance victims were centrist or liberal Peronists—including a great many trade unionists—or members of the centrist Radical Civic Union Party, the Christian Democratic Party, and various small socialist parties. Military and police assault teams also scooped into the darkness people who were friends, classmates, or coworkers of suspected terrorists.[35]

With regard to trade unionists, a recent study shows that the repressive apparatus systematically targeted activists of unions thought to be opposed to the government's economic policies.[36] Indirectly supporting this finding, another study argues that the regime's economic policies were driven by antiunion, anti-Peronist forces.[37] Alison Brysk cites evidence that 30 to 48 percent of the disappeared were workers.[38]

Jacobo Timerman, editor of the suppressed newspaper *La Opinion*, who became Argentina's most famous political prisoner, has recounted how psychiatrists as a group also became targeted.[39]

Religious activists were not exempt, especially if they were active in social ministries; dozens of priests and nuns, including two French nuns, were among those who fell victim to the terror.[40]

A regime-perceived affinity with antigovernment militants was sufficient cause for elimination. On the basis of my review of the file of disappearance cases of the American Embassy in Buenos Aires, as well as firsthand accounts and other credible case reports that reached me during my two years in the State Department's Bureau of Human Rights and Humanitarian Affairs (mid-1978 to mid-1980), I estimate that over half of the 9,000 victims of disappearance were not members of terrorist or guerrilla organizations. The official Argentine National Commission on the Disappeared has said: "We can state categorically . . . that they did not pursue only the members of political organizations who carried out acts of terrorism. Among the victims are thousands who never had any links with such activity."[41]

DOMESTIC OPPOSITION IN ARGENTINA

Domestic opposition to the junta increased but gradually in Argentina during the late 1970s, fueled, in part, by slowly growing public awareness of human rights abuses but also by economic discontent caused by the junta's radical shift from the welfare statism of the Peron era to full-scale laissez-faire capitalism at home and in foreign commerce. Hyperinflation was one result, leading to real declines in the income of the middle and poorer classes.[42] Economic problems reached the crisis stage in 1981, when, as David Rock points out, massive capital flight, bankruptcies, and a huge rise in foreign debt (from 14 percent to 42 percent of gross domestic product in 18 months) brought on a financial crisis and "thunderous economic collapse." Steel production fell 20 percent, manufacturing output by 22.9 percent, the gross domestic product by 11.4 percent, and real wages by 19.2 percent during 1981.[43]

Moreover, the unions were kept in check throughout most of the 1976–82 period by government intimidation and by the fact that, until 1981, the inflow of foreign capital and major growth in exports had maintained a certain minimal degree of health in the economy. Although the buying power of wages dropped, unemployment was usually in the 2 percent range.

The main Argentine political parties, the Justicialist (Peronist) and Radical Civic Union (centrist), were quiescent throughout the late 1970s, fearing, like many other Argentine groups, that criticism of regime terrorism would be seen as support for guerrilla terrorists. Some political party activists disappeared during this period; most others decided to keep their heads down. A notable exception was the Radical Civic Union leader Raul Alfonsin, a cofounder of the Permanent Assembly for Human Rights, the country's largest human rights organization. (Alfonsin was elected the first postjunta President of Argentina in 1983.) The junta failed to develop a popular political base of its own, leaving it with the prospect that, when the time eventually came to hand over power to civilians, it would be dealing with the same principal parties as before: Peronists and Radicals.[44]

Public opposition by the Catholic Church was slow to get under way, since the Church feared that high-profile militancy against the regime could encourage a revival of the Montonero and People's Revolutionary Army terrorism that had just wracked the country for three years and could even risk identifying the Church with these movements in the government's mind. One or two bishops began to speak out fairly early, however. Jacobo Timerman records in his prison memoir that some Catholic publications, including the magazine *Criterio*, joined the effort to press the military to wage the antiterrorist struggle within constitutional and legal norms, although he notes, "This activity in some instances succeeded in saving a life, although it never actually modified the course of events."[45] The Vatican lent early support to the cause of human rights through quiet diplomacy, and in early 1979 the Pope started to make public statements focusing on the disappearance issue in Argentina and Chile. The Vatican statements encouraged the Argentine hierarchy to take a more forthright public posture, which it did, albeit gradually. Catholic bishops and priests and Jewish rabbis were among the most active members of the Permanent Assembly for Human Rights. A Catholic bishop served as Vice President of the Assembly.

The Jewish community (about 500,000 of a total population of 25 million) was also divided on how to deal with state terrorism. Despite the fact that the disappeared and the state-of-siege detainees included a disproportionate number of Jews, the official leadership of the Buenos Aires Jewish community opted for a low-profile policy of quiet diplomacy; they told me on my 1979 visit that they feared that a more militant posture would simply fan the flames of anti-Semitism and cause more victims. A complicating factor was that Argentina had close and cordial relations with Israel and bought military equipment from the Israelis; Tel Aviv did not protest the Argentine repression.

EXTERNAL FACTORS IN THE ARGENTINE CASE

In any external effort to influence a government to change its human rights policies, bilateral and multilateral approaches are mutually reinforcing. Just as bilateral pressure is heightened if exerted by several countries, so multilateral activity is more effective when carried out through more than one channel. Moreover, these approaches should be maintained over an extended period—often several years—to demonstrate seriousness of purpose and the priority external actors attach to the human rights issue. In the case of Argentina, I am persuaded that the eventual halt in disappearances was due largely to this combination of sustained external pressures. Internal factors seemed to have less impact, because of the relatively low profile and low level of activity of the churches, unions, political parties, and press. Thus, most of the usual institutions through which popular resistance can be channeled either could not or would not take initiatives. Only the human rights organizations themselves took the risk. As the experience of the Mothers of the Plaza de Mayo illustrates, they began to have impact only when their story reached an international audience, through which their activity added to the external pressures on the military government.[46]

I am convinced that the combination of pressures from Western governments, the United Nations, the OAS, Amnesty International and other nongovernmental organizations, and the Vatican eventually made the regime understand that the human rights campaign was a serious priority of the international community and that it would affect Argentina's external relationships until the abuses stopped. Maintaining a policy of disappearance was not to be a cost-free exercise in terms of Argentina's ties with the world. The immediate cost was primarily in terms of a badly degraded image of the nation, an image that would take some time to repair; the immediate material costs were largely limited to the U.S. restrictions on military sales and assistance and on economic assistance.[47] Still, the latter were not trivial, and the Argentine junta was aware that they could be followed by similar actions by other Western states, some of which had already begun to follow the U.S. lead in refusing to support Argentine loan applications in the multilateral development banks. The regime thus had to consider the possibility that material costs could rise significantly. This helps explain why they fought so hard against being the target of any public human rights procedure in the United Nations, and why they worked so hard to hide within a consensus on the creation and renewal of the Working Group on Enforced Disappearances.

In the State Department, we believed that prompt intercession in disappearance cases worked fairly often in new cases because the central government—the entity with which we dealt, after all—had some interest in preventing a worsening of our already bad bilateral relations and of its own deteriorating international image. The regime had gone from attempting to explain disappearances as an effect of the war against terrorism ("There are always some missing in action after a battle," Argentine Army General (and later President) Bignone told me in April 1979) to stating that it would take measures to halt disappearances. By the time of my conversation with General Bignone, in fact, Argentine officials were making both statements simultaneously, thereby creating a bizarre situation in which they half-denied and half-accepted responsibility for the practice. It seemed that international pressure was beginning to have some effect.

Also, Argentina's hemispheric peers in the Organization of American States were growing more critical, and the publication of the report of the 1979 visit by the Inter-American Commission on Human Rights further raised public consciousness in Latin America, where it received considerable press attention. In April 1980 the military government felt constrained to publish a rebuttal of the report.[48]

Iain Guest cites an unnamed Argentine Foreign Ministry official's comment in October 1980 on the effectiveness of international human rights institutions: "We can predict adverse consequences from the machinery now in place in the international organizations. To counter this, we will need decisive support from the other countries." Guest adds that this comment "showed again that the very qualities that rendered the UN an object of contempt in the West—the delay in acting, the ponderous bureaucracy—made it an object of acute concern in Argentina."[49]

EFFECTIVENESS OF THE WORKING GROUP

On February 29, 1980, the UN Human Rights Commission created a mechanism that actually played a role in saving the lives of people marked for secret elimination by their governments.[50] Livermore and Ramcharan point out that during the first eight years of operation of the working group, "the total number of cases resolved or clarified [is] some 7 or 8 percent of all cases processed, some 25 percent of urgent cases." They acknowledge that, although this "remains small relative to the total caseload of the Working Group, the success rate is higher than that of any other body within the UN system, many of which have few procedures for dealing with individual cases in effective ways."[51]

In January 1981, the U.S. Mission in Geneva reported to the Department of State that "as the number of new disappearances declined significantly after the establishment of the Working Group, many Western observers believe the very fact of the Group's existence has helped to curb the practice.''[52] In June 1981, Thomas McCarthy, the UN official in charge of the staff supporting the working group, told me that ''there have been recent cases where the Working Group's rapid intercession seems to have been effective.''[53] A year and a half later, in December 1982, the Mission reported to the Department, ''The Working Group Chairman, Lord Colville (UK) recently told us that the number of new disappearances seems to be decreasing and that nearly all governments are cooperating with the Working Group.''[54]

Iain Guest has written that the publication in 1981 of the working group's first report ended an era:

The group had intervened to save lives. It had named governments, bypassed confidentiality, and taken information from people because they had suffered and not because they had been given ''consultative status'' [by ECOSOC]. . . . By taking up a theme as opposed to a country, it had also broken the mold of discriminatory, single country probes on Israel, South Africa, and Chile, and made the UN less ''selective.''[55]

The working group's ability to have a positive impact on the problem of new disappearances is attributable, in part, to its terms of reference and to the working methods it adopted. The former provide that it shall consist of five representatives of member states of the Commission, appointed by the chair, who would, once appointed, serve in their individual capacities and not as government representatives. This arrangement has the advantage of giving maximum freedom of action and flexibility to the group while keeping it responsible to a senior intergovernmental body. Thus, it can speak with the authority of the Human Rights Commission, but its members need not await instructions from their governments or from the Commission.

The working group defined its tasks in purely humanitarian terms. Its main objective is

to assist families in determining the fate and whereabouts of their missing relatives who, having disappeared, are placed outside the protective precinct of the law. . . . The Group's role ends when the fate and whereabouts of the missing person have been clearly established. . . . The Group's approach is strictly non-accusatory; it does not concern itself with the question of determining responsibility for specific cases of disappearance.[56]

The group is authorized to ''seek and receive'' information from all credible sources (i.e., that the group considers credible), including nongovernmental organizations, governments, intergovernmental organizations, and individuals. In a key phrase that authorizes the group to act rapidly on its own initiative, it is to ''bear in mind the need to be able to respond effectively to information that comes before it.'' The group is to address disappearances on a global basis; no country or region is mentioned by name in the resolution. It is to make a public report to the Commission, "together with its conclusions and recommendations," but it is given flexibility to determine how much should be in the report and how much should remain in the file cabinet (the group is to "bear in mind the need to be able to . . . carry out its work with discretion").[57]

The word "seek" in the phrase "seek and receive" is crucial; this word gives the group authority to demand information from governments about the location and status of a person believed to have been abducted by official forces. This, taken together with affirmation of the need for urgent action ("be able to *respond effectively*"), encouraged the group to adopt the practice of sending telegrams or telexes immediately upon receipt of a disappearance report from a relative, a generally reliable nongovernmental organization, a responsible press source, and so on. In the beginning, dispatch of such a telegram involved obtaining telephonic concurrence from all five members, but as there was consensus on every such telegram the members decided to streamline the procedure by letting the chair act in this matter on their behalf without prior consultation. In this way, the working group adopted a technique already employed with good effect by Amnesty International, which had instituted an "urgent action procedure" a few years earlier to respond to reports of torture. Nongovernmental human rights organizations are often the primary innovators of implementation techniques.

The working group has been blessed throughout the years with members whose courage and commitment to human rights have been matched by wisdom and sound judgment. Its first chairman, Viscount Colville of Culross (United Kingdom), led the group with distinction through the crucial early years. Jonas Foli (Ghana) was an outstanding member. They have been assisted by Secretariat staff of exceptional competence, sensitivity, and intelligence, including, in particular, Thomas McCarthy (United States), who for the crucial first four years was the senior professional responsible for supporting the working group and carrying on day-to-day operations, including the lifesaving urgent-action procedure.

The working group discovered that governments often responded promptly to their urgent-action cables. They did not, however, respond quickly—sometimes not at all—to the group's inquiries about people who had been missing for some months. The U.S. Government had a similar experience. Whenever the Department of State instructed one of our embassies officially to request a government to provide information about the whereabouts and situation of a missing person believed to have been taken into official custody, we received a prompt and positive response usually only in "current" cases—that is, of people who had been taken in the past few days or weeks. The more recent the event, the more likely we would receive a positive response, that is, a report that the individual was, in fact, in custody at a specific location and was going to be charged or released. From that moment, of course, the individual was protected from further danger of summary killing. He or she could be found and communicated with by family and attorneys and friends and supporters. The individual was no longer "disappeared" and thus no longer in a situation of absolute vulnerability to state power.

The problem with the older cases, we came to believe by 1979, was that most of the people had probably been killed. (However, there were recurring reports of secret detention centers in some countries where substantial numbers of long-missing individuals had recently been seen; in the case of Argentina, F. Allen Harris, the human rights officer at the American Embassy in Buenos Aires, and I were among those U.S. officials who found these reports credible and argued repeatedly for a prompt and serious investigation of them by U.S. or intergovernmental institutions. But we encountered skepticism and bureaucratic inertia. It was my view at the time, based on unconfirmed, but credible, information, that these secret camps and prisons held from several hundred to perhaps 1,500 disappeared persons. The regime frequently moved clandestine detainees and opened and closed secret centers—that much is certain. [58] Since the discovery of mass graves after 1983, we also know that, in fact, most of the disappeared were murdered at some time after their detention.) The Argentine, Chilean, and other governments that we approached for information concerning specific, long-disappeared individuals told us, typically, that the office responsible for handling such inquiries had checked with all police and military authorities and that no information was available on the person concerned or, sometimes, that the government understood that the individual had "gone abroad." (The latter assertion was rarely true, although, in fact, a tiny number of the disappeared did surface in foreign countries at one time or another.)

In Argentina, in a dozen or so cases in early 1979, prompt intercession by the American Embassy in Buenos Aires on behalf of someone just abducted led to pressure by the central military authorities on regional and local military and police commanders to acknowledge the detention. They did so, thereby halting in these cases the usual sequence of torture followed by killing. This enabled the Argentine junta to demonstrate its intention to seek a more cooperative bilateral relationship with the United States. At the same time, the rate of disappearances declined sharply from the 1978 rate of about 50 a month. Other concerned Western governments also made representations on behalf of individuals, and in September 1979 the InterAmerican Human Rights Commission (an expert-level body of the Organization of American States) made a long-planned and well-prepared two-week visit to Argentina. When the UN working group began to function in early 1980, the United States and other Western countries made it clear to the Argentine military that prompt and positive responses to working group inquiries were just as important to us as positive resolution of cases in which we had interceded on a bilateral basis.

I am persuaded that the sustained effort to join multilateral and bilateral pressure, carried on throughout the 1980s in countries where enforced disappearance had become a problem, contributed to the overall 25 percent success rate for current or recent cases reported by Livermore and Ramcharan. Before the advent of the working group, success stories were very rare.

In its 1988 report, for instance—covering 1987, the last of the eight years dealt with in the Livermore–Ramcharan essay—the working group transmitted to the 14 governments concerned 267 cases reported to have occurred in 1987, of which 215 were processed under the urgent-action procedure. [59] In 1989, the working group dealt with 721 new cases (those said to have *occurred* during the year, not the total of new reports), which it called "an alarming increase" over the 1988 figure of 400 and, *a fortiori*, over the 267 in 1988.[60] However, 400 of the new 1989 cases were in a single country, Peru. (Accounting for most of the others were Iran with 121, Guatemala with 40, and the Philippines with 36.)

The total declined in 1990, as the group dealt with 486 new cases, of which 232 were in Peru, with Colombia now in second place with 82 and Guatemala with 75.[61] Peru allowed the group to make an on-site visit in 1989, and, although the government did not formally respond to the group's recommendations, the over 40 percent decline in the number of new cases in 1990 and the further substantial decline in 1991—to 117, a 50 percent drop from the preceding year—suggest that the group's visit had a serious impact on Peruvian Government attitudes and actions.

In 1991, the total number of new cases worldwide dealt with by the working group rose to 636, but once again there was a concentration in a single country, this time Iraq, with 342. The urgent-action procedure was employed in 330 cases in 1991, resulting in clarification of 34 cases during the year.[62]

The number of cases reported to have occurred in the Philippines, where the working group made an on-site visit in 1991, declined from 36 in 1989 and 47 in 1990 to 5 1991.[63]

From 1980 through 1991, the working group dealt with a total of nearly 25,000 cases, an average of about 2,000 a year. The average for each of the last four of these years, however, was 528.

ASSESSMENT

One could say, of course, that the working group is a failure because it is unable to resolve 75 percent of the cases it undertakes under its most productive form of operation (its urgent-action procedure). But because there was, until establishment of the High Commissioner's office, no other agency within the UN system with the authority or ability to undertake this task, the real alternative was probably a much higher rate of failure. Of course, as I have acknowledged, the UN working group was far from the only entity trying to resolve cases of disappearance and to persuade regimes to halt the practice of disappearance. Governments, regional intergovernmental organizations, and nongovernmental organizations such as Amnesty International were all active on behalf of dis- appeared persons and interceded vigorously with the authorities in Argentina and other countries. Certainly, they had some positive impact on governments and thereby helped to resolve some individual cases. They also probably added to the overall pressure on offending governments to halt the practice. The UN working group added something new and important, however. For the first time, the entire international community of states put its political will behind a year-round multilateral implementation mechanism specifically designed to halt disappearances. When two or more entities are involved in a case, it is very difficult to attribute decisive influence to one rather than another. But the overall success rate rose impressively after the UN working group began to operate. It added a new, global dimension, and its "thematic" structure offered a less politicized approach to the issue that some violating governments may have found preferable to the generally more politicized approaches of other entities. In the case of Argentina, governments of considerable importance to the country, including the United States, the U.K., France, and Canada, were pressing the regime hard to account for the missing and to take steps to end disappearances. The Organization of American States was actively engaged, through the Inter-American Commission on Human Rights. Within Argentina, by 1979 at least eight domestic organizations were dealing with the issue. In addition to the Mothers of the Plaza de Mayo and the Permanent Assembly for Human Rights, they included Christian Service for Peace and Justice (of Nobel laureate Adolfo Perez Esquivel) and the Grandmothers of the Plaza de Mayo.[64] It is my deep conviction that they all helped. I am equally convinced that the UN working group added a very important dimension to these other efforts.

The working group continues to carry out its responsibilities on the basis of the Commission mandate, in coordination with the High Commissioner. The existence of a multilateral entity charged with this politically sensitive responsibility has been, for states, a valuable way to pursue an essentially humanitarian task that otherwise would not be performed by an agency responsible to the international community as a whole.[65]

I share the conclusion of Livermore and Ramcharan that

the Working Group has . . . helped to mobilize international public opinion . . . to exercise diplomatic influence in some countries, and to save lives in some circumstances. . . . [h]as broken new ground with its fact-finding procedures. . . . [i]s tangible proof that perseverance can result in effective international cooperation.[66]

Regional intergovernmental human rights machinery, which exists in some areas, has also been employed on occasion to deal with disappearances, especially in Latin America. If two or more intergovernmental organizations weigh in, that adds to the pressure on the government to respond quickly and positively. To repeat a point made earlier, if individual governments likewise make their views known directly to the responsible government, that also strengthens the prospects for success.

A government receiving representations from the UN Working Group on Disappearances is being asked to account to the community of states, of which it is a member, through an agency established by the community for a specific purpose. A state risks something, of course, by investigating enforced disappearances within its borders, especially when it knows or has reason to believe that a disappearance may have been caused by official forces. But by responding in a cooperative spirit, a government may at least control the damage to its reputation that often is already beginning to appear by the time the working group becomes involved. Reports of disappearances reach nongovernmental organizations, the domestic and international press, and other governments by a variety of channels. It is safer for a government to provide information to a multiregional agency responsible only to the intergovernmental entity that appointed it and of which the state is a member than to provide that information to the press, to a nongovernmental organization, or to another government, all of which might sensationalize their treatment of it or use it to attack the government concerned. It is also easier to use such an agency as an intermediary to pass information to relatives.

The combination of a well-conceived mandate, a clear, humanitarian purpose, the strong support of key states including parallel bilateral démarches, the wisdom of its members, and the competence of its staff has helped the working group to resolve a quarter of its most urgent cases and to register a significant advance in the process of increasing the capacity of international institutions to address humanitarian issues.

REVIEW

I conclude that the Working Group on Enforced Disappearances, the first of the Charter-based "thematic" mechanisms, made a valuable contribution during its first decade to the diminution of the practice of disappearance by the Argentine military regime as well as by governments elsewhere.

The next chapter concerns the Special Rapporteur on the Elimination of Religious Discrimination and Intolerance and includes a general appraisal of the strengths and weaknesses of the thematic approach to human rights issues.

NOTES

1. Thematic mechanisms also exist to address other abuses, such as torture, and throughout the 1980s and early 1990s there has been a trend toward creating more such special-purpose mechanisms. By March 1996 there were 13 thematic mechanisms.

2. General Assembly Resolution 33/173, adopted by consensus on December 20, 1978.

3. Patrick J. Flood, "U.S. Human Rights Initiatives concerning Argentina," in David Newson, ed., *The Diplomacy of Human Rights* (Lanham, MD: University Press of America, 1986), 129–39.

4. J. Daniel Livermore and Bertram G. Ramcharan, " 'Enforced or Involuntary Disappearances': An Evaluation of a Decade of United Nations Action," *Canadian Human Rights Yearbook 1989–90* (Ottawa: University of Ottawa Press, 1990), 217–30.

5. The figure of 600 is based on information from the UN Working Group on Chile, the *Vicaria de la Solidaridad* (Vicariate of Solidarity) of the Archdiocese of Santiago,

and the International Committee of the Red Cross. See UN document E/CN.4/1363, Feb. 2, 1980, esp. paras. 87–89. In 1991, the Chilean Commission for Truth and Reconciliation (the Rettig Commission) documented nearly a thousand cases of disappearance that resulted in death. Cited in Jack Donnelly, *International Human Rights* (Boulder, CO: Westview Press, 1993), 54.

6. In April 1979, F. Allen Harris, human rights officer at the American Embassy in Buenos Aires, showed this writer about 8,500 case files on which the embassy had acquired detailed and credible information. At that time, estimates of the number of disappeared persons by nongovernmental organizations ranged from 5,000 to 30,000. Amnesty International had already downgraded to 15,000 its earlier estimate of 30,000 disappearances. The embassy files eventually reached about 9,000 cases, a figure subsequently corroborated by independent investigations conducted by the InterAmerican Commission on Human Rights of the Organization of American States (1979) and, after the restoration of democratic governance in Argentina, by the official Argentine National Commission on Disappeared Persons. The UN Working Group on Disappearances used the same figure. Other sources continue to insist that the number is probably higher— perhaps much higher, although they do not offer hard evidence to support this contention. See, for instance, Alison Brysk, *The Politics of Human Rights in Argentina* (Stanford, CA: Stanford University Press, 1994), 37–40, 70–72, 216 (n. 48).

7. For a thoroughly researched, well-documented, sympathetic account of the Argentine human rights movement, see Brysk, *The Politics*. For an extensive, if highly partisan, appreciation of the Mothers of the Plaza de Mayo, see Marguerite Guzman Bouvard, *Revolutionizing Motherhood: The Mothers of the Plaza de Mayo* (Wilmington, DE: SR Books, 1994).

8. In 1976, the military government tried to choke off preliminary action by the expert-level UN Human Rights Subcommission on Discrimination and Minorities. Antonio Cassese, then a member of the Subcommission, recounts blatant attempts at intimidation by the Argentine Ambassador in Geneva (Antonio Cassese, *Human Rights in a Changing World* [Philadelphia: Temple University Press, 1990], 128–29).

9. Joseph S. Tulchin, *Argentina and the United States: A Conflicted Relationship* (Boston: Twayne, 1990), xv–xvi, 88–91.

10. Ibid., 92–93.

11. Ibid., 95.

12. Ibid., 143.

13. Ibid., 141–42.

14. Livermore and Ramcharan, " 'Enforced,' " 220. See also David Forsythe, *The Internationalization of Human Rights* (Lexington, MA: Lexington Books, 1991), 65–69.

15. There is a minor exception to this statement: member states of the Commission also had access to a periodic summary list of complaints received by the Secretariat. These, too, were UN-confidential. The lists contained little information about the substance of the complaint and served primarily a record-keeping purpose.

16. Iain Guest, *Behind the Disappearances: Argentina's Dirty War against Human Rights and the United Nations* (Philadelphia: University of Pennsylvania Press, 1990), 232.

17. Report of the Special Rapporteur on Human Rights in Chile, UN document A/34/583, November 21, 1979, paras. 1–13.

18. Tulchin, *Argentina*, 146–47.

19. Ibid., 148–49.

20. See, for instance, Juan Carlos Torre and Liliana de Riz, "Argentina since 1946," in Leslie Bethell, ed., *Argentina since Independence* (London: Cambridge University Press, 1993), 324–27; David Rock, *Argentina 1516–1982: From Spanish Colonization to the Falklands War* (Berkeley: University of California Press, 1985), 352–66; Tulchin, *Argentina*, 134–39. But Brysk, *The Politics*, 32, asserts that the Montonero and People's Revolutionary Army guerrillas "never posed a serious threat to the territorial or institutional integrity of the state" and that whatever threat did exist "had substantially diminished before the 1976 coup."

21. Jacobo Timerman, *Prisoner without a Name, Cell without a Number* (New York: Alfred A. Knopf, 1981), 101–2.

22. Tulchin, *Argentina*, 155. Also see Brysk, *The Politics*, 33.

23. Guest, *Behind the Disappearances*, Chs. 14–18, contains a comprehensive account of the operations of Argentine diplomats at the United Nations in New York and Geneva during the period under review.

24. Ambassador Kirkpatrick is best known for her 1979 *Commentary* article, "Dictatorships and Double Standards," which then-candidate Reagan said had a formative effect on his view of an appropriate U.S. human rights policy. Also see Forsythe, *The Internationalization*, 126–29.

25. U.S. Mission Geneva telegram 1645, Feb. 18, 1981.

26. U.S. Mission Geneva telegram 1542, Feb. 16, 1981.

27. Memorandum to Warren Hewitt, Director of Human Rights Affairs, Bureau of International Organizations, Dept. of State, Nov. 5, 1980, transmitting and commenting on UN Note No. G/SO 214 (3-3-8) concerning Resolution 18 (XXXIII) of the Subcommision on Prevention of Discrimination and Protection of Minorities on the terms of reference of the Working Group on Disappearances. In 1982 the Human Rights Division was renamed the Human Rights Center, an administrative change intended to raise its status within the UN bureaucratic structure. The change had little impact on the Center's influence within the United Nations or its prestige among member states.

28. Geneva telegram 2796, Mar. 17, 1981.

29. For instance, U.S. Mission Geneva telegram 11211 of Aug. 19, 1980 to the Department of State: "UN Human Rights Division Director told Mission . . . Working Group prefers private session this time because of sensitive and controversial nature of material to be considered. WG plans to invite NGO's and other interested parties to appear. . . . WG would probably hold a third session later. . . . WG would decide whether this session would be public or private. . . . [h]e expects the WG's report to the UNHRC to be public."

30. Geneva telegram 12616, Dec. 24, 1981.

31. Tulchin, *Argentina*, 150; see also Gaddis Smith, *Morality, Reason, and Power: American Diplomacy in the Carter Years* (New York: Hill and Wang, 1988), 128–29.

32. Tulchin, *Argentina*, 148.

33. Cited in Torre and de Riz, "Argentina since 1946," 328.

34. Cited in Martin Edwin Andersen, *Dossier Secreto: Argentina's Desaparecidos and the Myth of the "Dirty War"* (Boulder, CO: Westview Press, 1993), 184.

35. Rock, *Argentina*, 363, 367. See also Ronald Dworkin, ed., *Nunca Mas: The Report of the Argentine National Commission on the Disappeared* (New York: Farrar, Straus, and Giroux, 1986), cited in Brysk, *The Politics*, 39, 202–3 (n. 123).

36. David Pion-Berlin and George Lopez, "Of Victims and Executioners: Argentine State Terror, 1975–79," *International Studies Quarterly* 35, March 1991, 63–86.

37. Juan M. Villareal, "Changes in Argentine Society: The Heritage of the Dictatorship," in M. Peralta-Ramos and Carlos Waisman, eds., *From Military Rule to Liberal Democracy in Argentina* (Boulder, CO: Westview Press, 1987), 69–97.

38. Brysk, *The Politics*, 203 (n. 106), 246 (n. 26).

39. Timerman, *Prisoner without a Name*, 98.

40. Cited in Brysk, *The Politics*, 40, 203 (n. 129).

41. Ibid., 202–3 (n. 123).

42. See, for instance, Monica Peralta-Ramos, "Toward an Analysis of the Structural Basis of Coercion in Argentina: The Behavior of Major Fractions of the Bourgeoisie, 1976–83," in Peralta-Ramos and Waisman, *From Military Rule*, 39–69.

43. Rock, *Argentina*, 373–74.

44. Torre and de Riz, "Argentina since 1946," 336.

45. Timerman, *Prisoner without a Name*, 100.

46. Guzman Bouvard, *Revolutionizing Motherhood*, 82, 86–87.

47. Smith, *Morality*, 128–29.

48. Government of Argentina, *Observaciones y Comentarios Criticos del Gobierno Argentino al Informe de la CIDH sobre la Situacion de los Derochos Humanos en Argentina* (Buenos Aires: Circulo Militar, 1980).

49. Guest, *Behind the Disappearances*, 238.

50. UN Human Rights Commission Resolution 20 (XXXVI), Feb. 29, 1980.

51. Livermore and Ramcharan, " 'Enforced,' " 226–27.

52. U.S. Mission Geneva telegram 108, Jan. 6, 1981.

53. Memorandum from the writer to Warren Hewitt, Director of the Office of Human Rights, Bureau of International Organizations, Department of State, June 30, 1981.

54. U.S. Mission Geneva telegram 12546, Dec. 29, 1982.

55. Guest, *Behind the Disappearances*, 234.

56. United Nations Secretariat, *Yearbook on Human Rights for 1988* (New York: United Nations, 1992), 98.

57. UN Human Rights Commission resolution 20 (XXXVI), Feb. 29, 1980.

58. The report of the Argentine National Commission on the Disappeared subsequently documented the existence of these camps, their number (340), and the fact that they shifted location (Brysk, *The Politics*, 70, 208 [n. 56]).

59. Report of the Working Group to the Human Rights Commission, E/CN.4/1988/19 and Add. 1).

60. E/CN.4/1990/13.

61. E/CN.4/1991/20.

62. E/CN.4/1992/18, at paras. 5, 53, and 72.

63. E/CN.4/1992/18.

64. For a thorough account of the Argentine human rights movement, see Brysk, *The Politics*.

65. The Central Tracing Service of the International Committee of the Red Cross, which might at first be considered an exception to this statement, focuses on locating prisoners of war and civilians displaced by war and is therefore not generally able to act in cases of enforced disappearance by states against their own inhabitants in peacetime.

66. Livermore and Ramcharan, " 'Enforced,' " 230.

5

Special Rapporteur on the Elimination of Religious Discrimination and Intolerance

BACKGROUND

Efforts to deal internationally with state-sponsored religious discrimination and intolerance have a long history. In the sixteenth century, for instance, some European states obtained rights to protect their nationals in the Ottoman Empire, and in the eighteenth century the Ottomans promised Russia to protect the Christian religion and churches within the Empire. In East Asia there is evidence of a tradition of equal protection of foreigners irrespective of religion. The Congress of Vienna (1815) provided for religious freedom and civil equality of believers of different Christian faiths in the Swiss Confederation. In some of the post–World War I treaties, states undertook to accord legal equality, including equal civil and political rights, to members of religious minorities, under the guarantee of the League of Nations.[1]

The atrocities committed during the Second World War against believers and entire religious communities were powerful arguments that more needed to be done on the international level. For those in the West, the systematic persecution of religion in Communist states was another strong incentive to improve efforts to protect religious freedom through international measures. These experiences led first to the incorporation of a strong affirmation of religious freedom as a fundamental human right in the Universal Declaration of Human Rights[2] and, later, to an equally strong legal formulation of this right in the International Covenant on Civil and Political Rights.[3]

Because many members of the international community saw that these measures would not suffice, they initiated further steps within the United Nations toward better safeguarding religious freedom. These steps, including studies by the Human Rights Commission's Subcommission on Prevention of Discrimination and Protection of Minorities and the Human Rights Commission itself, eventually led to the adoption in 1981 by the Commission, and then by the General Assembly, of a Declaration on the Elimination of All Forms of Intolerance and of Discrimination Based on Religion or Belief.[4]

ESTABLISHMENT OF THE SPECIAL RAPPORTEURSHIP

With the standard-setting phase of the work complete, some member states urged the United Nations to turn to methods of implementation. This writer joined that effort. In a letter of July 23, 1981, to the Department of State, I urged the Department

to focus more intensively in the UN on the issue of religious persecution in the USSR and other Communist countries. Now that the Commission has approved the Draft Declaration . . . we have an international standard against which Soviet conduct can be measured and legitimately evaluated in UN forums.[5]

In December 1982, the United States formally requested the Human Rights Commission to inscribe on its agenda an item entitled "Implementation of the Declaration on the Elimination of All Forms of Intolerance and of Discrimination Based on Religion or Belief."[6] Acting under this new agenda item, in 1983 the Commission requested the Subcommission on Prevention of Discrimination and Protection of Minorities to study contemporary manifestations of intolerance or discrimination, using the Declaration as a benchmark, and to recommend measures to combat these problems.[7] On the basis of the Subcommission report, the Commission decided in 1986 to appoint a Special Rapporteur to implement the Declaration:[8]

The mandate, approved by the Commission and ECOSOC in 1986, authorized the Rapporteur

to examine . . . incidents and [governmental] actions and to recommend remedial measures . . . seek credible and reliable information from Governments, as well as specialized agencies, intergovernmental organizations and non-governmental organizations, including communities of religion or belief . . . [and] in carrying out his mandate, to bear in mind the need to be able to respond effectively to credible and reliable information that comes before him and to carry out his work with discretion and independence. . . . [and] to report [to the Commission on] the occurrence and extent of incidents and actions inconsistent with the provisions of the Declaration, together with his conclusions and recommendations.[9]

The rapporteur, Angelo Vidal d'Almeida Ribeiro of Portugal, issued his first report in 1987.[10] In this document, he clearly opted for a cautious approach for the first year of his mandate, limiting his remarks to general aspects of the subject of religious discrimination and intolerance.

In his second report,[11] Ribeiro became more specific, noting that his mandate called upon him to ''bear in mind the need to respond effectively to credible and reliable information that comes before him,'' language drawn from the terms of reference of the Working Group on Enforced Disappearances.[12] As in the latter case, this carefully phrased grant of authority was intended to stimulate an activist approach by the rapporteur. Thus, in addition to asking for information from all governments, UN bodies, specialized agencies, and interested intergovernmental and nongovernmental organizations, Ribeiro addressed specific requests to the governments of Albania, Bulgaria, Iran, Pakistan, Turkey, the USSR, and Burundi for ''comments on information concerning incidents and measures which appeared to be inconsistent with the Declaration.'' In his report, Ribeiro said this was a new phase of his work and noted that

this procedure provoked a reaction from the authorities concerned in certain cases and led to a reply from them. [He] welcomed this constructive approach and the openness shown by certain countries, which gave him reason to hope that Governments would take a growing interest in the issues within his frame of reference and their solution.[13]

PROBLEMS WITH IMPLEMENTATION

But the rapporteur stayed on this level of extreme caution through the next few years, never really engaging states on the level of concrete cases. Unlike the Working Group on Disappearances, the record does not show that any concrete cases of religious persecution were resolved. Nor does it contain any reference to on-site visits by the rapporteur to places where persecution or discrimination was alleged to be taking place or even to attempts to conduct such visits. Instead, his reports are filled with general comments on problems connected with the exercise of religious freedom and with broad, abstract recommendations for improvement.

For instance, his 1990 report to the Commission dwelt at length on the advantages and disadvantages of the idea of drafting a convention on the elimination of religious discrimination and intolerance as a follow-up to the 1981 Declaration.[14] The United Nations has followed this sequence in several other human rights standard-setting exercises, that is, first defining rights and responsibilities in a declaration, then crafting a binding legal instrument. Supporters of this approach start from the premise that a state is more likely to respect a particular human right when it has formally accepted a specific legal obligation to do so. Moreover, they say, the text of a convention usually spells out more precisely the nature of a state's obligations. Third, some have also felt that, because a law is meant to be carried out, enactment of a convention brings with it an impetus to create implementation machinery and for that machinery to be efficacious. This line of thinking was shaped by the experience of the framers of the Universal Declaration, who had tried and failed to get approval for simultaneous approval of a binding instrument and who felt that the lack of such an instrument was the principal obstacle to improving implementation.[15]

The first premise has been thrown into question by the development through state practice, as well as decisions of the International Court of Justice, of the doctrine that the Universal Declaration has become part of binding customary international law. In this view, the Declaration spells out in precise terms the Charter provisions on human rights, which are, like the rest of the Charter, binding on all member states. Also, on numerous occasions the community of states has referred explicitly in other documents to the Declaration as having binding character. I find these arguments persuasive. Potentially, other declarations adopted by the General Assembly on human rights subjects could also acquire the status of customary law.[16]

Second, since the mid-1970s General Assembly declarations on human rights have tended to specify state obligations in increasingly concrete terms. It would be difficult for a state to claim that it did not know what obligations it had undertaken to eliminate governmentally sponsored religious persecution, because the text of the Declaration contains this information. It is true that, before a declaration acquires the force of customary law, obligation is political rather than legal. On a foreign policy basis, a state accepts obligations contained in a declaration through the act of voting for, or joining in, consensus adoption of the text by the General Assembly. Before that stage, states have had ample opportunity to put their own stamp on the document through participating in the typically multiyear drafting and amending process, regularly submitting written comments to the Secretary-General for circulation to all states, oral statements at UN meetings, and the like. Even if we grant that all of this constitutes "only" a political, and not a legal, obligation, I would hold that it amounts to an extraordinarily strong and serious form of political obligation to which other states and the community of states can hold a state politically accountable. In the case of a convention, a state must actually sign and then formally accede to the document in accordance with its own constitutional procedure, usually taking months or even years, with opportunities for filing reservations and understandings and other calibrations of acceptance. This constitutes full international *legal* obligation.

What one gains in level of commitment one can lose in coverage; usually, few states become parties to a convention in the early years, and meanwhile there is a need to protect the substantive right—in this case, religious liberty—in all places.

Third, the implementation machinery set up by conventions, such as the two Covenants, is more limited in several respects than the system of special rapporteurs created by Charter-based organs to implement declarations. I argued in Chapter 3 that the latter have more impact.[17] The worldwide scope and flexible mandates of Charter-based agents contrast with the narrower focus of treaty-based mechanisms, which apply only to states parties and which consist largely of examination by an international panel of nongovernmental experts of periodic reports prepared by the states themselves.

According to Reed Brody and David Weissbrodt, "It is precisely the individual initiative and independence of the [Commission-appointed special] Rapporteurs which make them effective in protecting human rights."[18] If this is so, then it is regrettable that the rapporteur on religious discrimination has not emulated the urgent-action approach of his counterparts in the other thematic procedures and has chosen instead to dwell at such length on the legalistic issue of a possible convention. Theo van Boven, who had been charged by both the Commission and, separately, by its expert-level Subcommission on Prevention of Discrimination and Protection of Minorities to examine and report on the possibility of a convention, concluded that "we should not rush into such an exercise and perhaps should wait until the Human Rights Committee, the body that monitors the implementation of the Covenant [on Civil and Political Rights] has formulated its general comments with respect to Article 18."[19]

More important, van Boven pointed out that

the exercise of religious liberty does involve other human rights . . . [such as] the right to physical and mental integrity . . . to peaceful assembly and association . . . to freedom of opinion and expression . . . not to be subjected to arbitrary arrest and detention . . . to leave one's country and return to it . . . to education, and so forth. Indeed, many aspects of religious liberty have little or no meaning if other human rights are not effectively secured.[20]

This being the case, one wonders why the rapporteur did not intercede more vigorously and more often in cases where the state's motive in violating one of these other rights was directly connected with the religious beliefs or practices of the victim. Van Boven acknowledged that some instances of religious intolerance or discrimination are caused by nonstate actors and are thus beyond the scope of UN supervisory mechanisms, which "rely solely on the accountability of governments," and he gave the rapporteur credit for taking due notice of these nongovernmental problems. Van Boven also called for efforts by religious communities themselves to build understanding, respect, and tolerance.[21]

By the time of his fifth report to the Commission (1991), Ribeiro had moved a bit further toward specifics. He said he had communicated with 21 governments during the preceding year concerning complaints of religious persecution. He described the reported incidents and included any replies received from the governments concerned. The document included reports of numerous incidents in Iran and China.[22]

In his 1992 report, Ribeiro continued along the same line, expressing "concern at the persistence of the allegations, stating that they ranged from extrajudicial killings of clergy members to the prohibition of specific manifestations relating to a particular religion or belief."[23] He again cited countries by name and incorporated their replies, if any, to the allegations against them. Once again, though, he placed emphasis on the idea of preparing a "separate binding international instrument."

As I noted earlier, I have been unable to find evidence that the rapporteur made any on-site visits during the first six years of his mandate or that he even tried to do so, despite the fact that financial provisions had been made for this. Having mentioned Iran as a particularly egregious case, for example, one wonders why he did not seek permission to visit—the host government sometimes acquiesces in such visits in order to show its own side of the story or at least to balance the negative information reaching the United Nations from refugees, opposition political groups, or nongovernmental human rights organizations. The Iranian Government might have refused permission, but it would have had to give a reason; and by 1990 it might have said yes, as it was then willing to allow visits by the Commission's special rapporteur on Iran (Chapter 7).

In the annex to the annual report of the Human Rights Commission, the Secretariat states the financial implications of every resolution adopted at that session. In 1990, the Secretariat estimated that the rapporteur would undertake four field missions during the two years of his mandate, in addition to the usual three round-trips to Geneva per year to prepare his report and a fourth trip to present the report to the annual Commission session. The document provides for three Secretariat staff to ''gather information, compile and analyze material, prepare and help conduct the field missions and prepare the final report.''[24] But it does not appear that Ribeiro availed himself of the resources available for field missions.

The General Assembly seems not to have been wholly satisfied with this state of affairs, because there is a noticeable shift in tone and content from the 1991 to the 1992 Assembly resolutions on the subject.[25] In 1992, for instance, the Assembly included a new preambular paragraph:

Alarmed that serious instances, including acts of violence, of intolerance and discrimination on the grounds of religion or belief occur in many parts of the world, as evidenced in the report of the Special Rapporteur of the Commission on Human Rights, Mr. Angelo Vidal d'Almeida Riberio . . .

Previous resolutions had not used words like ''alarmed,'' nor had they mentioned Ribeiro by name. But more important was a new operative paragraph:

[The General Assembly]
11. Encourages Governments to give serious consideration to inviting the Special Rapporteur to visit their countries so as to enable him to fulfill his mandate even more effectively.[26]

It would appear that the Assembly felt that the time had come for this rapporteur to take more initiative and to establish a UN human rights presence, albeit temporarily, in places where the rights with which he is concerned were being violated. His thematic and geographic counterparts were, of course, already doing this.

The rapporteur had a mandate as strong as that of the other thematic mechanisms, and he had the financial and staff resources to carry it out. That he moved so slowly and cautiously from 1986 to 1992 (the period covered in this study) is difficult to explain from the available documentation and scholarly literature. Surely the rights he was called upon to monitor were no less important than those dealt with by other mechanisms. Indeed, as van Boven has pointed out, they are inextricably intertwined. The enforced disappearance, summary execution or threat thereof, or torture or other serious abuse of someone on religious grounds could have stimulated a response by this agent in addition to action by other thematic mechanisms and by the country rapporteur. While Ribeiro pulled fewer punches in his annual reports as years went on, naming governments and describing incidents in detail, he does not appear to have believed that either an urgent-action procedure or field visits were appropriate.

This appears to be a case where the energy and style of the individual have made a difference in the effectiveness of the mechanism. There is more to tell about the Working Group on Enforced Disappearances than about the Rapporteur on Religious Discrimination because the working group attempted and accomplished so much more. The story of the Rapporteur—when contrasted with that of the working group—gains impact from its very thinness.

SOME ELEMENTS OF EFFECTIVENESS OF THEMATIC MECHANISMS

B. G. Ramcharan, one of the most insightful participants in, and scholars of, the UN human rights system, has set forth the advantages and disadvantages of the thematic procedures. His overall conclusions are worth repeating, as we prepare to turn our attention to country-specific mechanisms:

The thematic approach enables the examination of global dimensions of violations . . . [and] enables specific situations of violations to be dealt with through the angle of a global examination [as well as] the identification of global strategies of action and of further standards which may be needed in the area being dealt with. . . . [It] has also in some instances been successful in developing an urgent action dimension.

[However, it] . . . could . . . lead to excessive generalization about problems and take the examination away from concrete issues . . . [or] to insufficient attention being paid to a particular case or situation and thus detract from the quality of protection offered . . . [or] lead to insufficient pressure being brought to bear upon particular governments, as their situations are ranged among several other situations of a similar nature, on a global basis.

[It] has the merit of giving the United Nations access to a problem . . . usually does not result in the dramatic elimination of the problem but in nearly every instance it has some mitigatory effect and cumulatively, in the long-term, does contribute to the containment and possibly the elimination of the problem. . . . [and] protection is afforded to some individuals and this is always worthwhile, for a life saved . . . is justification in and of itself.[27]

In evaluating the effectiveness of thematic mechanisms, I believe several points have particular relevance. What follows applies equally to the various individual thematic rapporteurs (by 1996 there were 12 of them) and to the Working Group on Disappearances, although I use the term "thematic agent" for the sake of simplicity. First, the number of cases dealt with by the agent is bound to rise during the first few years of operation, as more and more individuals and groups learn of his or her existence. This is a slow process, because unfortunately the UN human rights structure is only beginning to include a network of field offices and outreach activities capable of informing large and far-flung populations or of acting as points of contact for victims of human rights abuse, and the press and media do little to promote awareness of these new instruments.[28] While nongovernmental human rights organizations help get the word out and act as conduits for many of the cases that reach Geneva, they cannot do the whole job. Awareness of new thematic mechanisms also spreads more slowly than awareness of country-specific mechanisms because of the latter's clearly defined geographic scope.

Especially in the early years, a thematic agent might not know about certain incidents, which therefore would not figure in his or her annual reports to the Human Rights Commission. As the years go on, the number of reported cases is likely to rise—but this does not mean that there are more and more violations. It means that more are being reported, including incidents that took place some years earlier.

Second, a rise in caseload also means that the international community has found a way to convert its *potential* influence on human rights issues into an actual operating mechanism that seeks to exercise influence in an increasing number of concrete situations. An active agent is engaged with governments, and they are engaged with him or her—they accept the obligation to talk with the agent, to provide a response, to supply information, sometimes to explain what they are doing and have done, and to explain why they are, or are not, acceding to his or her appeals. The thematic agent has become a factor that governments take into account, to one degree or another, at various stages of their decision-making processes. This mechanism gradually becomes accepted as a normal, legitimate part of the international context within which a government operates.[29]

Thus, up to a point, a rise in the number of cases dealt with by a rapporteur can be seen as evidence of increasing impact. A truly effective thematic mechanism should, of course, be able to promote an eventual decline in the specific category of abuse with which it is concerned (disappearance, torture, religious discrimination, etc.) and to help at least some actual victims as it moves toward this goal. It is highly unlikely to be able to achieve total eradication of an abuse; human rights violations are not like smallpox—one cannot simply find the right vaccine and inject everyone. They arise from defects of the will or of the heart— and the cure is probably never final or universal. Still, sometimes the international community has come close: chattel slavery is virtually gone from the earth.

Third, an increase in caseload is a sign that people have enough confidence in the institution responsible for combating a particular abuse to turn to it for intercession and to provide it information. If they stopped doing these things, it would mean either that there was no longer a problem or that no one took the mechanism seriously anymore.

But how long can a period of gradually increasing caseload last before one can determine that a mechanism has succeeded or failed? This is not easy to say. Because many of the countries where serious abuses occur have poorly developed communications systems and press and media facilities, the lag time between incident and report may affect the rise and fall of caseloads as much as the actual rise and fall in violations.

In its paper for the 1993 World Conference on Human Rights, "Facing up to the Failures," Amnesty International charged that "experts [of the thematic mechanisms] are swamped with an ever-increasing flood of cases but have been unable to have any significant impact on these practices which are a blatant contradiction of the most fundamental internationally-recognized human rights norms."[30] The charge that they have no significant impact is too harsh, particularly in light of the record of the Working Group on Disappeared Persons. But Amnesty International was here building the case for its proposal for a Special Commissioner for Human Rights (a post very much like that of the High Commissioner, which was eventually endorsed by the Conference—see Chapter 8), and in the process it undervalued the contribution of the thematic mechanisms, which are in a true sense immediate precursors of the High Commissioner. Both their accomplishments and their shortcomings have important teaching value for the work of the new office.

REVIEW

In this chapter I briefly reviewed the history of international efforts to protect religious liberty, including efforts within the UN system to set clear standards and to establish implementation machinery—specifically, the post of Special Rapporteur on the Elimination of Religious Discrimination and Intolerance. I then looked more closely at the mandate of the rapporteur and at the way he has carried it out. I concluded that, although the problem with which he deals is less case-specific and less infused with a sense of life-and-death urgency than that addressed by the Working Group on Disappearances, it nevertheless lends itself to urgent-action procedures, on-site visits, and intercession in individual cases. For reasons probably attributable in large measure to the personality and style of the rapporteur, the mandate has been carried out in a generally passive and abstract way, with much time and energy devoted to the nonoperational question of whether to prepare an international convention on the topic.

The chapter also summarizes the advantages and disadvantages of the thematic approach to multilateral protection of human rights, outlining the difficulties in coming to firm conclusions on the overall utility of these procedures vis-à-vis country-specific approaches but pointing to some of the factors that need to be taken into account in reaching a conclusion on the matter.

NOTES

1. B. G. Ramcharan, *The Concept and Present Status of the International Protection of Human Rights* (Dordrecht, Netherlands: Martinus Nijhoff, 1989), 10–14, 196–200; R. J. Vincent, *Human Rights and International Relations* (Cambridge: Cambridge University Press, 1986), 44–45.

2. Article 18: "Everyone has the right to freedom of thought, conscience and religion; this right includes freedom to change his religion or belief, and freedom, either alone or in community with others and in public or private, to manifest his religion or belief in teaching, practice, worship and observance."

3. Article 18: "1. Everyone shall have the right to freedom of thought, conscience and religion. This right shall include freedom to have or to adopt a religion or belief of his choice, and freedom, either individually or in community with others and in public or private, to manifest his religion or belief in worship, observance, practice and teaching. 2. No one shall be subject to coercion which would impair his freedom to have or to adopt a religion or belief of his choice." (Paragraph 3 enumerates the permissible limitations on these rights, and paragraph 4 affirms parents' rights to ensure the religious and moral education of their children.)

4. General Assembly Resolution 36/55 and annex.

5. Letter to Warren Hewitt, Director of the Office of Human Rights Affairs, Bureau of International Organization Affairs, July 23, 1981.

6. Diplomatic note No. 130 from the U.S. Mission in Geneva to the United Nations Secretariat, Dec. 9, 1982.

7. Human Rights Commission Resolution 1983/40.

8. An excellent survey of the development of UN engagement with the issues of religious discrimination and intolerance can be found in Theo van Boven, "Advances and Obstacles in Building Understanding and Respect between People of Diverse Religions and Beliefs," *Human Rights Quarterly* 13(4) (1991), 437–52.

9. Human Rights Commission resolution 1986/20.

10. E/CN.4/1987/35.

11. E/CN.4/1988/45 and Add. 1 and Corr.1.

12. Human Rights Commission Resolution 1987/15.

13. *UN Yearbook on Human Rights for 1988* (New York: United Nations, 1992), 85.

14. E/CN.4/1990/46.

15. A. H. Robertson and J. G. Merrills, *Human Rights in the World*, 3d ed. (Manchester: Manchester University Press, 1989), 25–27.

16. This issue is dealt with at length by Theodor Meron in *Human Rights and Humanitarian Norms as Customary Law* (New York: Oxford University Press, 1989). See also Louis Henkin, *The Age of Rights* (New York: Columbia University Press, 1990), 18–21; Hurst Hannum, "Human Rights," in Oscar Schachter and Christopher Joyner,

eds., *United Nations Legal Order*, Vol. 1 (Cambridge: Cambridge University Press, 1995), 319–48.

17. See Chapter 3. For another extended discussion of the differences between these types of implementation mechanisms, see Theo van Boven, " 'Political' and 'Legal' Control Mechanisms," in A. Eide and B. Hagtvet, eds., *Human Rights in Perspective* (Oxford: Blackwell, 1992), 36–60.

18. R. Brody and D. Weissbrodt, "Major Developments at the 1989 Session of the UN Commission on Human Rights," *Human Rights Quarterly* 11(4) (1989), 602.

19. Van Boven, "Advances and Obstacles," 445. He added that any binding instrument should take the form of a protocol to the covenant rather than a separate document and that it should utilize the existing implementation procedures of the covenant.

20. Ibid., 446.

21. Ibid., 447.

22. E/CN.4/1991/56.

23. E/CN.4/1992.

24. E/CN.4/1990/94 Add. 1.

25. General Assembly Resolutions 46/131 and 47/129, respectively. Both were adopted without a vote.

26. General Assembly Resolution 47/129.

27. Ramcharan, *The Concept*, 192–93.

28. Former UnderSecretary-General Jan Martenson was a notable exception to this statement. Martenson deserves credit for injecting genuine vigor into this effort during his tenure (1988–93), including the vast project of preparing for the 1993 World Conference on Human Rights. Since 1994, the High Commissioner for Human Rights, Jose Ayala Lasso, has established several long-term field missions in troubled areas, including Burundi, Rwanda, the former Yugoslavia, Colombia, Cambodia, Malawi, Zaire, and Abkhazia/Georgia.

29. In the case of a country-specific rapporteur, it is precisely the eventual removal of the mechanism that contributes to a sense of a return to normalcy in a state's international life.

30. Amnesty International, "Facing up to the Failures: Proposals for Improving the Protection of Human Rights by the United Nations," Apr. 5, 1993, A/CONF.157/PC/62/ Add. 1, 8.

6

Special Rapporteur on Chile

Early in the regime of President Pinochet, the United Nations established a Chile-specific mechanism to press the military government to halt human rights abuses, and the United Nations demonstrated willingness to sustain its efforts until restoration of full respect for human rights over 15 years later. The UN campaign was only one of several factors influencing human rights practices, and it was not the most important. But among external factors, I think it is fair to say that it played a meaningful role and made a contribution to the eventual outcome. A by-product of this effort—one of the first attempts by a political organ of the United Nations to influence the human rights situation in a specific country—was the gradual strengthening of the political will of states to utilize the United Nations for human rights purposes. This chapter examines the operation of the Chile-specific UN human rights mechanism against the historical background of the Allende regime, its violent overthrow, the policies followed by the Pinochet junta, and the domestic and international factors that helped shape the junta's human rights practices over a period of years.

POLITICAL PARTIES AND ELECTIONS

For over four decades before 1973, Chile had been free of the military and civilian dictatorships, political instability, and human rights abuses that had plagued many other Latin American states. Political change took place through periodic democratic elections, and the military did not see itself as entitled to settle the political fate of the nation.[1]

Prolonged domestic peace enabled the growth of a prosperous economy. Chileans enjoyed one of the highest standards of living in Latin America, and this prosperity was more evenly distributed than in most countries of the region.

However, a slowdown in the rate of economic growth in the 1960s contributed to a sense that too many of the benefits of economic growth were beginning to be reaped by too few, with the poor, particularly in urban areas, being deprived of their fair share. A sense of resentment toward foreign investors and their governments also began to make headway. These feelings found political expression in increased support for leftist political parties, which, of course, did their part to profit from this discontent.

The Chilean Left took three main organizational forms: a pro-Soviet Communist Party, a Socialist Party, also sympathetic to the USSR but favoring more radical changes at a faster pace than the Communists, and the guerrilla Movement of the Revolutionary Left. Julio Faundez notes that Marxist parties had held an established niche in Chilean political life since 1932. Of the eight Chilean governments between 1932 and 1973, they had participated in five at cabinet level.[2]

In the center was the Christian Democratic Party, which favored a proactive policy of significant social and economic reform but opposed full state socialism. They sought a new approach to maintaining control over foreign economic interests without alienating them. The Christian Democrats also strongly opposed Soviet geopolitical ambitions.[3]

On the right, the conservative National Party—formed in 1966 from the merger of the traditional Conservative and Liberal Parties—represented the status quo and espoused a platform of free market economics and an anti-Soviet foreign policy.

For the 1970 presidential election, Salvador Allende of the Socialist Party led a Socialist-Communist "Popular Unity" electoral front. Radomiro Tomic was the candidate of the then-ruling Christian Democrats, and former President Jorge Alessandri represented the National Party. In the previous election (1964), Allende had challenged incumbent President Edouardo Frei and received 39 percent of the vote to Frei's 56 percent. (The Right fielded only a minor candidate.) With the popular centrist Frei ineligible for a third consecutive term in 1970, his party nominated the relatively unknown Tomic, an activist on the party's left wing. Alessandri decided to run again to ward off the possibility of a Socialist-Communist victory and also because he thought Tomic was an unacceptably leftist alternative. Alessandri nearly succeeded: the result was very close—Allende 36 percent, Alessandri 35 percent, Tomic 29 percent.[4]

As no candidate had received the required minimum of 40 percent, the Chilean Congress had to elect the President from the top two candidates. This had happened before in Chile, and the Congress had established the practice of following the order of the popular vote. The Christian Democrats—the largest group in Congress—decided to follow this tradition and to back Allende, who was thereupon elected.

Faundez argues that, had Christian Democratic legislators chosen instead to support Alessandri, there would have been a bloody confrontation that the Left was likely to win.[5] However, I disagree, because, first, as Faundez himself notes, the election of Alessandri would have been perfectly constitutional and thus seen by most citizens and groups as legitimate, despite the fact that it would have broken with the tradition of electing the front-runner. Second, the closeness of the vote takes away any argument that Allende had a popular mandate. He received a smaller percentage of the vote than he had gotten six years earlier; only the distribution of the vote among the other candidates had changed this time sufficiently to give him a very narrow plurality, not any groundswell of support for him or his coalition. Although Faundez points out that two-thirds of the electorate voted for stepped-up economic reform, it is also true that almost two-thirds voted for non-Marxist candidates over an avowed Marxist. The Congress could have concluded that a majority of the people might as well have chosen Alessandri as Allende in a two-candidate race—certainly a plausible hypothesis—and in my view it is unlikely that a prolonged, serious confrontation would have resulted had the Congress elected Alessandri.[6]

THE ALLENDE ADMINISTRATION AND THE PINOCHET COUP

Allende's government was troubled from the start by its lack of majority popular support. There were sporadic public protests over economic dislocation and perceived threats to civil freedom. The Popular Unity government actually made slight gains in the March 1973 Congressional elections, the first real, nationwide test of the government's popular support. While this still left the opposition with solid majorities in both houses (30–20 in the Senate, 87–63 in the Chamber of Deputies), Edy Kaufman says that the significance of the results is that they disappointed opponents who had hoped for a two-thirds majority in order to impeach Allende. The Right then saw no way to replace Allende before his term ended in 1976. Kaufman also notes that the Left's gains in 1973, albeit small, encouraged the government to take a harder line on some economic issues, thereby polarizing the political situation. General Augusto Pinochet and civilian rightists began to prepare for a coup.[7]

In September 1973 the armed forces, led by Pinochet, overthrew Allende in a bloody coup, which was followed by a period of repression so massive and violent that it quickly put the Chilean human rights situation on the global agenda. During the first months of military rule, there were hundreds of disappearances,[8] widespread torture, and thousands of arbitrary arrests.

Domestically, the military government encountered no serious opposition during the first two years. In the economy, the regime's shift to laissez-faire capitalism led to a rise in investment and production. This growth was aided by the decision to reopen the Chilean economy to foreign investment and to strengthen ties with multinational corporations and banks.[9] On the political and human rights side, arbitrary detention became institutionalized under a series of state-of-siege decrees renewed every six months. All democratic political and union activity was outlawed, meetings were banned, and the press was increasingly subject to censorship. The political parties continued to exist but were perforce quiet during this period. The Left was too afraid to take an active stance, and the Right tended to support the junta. The Christian Democrats trod cautiously but criticized the regime as often and as boldly as circumstances would allow.

THE CATHOLIC CHURCH AND THE JUNTA

The Catholic Church had for some years been a leading force for social reform in Chile—indeed, it was regarded as one of the most socially committed churches in Latin America, dedicated to carrying out the Second Vatican Council's appeal to exercise a "preferential option for the poor." This commitment extended from Cardinal Raul Silva of Santiago, through the Bishops' Conference, to the parish level.[10]

Only 3 of the country's 30 bishops actually welcomed the Pinochet coup, calling it a necessary step to save the country from anarchy and social collapse; the others and most priests and nuns simply stayed out of the political fray at first, focusing instead on the Church's traditional ministries and on its social mission among the poor. But even during this early period, Cardinal Silva as well as other bishops and priests often interceded privately with the authorities on behalf of individual victims of disappearance, torture, or prolonged arbitrary detention.[11]

Under the leadership of Cardinal Silva, already in 1973 Catholic, Protestant, and Jewish religious leaders established the Committee of Peace to assist victims of human rights abuse, help families of the imprisoned keep in touch with their relatives, provide material help to families in the form of food, clothing, and money, organize work projects for some of those summarily fired by the new regime (or help them try to get their jobs back), and assist students to gain admission to universities abroad. It also documented human rights cases and brought them to the attention of governments and international organizations as a way to put pressure on the junta to halt violations.

Two years later, Pinochet pressed successfully for the dissolution of the Committee on the grounds that it was being used by Marxist-Leninists, but the Catholic Church quickly reestablished it under a different name: the Vicariate of Solidarity. To avoid reopening the issue of exploitation by Marxist-Leninists, the Vicariate decided to restrict the sending of information abroad. The junta continued to exert pressure on the new organization, although it did not move to suppress it directly. Among its many activities, the Vicariate petitioned the Supreme Court to appoint a special investigating judge to inquire into cases of disappeared persons; the request was denied. The regime subsequently deported one of the Vicariate's lawyers and arrested another.[12]

Writing five years after the coup, Robert Alexander said that "the Roman Catholic Church must be classified as part of the opposition. . . . It has consistently criticized the regime's policies, particularly its handling of the economy and its violations of human rights." He added, however, that both sides had sought to avoid any sharp confrontation.[13]

While there may be some basis for this last comment, there is also evidence that the confrontation at times became sharp indeed. In 1974, the year after the coup, the Chilean bishops issued a fairly moderate statement calling for "unrestricted respect for human rights as formulated by the United Nations and the Second Vatican Council," noting that their violation was standing in the way of national reconciliation.[14] But as the apparatus of repression became more and more systematic and institutionalized, the Church itself became a target. Bishops, priests, and nuns—especially those engaged in social-action ministries—were accused of supporting (or being) Communists or other subversives. Arrests of clergy began to mount. Some foreign priests were expelled, and others were pressed to leave the country; over 300 priests went into forced or voluntary exile. Pinochet appointed a military officer to run the Catholic University of Santiago. Bishops were denounced and harassed and sometimes detained by the police for short periods.

In response to these acts and to the continuing pattern of official oppression of human rights, in 1975 the Church shifted to a more "prophetic" stance on social and political issues, publicly denouncing human rights abuses and the regime's disregard of the problems of the poor as well as its persecution of the Church.[15] In a 1977 statement, the bishops even called for formation of a new national political consensus on the basis of which new constitutional laws could be enacted, a bold position that drew from the Justice Minister the comment that the bishops were "useful fools getting themselves mixed up with politicians and Marxists." But the contest between Church and State was hardly one-sided: when the bishops protested the minister's remark, the minister resigned.[16]

EXTERNAL CRITICISM

Robert Alexander notes that Chile's reaction to external criticism and to cooperation with international bodies went through several phases. In the weeks and months following the coup, the regime allowed many official and unofficial missions to visit Chile, to speak with government leaders, and even to interview prisoners and residents of refugee camps. But this did not produce the effect desired by the junta, namely, to quiet criticism, because many of the visitors were, as Alexander put it, "horrified by what they saw."[17]

After the UN General Assembly adopted its first resolution condemning violations in Chile in November 1974 by the lopsided vote of 63 to 9, with 21 abstentions, the junta decided that since an open-door policy seemed to increase the volume of denunciations, closing the door should have the opposite effect. At about the same time, the regime picked up a theme it had occasionally used earlier and launched a systematic propaganda campaign to refurbish its image by alleging that all foreign criticism emanated directly or indirectly from the world Communist movement.[18]

Alexander observes that the junta's critique of foreign pressure was not baseless. There had been a great deal of uninformed and thus exaggerated sympathy for Allende in some Western countries, particularly in Europe, where he was often seen as merely a socialist reformer despite the fact that his party stood to the left of the Communists as well as the fact of his growing ties with the USSR. Moreover, Moscow and its satellites did indeed mount a substantial anti-Pinochet propaganda campaign from the early days after the coup.[19] Alexander says that a few of the charges against the regime were simply unfounded. But he maintains—accurately, in my opinion—that the junta's sustained efforts to belittle all of them as Communist propaganda did not succeed where it counted, that is, with governments and publics of countries particularly important to Santiago.

James Whelan presents a different perspective on Chile's response to criticism from abroad. Prefacing his treatment with a lengthy pro-Pinochet quote from Henry Kissinger (sample: "Was [the coup's] crime in its methods, or in its position on the right . . . ? [w]hy [must] conservative governments like Chile's be reformed by ostracism?"), Whelan devotes several pages to explaining and justifying the junta's actions. He praises the regime (properly, in my view) for permitting early visits by representatives of the International Committee of the Red Cross, Amnesty International, the InterAmerican Commission on Human Rights, and the UN High Commissioner for Refugees. But when the Inter Parliamentary Union was denied the opportunity to visit former Chilean congressmen in prison, Whelan's only comment was, "Only a small handful of members of Allende's coalition fit that description."[20]

Whelan wrote that "the attacks on Chile increased in intensity and ferocity" and even called the campaign against human rights abuses in Chile a "worldwide pogrom."[21]

In March 1975, the UN Human Rights Commission decided to set up an ad hoc working group to investigate and report to the Commission and the General Assembly on the human rights situation in Chile and to make recommendations for improvement. This was one of the earliest efforts by a UN political body to grapple with a concrete human rights situation.[22]

The Chilean case acquired this high "UN profile" and relatively assertive attention for several reasons. First, the Soviet Union leaped on the issue for obvious ideological and geopolitical reasons. It was able to exploit for propaganda purposes the violence and bloodshed of the coup and its aftermath. Second, the excesses of the Pinochet regime were widely publicized by the international press. The large number of detainees, tortures, and disappearances shocked people who had not expected to see this in a country with Chile's tradition of respecting human rights. Third, the United States was reeling from the just-concluded Vietnam War and the still-boiling Watergate crisis and at that time was interested only in superpower diplomacy and in the Middle East—the latter of which conveniently burst into flames again right after the coup in Santiago, raising U.S.–Soviet tensions and monopolizing U.S. official attention for several weeks. Fourth, the United States was not riding a wave of popularity in the UN, and vice versa. The Soviets had a clear field to exploit the Chile issue.

Meanwhile, inside Chile the repressive fury continued through 1975 with little letup. Credible reports of abuse continued to reach nongovernmental human rights organizations and governments, and through them the United Nations, at an alarming rate.

In mid-1975 the junta first granted and then revoked permission for the working group to make an on-site visit to Chile. It justified the revocation on the grounds that the United Nations had provided insufficient guarantees that the government would have an opportunity to review and rebut allegations.[23]

In Chile, the steady drumfire of criticism by the Church from 1975 on and by some of the braver political figures and journalists lent indirect support to the United Nations' efforts to gain access by the working group. So, too, did the increasing level of concern expressed directly by European countries of importance to Chile—France, Italy, West Germany, and the United Kingdom.

In the United States, even an Executive Branch sympathetic to Pinochet for geopolitical reasons could not stop Congress in 1975 from cutting off credits or grants to the Chilean Government for arms purchases. In June 1976 Secretary of State Henry Kissinger, who generally sought to exclude human rights concerns from U.S. foreign policy, acknowledged at the General Assembly of the Organization of American States that "the condition of human rights as assessed by the OAS Human Rights Commission has impaired our relationship with Chile and will continue to do so."[24]

Kissinger probably attributed the assessment of the rights situation to the OAS commission rather than to an independent U.S. appraisal in order to provide cover for his criticism of a government with which he thought we should maintain good relations. But it also had the effect of enhancing, even to a slight degree, the prestige and credibility of international human rights institutions.

The junta's relationships with Western European countries also suffered badly as a result of its human rights policies. Italy even refused to recognize the junta for almost a year after its seizure of power. France, West Germany, the U.K., Italy, Belgium, and the Netherlands declined to support a World Bank loan for Chile in December 1976, following the earlier lead of the Scandinavian countries in the multilateral development banks. The loan went through anyway, but a strong political signal had been sent. Also, starting in 1974 most Western nations regularly voted for UN resolutions condemning Chilean human rights violations.

By the mid-1970s, then, Chile's economic opening to the world and its consequent enjoyment of resource inflows were accompanied by growing political isolation. Many governments suspended diplomatic relations or lowered the level of their representation in protest against the continuing wave of human rights violations: France, Sweden, Colombia, Venezuela, and Belgium were among those who took this step. The U.K. followed suit in 1975 after the secret police tortured Sheila Cassidy, a British physician who had treated suspected guerrillas.[25]

The junta's relations with Latin American nations were also troubled—particularly with Mexico and Venezuela but also, after Chile's December 1976 withdrawal from the Andean Pact, with Bolivia, Peru, Ecuador, and Colombia.[26]

Human rights pressure on the Chilean government continued to build within the Organization of American States, as its expert-level Inter-American Commission on Human Rights (IACHR) steadily took a more active stance on abuses in the hemisphere, including, of course, in Chile, which had already been the subject of a special IACHR mission and report in 1974.

The U.S. attitude was particularly important because of its role as a Hemispheric and Western leader and because of its close economic and security ties with Chile. As mentioned before, the Nixon and Ford administrations were prepared, for the most part, to overlook abuses in Chile because of Pinochet's anti-Soviet stance. They did not want to let the rights issue interfere with our bilateral relations or operate in a way that would weaken Pinochet. In Congress, however, human rights advocates took a different view. For them, it was no longer enough to denounce abuses in the Soviet Bloc while remaining silent and indifferent to serious violations in allied states.

Recognizing that the incoming Carter administration would likely take a different approach from that of its predecessors, the junta released 300 political prisoners shortly after the U.S. election. However, this act did nothing to diminish new abuses by the security forces or to change the repressive character of the system.

President Carter shifted U.S. policy in several ways. For instance, the new administration was not nearly as reticent in its public criticism of the junta's abuses. In May 1977 the administration made the symbolic gesture of receiving ex-President Frei at the White House and Allende's ex-Foreign Minister Almeyda at the State Department. The Pinochet regime thereafter began to receive strong diplomatic representations regularly from the Executive Branch. Secretary of State Cyrus Vance and his deputy Warren Christopher engaged in active promotion of human rights on a continuous basis. The new Bureau of Human Rights and Humanitarian Affairs, led by Assistant Secretary Patricia Derian, quickly took a leadership role within the Department and the wider foreign affairs community on a broad range of human rights–related issues, including military and economic assistance and sales and U.S. voting practices in the multilateral development banks. Within international organizations, this led to active U.S. support for resolutions in the UN and the OAS condemning rights violations in Chile.

With regard to Chile, Joseph Tulchin and Augusto Varas grant that the Carter policy on human rights saved lives but that the policy was not implemented "coherently and consistently with adequate political and diplomatic tools to achieve its goals."[27] They state that "there is no question that the U.S. policy saved Chilean lives. But the policy as enacted did not accomplish its stated goals. U.S. sanctions for human rights violations also harmed U.S. relations with the military and the right."[28] What they do not say is that saving Chilean lives *was* one of the stated goals of U.S. policy. But the paragraph from which this quotation is taken and the one following make clear that the main "stated goal" to which they refer is the restoration of democracy in Chile. Here I believe the authors' comment is closer to the target, in the sense that a policy of bilateral criticism and of increasing political distance is not by itself the most likely to achieve redemocratization in the short run.[29]

Chile's increasing isolation and consequent loss of prestige during the 1970s and early 1980s could also be seen in the fact that many heads of state no longer included Santiago on their itineraries. During the six years of the second Frei administration (1964–70), ten heads of state came to Chile from various parts of the world; by contrast, during the first eight years of the junta (1973–81), only four heads of state visited, all of them from South America.[30]

Chile's growing isolation led it to seek new ties with countries that had never held much importance for it—such as Arab states and South Africa. For all its fervent antiCommunism, the regime took steps to improve its relations with the People's Republic of China and with Pol Pot's Cambodia.[31]

Also, although Chile faced no significant external military threat (except briefly during the Beagle Channel dispute with Argentina in late 1978) and therefore had no need for a substantial defense establishment, the U.S. arms embargo and similar restrictions by France, West Germany, and the U.K. steadily took their toll on the capabilities of the Chilean armed forces. By the end of the decade, the regime's military power vis-à-vis its neighbors had dwindled, a further reason for the drop in Chile's prestige.[32]

At the United Nations, heavy criticism continued unabated. Heraldo Munoz described the regime's international position in the late 1970s:

[There was] deterioration of national prestige, an intangible element of power of special importance to countries which, like Chile, do not have great political or economic resources . . . isolation means that the . . . government is not able to satisfy national objectives in the world with the same ease and success as its predecessors.[33]

Moreover, the regime was forced to conclude that its best efforts to improve its image by other means had failed; Operación Verdad (Operation Truth), a well-financed propaganda campaign that included large, paid advertisements in major newspapers in the United States and Western Europe, yielded few positive results.[34] When Pinochet decided to seize a human rights banner himself, he did so clumsily: he waited until just before the fall of Saigon in May 1975 to condemn North Vietnam for human rights abuses.[35]

THE REGIME SHIFTS COURSE REGARDING THE UNITED NATIONS—FOR AWHILE

Hoping to end Chile's growing political isolation, in April 1978 newly appointed Foreign Minister Herman Cubillos launched a reorientation of Chilean foreign policy. Among the first concrete signs of the new approach was the decision to invite the Human Rights Commission's ad hoc working group to visit the country. Pinochet had won a plebiscite on his rule earlier that year and probably felt secure in reopening the door to outside critics.

Thus, after stonewalling the working group for three years, the government finally allowed it to visit Chile in 1978 (the first on-site visit ever made by a UN human rights body)—believing, it said later, that granting permission for the visit would end the United Nations' active concern with the human rights situation there.

In its reports later that year to the General Assembly and in early 1979 to the Human Rights Commission, the working group noted improvement in some aspects of the situation but called attention to the persistence of other very serious abuses.[36] In March 1979, the Commission decided to replace the group with a special rapporteur having a similar mandate and with a separate appointee to study and report on the fate of disappeared persons in Chile.[37] The Chilean Government reacted sharply, accusing the United Nations of deception:

Chile had every right to expect that the *ad hoc* and therefore arbitrary procedure hitherto applied by the United Nations would be terminated, since it fully complied with its undertaking by agreeing to the visit by the *Ad Hoc* Working Group and affording it every facility for the performance of its task. . . . Instead, showing utter contempt for the good faith of Chile . . . the Commission . . . is establishing . . . new *ad hoc* procedures. . . . [s]ince these procedures have no legal basis in the United Nations system and do not have the endorsement of Chile, they will have no legal or moral force.[38]

Pinochet thus attempted to blunt further UN efforts by appealing again to nationalist sentiment—Chilean honor was at stake; Chile would not be bullied; Chile had done its part and would refuse to be singled out for unfair treatment.

LEGAL ISSUES AND POLITICAL ISOLATION AT THE UNITED NATIONS

Its fulminations against the legality of the UN decision to establish the special rapporteur notwithstanding, there are good arguments for the view that validly established, Charter-based human rights mechanisms and procedures are legally binding on all member states.[39] As B. G. Ramcharan put it:

As a corollary of its membership in the international community, every state is under a duty to respect the human rights and fundamental freedoms of every human being and to subject itself to legitimate measures of international scrutiny that the international community is entitled to utilize to ensure protection of human rights and fundamental freedoms and, if necessary, to develop new forms of action.[40]

If such a duty exists as a corollary of membership in the international community, then it clearly goes with being a member of the United Nations and thereby comes under the provisions of the Charter, which are binding on all member states. While few provisions of international law are self-enforcing, they are all *intended* to be observed; the community of states has the right to decide upon means that are appropriate and effective to achieve that goal. States, which have an obligation to observe the law, thus also have a duty to cooperate with legally established implementation mechanisms. A refusal to cooperate creates a *new* question, that is, of possible next steps the community might wish to consider taking to achieve observance. But the *legal right* of the international community to attempt to ensure implementation of legally proper decisions is not then the issue.

The Chilean authorities became aware that the process of singling out could lead to extreme diplomatic isolation, as it had in the case of South Africa and Israel.[41] It could also lead to economic sanctions by member states [42] as well as by the United Nations itself and perhaps, as in the case of South Africa, to loss of voting rights in the United Nations. When Chile's rulers realized that they could not avoid UN scrutiny altogether, they pleaded to be considered under existing universal procedures—by which they meant, first of all, the closed-door hearings conducted under ECOSOC Resolution 1503 (1970) and, second, the tame report-examination procedure of the Human Rights Covenant.[43]

The special rapporteur, Judge Abdoulaye Dieye of Senegal, responded that it is for the competent organs of the United Nations, acting under the Charter,

to utilize for each situation such methods or procedures as it considers best suited to deal with that situation. A government cannot, therefore, legitimately claim that the situation in its country should be examined under any particular procedure or procedures, or under one procedure to the exclusion of others. The decision in each case is a matter for the United Nations.[44]

THE REGIME DECIDES TO COOPERATE AGAIN—A FEW YEARS LATER

Although the Pinochet Government did not permit Judge Dieye to visit Chile, it did allow his successor, Justice Rajsoomar Lallah of Mauritius, to make three visits: in December 1985, March 1987, and December 1987. Judge Dieye had angered the regime by his blunt criticism to the point of becoming personally unacceptable, but other factors were also at work in the decision to receive Lallah. I believe that the decision is attributable primarily to the fact that the regime was tired of being treated as an international pariah, that it felt it had halted most of the bloodier abuses that had drawn international fire, and that it probably thought it could therefore count on a moderately favorable report. As early as 1981, in another attempt to end its political isolation, Rene Rojas, Foreign Minister Cubillos' successor, said that Chile "wanted to be present, if possible, in all international events, to show that Chile is a progressive country, a lively, creative, imaginative country."[45] However, this expression of a desire for a better image did not immediately produce a new invitation to the United Nations to visit.

Chile's steady economic advance of the mid-and late 1970s had been based on a policy of reprivatization of the hundreds of enterprises nationalized by Allende (plus a few of those acquired earlier under Frei), very low import tariffs, an open door to foreign investment, a controlled exchange rate, and massive foreign borrowing. The copper industry was the only major economic sector retained by the government. The heavy inflow of foreign capital and cheap imported goods gave Chileans a sense of prosperity during these years. This era of good feeling, combined with an appeal to nationalist sentiments, enabled Pinochet to win a popular vote of confidence in a plebiscite in January 1978. The occasion for the plebiscite was the latest UN condemnation of the regime for human rights violations.[46] The result strengthened Pinochet's position; it also contributed to the decision to permit the working group to make an on-site visit later that year. The fact that a dictator decided to hold a plebiscite on the occasion of a UN human rights resolution shows that he was beginning to take the United Nations more seriously; he chose to fight the external criticism rather than ignore it. Pinochet won the immediate battle in 1978, but in the process he tacitly acknowledged that the war for Chile's international image was important enough to be waged vigorously.

The prolonged period of economic expansion that had produced a rise in living standards in the 1970s had strengthened Pinochet's domestic base to the point that he felt able to resist external criticism most of the time until the mid-1980s. His victory in the 1978 plebiscite also encouraged him to proceed along this course, as did the election in 1980 of Ronald Reagan. The Reagan administration quickly reversed former President Carter's ban on Export-Import Bank financing of projects in Chile, invited Chile to resume participation in hemispheric naval exercises, obtained a loosening of the Humphrey–Kennedy Amendment restricting military and economic assistance and arms sales, and sent Ambassador Jeane Kirkpatrick—a member of the Cabinet—on an official visit to Chile.

There was still substantial criticism from Western Europe in the early 1980s, however. While the Thatcher government had moved to rebuild a more normal relationship with the regime after 1979, France stepped up its criticism after the election of Mitterrand in May 1981. Italy and the Scandinavian countries continued their steady public critique, and the UN Human Rights Commission and the General Assembly adopted condemnatory resolutions year after year, with strong support from developing countries as well as most Western states.

In 1980 the standard of living, based so heavily on the influx of foreign money and goods, was still high enough to enable Pinochet to win a second plebiscite, this time on a new constitution that guaranteed him another eight years in office, with a new plebiscite on his tenure to be held in 1988. But the economy was just beginning to enter a period of serious decline. By mid-1982 it was in an authentic crisis, with interest rates over 40 percent, labor costs rising due to indexation, declining exports, huge trade deficits, and falling copper prices. The result was a 14 percent drop in gross domestic product (GDP) in 1982 and a whopping 30 percent unemployment rate.[47] These developments led to increasingly widespread domestic hardships and sparked public protests.[48]

These economic difficulties continued through the 1980s. Meanwhile, U.S. policy underwent another change. The first Reagan administration, as I have noted, sought to achieve its goals by embracing the Pinochet regime and overlooking its faults. Tulchin and Varas credit the second Reagan administration with finding the right approach, that is, of timing a positive approach to bilateral relations with moves by domestic forces "to achieve development through democratic consensus."[49] They acknowledge that internal political developments helped make such a policy feasible; in particular, by the mid-to-late 1980s most Chilean political parties were beginning to agree that it was more important to pool their resources against the regime than to continue the interparty programmatic battles that had grown so bitter in the 1960s and 1970s. Tulchin and Varas do not mention, however, the symbolically important shift in U.S. policy in 1985 once again to a policy of voting in favor of UN human rights resolutions criticizing Chilean human rights practices. I believe this step added to the junta's perception that the costs of their policies were rising and that there might be an advantage in renewing cooperation with the United Nations.

Writing in the same volume as Tulchin and Varas, Chilean Ambassador Carlos Portales notes that the Chilean opposition began in the mid-1980s to "take advantage of the liberalization process—the government response to the *protestas* and foreign influence."[50] This suggests that the junta had decided that the combination of a prolonged economic crisis, domestic unrest, and mounting external criticism added up to a situation pointing toward a reevaluation of its policy toward cooperating with UN human rights institutions. Portales says that

from 1983 to the 1988 plebiscite . . . the policies of foreign powers—particularly those of the United States—sought to favor a gradual and peaceful process of transition to democracy. . . . External influences limited the arbitrary policies of the military government and induced liberalization."[51]

Receiving the new UN special rapporteur might help the regime gain a favorable report, which would improve its international image, which might, in turn, help it gain the international economic support it needed to rebound from its protracted economic crisis. It might also help Pinochet win the plebiscite scheduled for 1988, in which voters were to be asked whether they wanted him to remain in office.[52] The Chileans gave Justice Lallah a mixed reception. For instance, he recounted in his 1988 report to the General Assembly that

[s]everal competent representatives of the military courts did not respond promptly or in a proper manner to his request for a hearing . . . [nor did] the Director-General of the National Information Agency . . . [or] representatives of the ordinary courts who were

investigating important complaints of human rights violations . . . with the result that he was obliged to make direct contact, at very short notice, with the various civil judges and magistrates, who did allow the Special Rapporteur to interview them.[53]

Notwithstanding these complaints, Lallah acknowledged that the government "gave . . . all the necessary facilities for carrying out his mission. The Special Rapporteur himself drew up his program of work and put it into practice . . . without any interference from the Government."[54] He even gave the government credit for a "tendency or willingness . . . to improve its performance with regard to political freedom. . . . For example, the political parties had been able to emerge from banishment." On the other hand, military court investigations had become "an especially odious and unjust instrument of oppression," and the press continued to live in a climate of intimidation.[55] Nevertheless, the overall tone of the report was positive.

THE END OF SPECIAL UN ATTENTION TO CHILE

After the opposition victory in the 1988 referendum, Pinochet decided to negotiate a gradual return to democratic rule; however, he insisted on remaining as head of the armed forces, an arrangement the opposition reluctantly had to accept as the price of a free political process. In December 1989, a 17-party opposition coalition led by Patricio Aylwin won a free election. The new government began immediately to restore civil and political rights. By early 1990, the rapporteur on Chile was able to recommend the abolition of his post and, simultaneously, the removal of the special item on Chile from the agenda of the Human Rights Commission. The Commission adopted these recommendations by consensus.[56]

In 1991, the Commission heard a final, very positive report on the state of human rights in Chile by the new Chilean UnderSecretary for Foreign Affairs, Edmundo Vargas Carreno, a Christian Democrat who, while in exile from the Pinochet regime, had served for several years as Executive Secretary of the Inter-American Commission on Human Rights. The Inter-American Commission had issued several reports seriously criticizing the abuses of the Pinochet regime.

Acknowledging the importance of external human rights criticisms, Ambassador Portales wrote that

transition to democracy will lead to the reassertion of a positive Chilean foreign policy. The country should be able to leave behind sixteen years of indictment for human rights abuses and repressive policies and recover a place in the international community.[57]

ANALYSIS

In 1978 Robert Alexander noted that the junta had "suffered from a kind of international quarantine ever since its establishment in September 1973. Its many efforts to deal with this situation . . . more often than not intensified Chile's isolation."[58] Munoz, Tulchin, Varas, Alexander, and Portales all explore the implications of Chilean isolation for various aspects of the regime's policy. This growing sense of isolation and Chile's economic downturn help explain why, in the mid-1980s, Chile stopped making strenuous efforts to ward off UN involvement in its human rights situation. The mutually reinforcing dynamic of steady multilateral and bilateral pressure, the discomfort of political isolation, domestic economic difficulties, and growing internal demands for freedom and an end to repression eventually combined to bring about a fundamental reorientation of Chilean human rights policies and its attitude toward cooperation with UN human rights efforts.

This does not mean that the UN special rapporteur's efforts alone played a decisive role in modifying the internal human rights situation in Chile. That would be claiming too much for a single source of pressure. But the regime recognized that the UN human rights structure and campaign were an integral and important part of the external environment within which Chile exists and functions. For the sake of Chile's own national interests, the government finally decided that it should seek some sort of accommodation with this important actor in the universe of actors—states, international organizations, nongovernmental organizations, and economic institutions—whose activities impinge positively or negatively on Chile's interests. The international environment consists of intangible as well as material factors that affect interests, and national interests themselves have intangible as well as material elements. Among the intangible elements are a country's image—how it is seen by other members of the community of states in terms of ethical categories, including a state's observance of community standards in human rights. The human rights category is now one of the half-dozen or more most important external factors that a government must take into account in weighing how best to promote its interests in the world of states.

The states that are prepared to condemn in the United Nations a government's human rights abuses are entities with which the target state must deal in other ways important to it. The same states trade with it, conduct joint military exercises, vote on loans in the multilateral development banks, sell military equipment, and maintain air links, financial agreements, taxation treaties, tourism arrangements, and a host of other ties, all of which can be weakened or strengthened or suspended. Most states eventually decide that their interests vis-à-vis the community of states are better served by cooperating with international human rights mechanisms. These mechanisms, in turn, can have a positive moderating influence on state behavior in human rights. This is most likely to happen when multilateral human rights pressure is sustained for several years and when it is paralleled by bilateral initiatives aiming at the same goals and by domestic human rights pressure.

A target state that believes the United Nations' interest is transitory or shallow is likely to ignore UN implementation mechanisms (after protesting their creation) in the belief that they can be swept away after a year as international attention shifts to other crisis areas. When, however, political will is sustained over several years, a state is inclined to recalculate the advantages and disadvantages of intransigence. Pressures on the Pinochet regime came directly from states, through bilateral channels, as well as through the United Nations. The United States (during the Carter administration), the United Kingdom (especially under the Labor government), France, Italy, and Spain exercised important bilateral pressure on Chile during the late 1970s and 1980s, reducing or halting economic aid and military sales and refusing to vote for loans for Chile in the World Bank (as a way of sending a political signal; no loan was ever defeated, although some votes were close). In the United States the second Reagan administration returned to a more active pro-human rights stance toward Chile. Nongovernmental organizations kept up a steady flow of public pressure on Chile throughout this period, and the Organization of American States also took the regime to task on several occasions for human rights violations. This combined and sustained pressure, in which the UN Human Rights Commission and its special rapporteurs on Chile played a particularly high-profile role, eventually led to the end of repression.

REVIEW

Pinochet's 1973 coup and its bloody aftermath stimulated an unusually rapid, high-profile reaction and institutional response within the United Nations. The regime at first reacted with intransigence and then in 1978 accepted an on-site visit by the Human Rights Commission Working Group on Chile, after which it renewed its hard-line stance for five years, then decided to resume cooperation with the United Nations. The chapter recounts this history in the light of the work of the first and second special rapporteurs and the reaction of the Chilean regime to their efforts. I conclude that, over time and together with other domestic and international factors, the United Nations made an important contribution to the evolution of the human rights situation and to Chile's willingness to cooperate with the international community.

The next chapter looks at a similar set of issues and UN responses concerning the fundamentalist Moslem regime in Iran.

NOTES

1. For a thorough and careful study of the role of the military in the decades before the Pinochet coup in 1973, see Frederick M. Nunn, *The Military in Chilean History* (Albuquerque: University of New Mexico Press, 1976), particularly Chs. 11 and 12. See also the brief, but perceptive, comments on this subject by Gilbert Merkx in his Foreword to Gennaro Arriagada, *Pinochet: The Politics of Power* (Boston: Unwin Hyman, 1988), vii–ix.

2. Julio Faundez, *Marxism and Democracy in Chile: From 1932 to the Fall of Allende* (New Haven, CT: Yale University Press, 1988), 2.

3. In 1970 the Christian Democratic Party moved leftward in an effort to take support away from the Socialists and Communists, who were then gaining in popular strength. For a concise history of centrist parties in Chile, see Timothy Scully, "Reappraising the Role of the Center: The Case of the Chilean Party System," Kellogg Institute Working Paper No. 143 (Notre Dame, IN: Helen Kellogg Institute, University of Notre Dame, September 1990), esp. 32–34.

4. Edy Kaufman, *Crisis in Allende's Chile: New Perspectives* (New York: Praeger, 1988), 185. Also, Faundez, *Marxism*, 179.

5. Faundez, *Marxism*, 180.

6. Kaufman, *Crisis*, 185.

7. Ibid., 185–87. Also, on the government's new, harder line, Faundez, *Marxism*, 2.

8. The UN Working Group on Chile determined that at least 600 disappearances occurred during the period 1973–79; most of these took place in the first year or two of the Pinochet regime. This figure of 600 was also used by the *Vicaria de la Solidaridad* (Vicariate of Solidarity) of the Archdiocese of Santiago and the International Committee of the Red Cross. See UN document E/CN.4/1363, Feb. 2, 1980, esp. paras. 87–89. In 1991, the Chilean Commission for Truth and Reconciliation (the Rettig Commission) documented nearly a thousand cases of disappearance that resulted in death. Cited in Jack Donnelly, *International Human Rights* (Boulder, CO: Westview Press, 1993), 54. See also Chapter 4 of this study.

9. Karen L. Remmer, *Military Rule in Latin America* (Boston: Unwin Hyman, 1989), 157–59.

10. Julio Samuel and Arturo Valenzuela, "Political Processes in an Authoritarian Regime: The Dynamics of Institutionalization and Opposition in Chile, 1973–80," in Julio Samuel and Arturo Valenzuela, eds., *Military Rule in Chile: Dictatorship and Opposition* (Baltimore: Johns Hopkins University Press, 1986), 214–16.

11. Brian H. Smith, "The Catholic Church in Opposition," in Samuel and Valenzuela, *Military Rule*, 270–97, esp. 277–82.

12. Robert J. Alexander, *The Tragedy of Chile* (Westport, CT: Greenwood Press, 1978), 368–69.

13. Ibid., 367.

14. Cited in ibid., 369.

15. Smith, "The Catholic Church," 277–82.

16. Alexander, *Tragedy*, 370.

17. Ibid., 372–73.

18. Ibid.

19. Western Marxists enthusiastically supported this effort. See, for instance, Ian Roxborough, Philip O'Brien, and Jackie Roddick, *Chile: The State and Revolution* (London: Macmillan, 1977).

20. James Whelan, *Out of the Ashes: Life, Death and Transfiguration of Democracy in Chile, 1833–1988* (Washington, DC: Regnery Gateway, 1989), 698–700.

21. Ibid., 700–702.

22. Ibid. states erroneously on 699 that the working group was established in 1974 and on 701 that its report was voted on in November of that year. On 700 he uses the correct date, 1975. The other early country-specific efforts by the United Nations concerned South Africa and Israel.

23. Ibid., 700.

24. Quoted in Alexander, *Tragedy*, 377.

25. Heraldo Munoz, "Chile's External Relations under the Military Government," in Samuel and Valenzuela, *Military Rule*, 307–9.

26. Alexander, *Tragedy*, 380.

27. Joseph S. Tulchin and Augusto Varas, Introduction, *From Dictatorship to Democracy: Rebuilding Political Consensus in Chile* (Boulder, CO: Lynne Rienner, 1991), 3.

28. Ibid., 3–4.

29. Ibid., 4–5. In fact, democratization was not achieved during the four years of the Carter administration nor during the four years of the first Reagan administration, which involved a full reversal of the Carter policy and an embrace of the junta; Tulchin and Varas skip over the 1981–85 period, resuming their narrative with the second Reagan administration, when a variety of international and domestic factors came together to permit the redemocratization process to get under way. Because democratization is not the focus of this study, I address these factors only briefly.

30. Samuel and Valenzuela, *Military Rule*, 310.

31. Alexander, *Tragedy*, 375.

32. *Proceedings of the U.S. Naval Institute*, Fall 1982, cited in Munoz, "Chile's External Relations," 310.

33. Munoz, "Chile's External Relations," 319, n. 1.

34. Ibid., 314.

35. Ibid., 317.

36. UN Documents A/33/331 (1978) and E/CN.4/1310 (1979).

37. The functions of the latter were subsequently assigned to the special rapporteur and to the Commission's Working Group on Enforced or Involuntary Disappearances.

38. Text included in the report to the 34th Session of the General Assembly by the special rapporteur, Judge A. Dieye (Senegal), A/34/583, paras. 1–13, cited in Theo van Boven, " 'Political' and 'Legal' Control Mechanisms: Their Competition and Coexistence," in A. Eide and B. Hagtvet, eds., *Human Rights in Perspective* (Oxford: Blackwell, 1992), 51–52.

39. van Boven, " 'Political,' " 46–52. See also Louis Henkin, *The Age of Rights* (New York: Columbia University Press, 1990), 23, 55–56.

40. B. G. Ramcharan, "Strategies for the International Protection of Human Rights in the 1990s," *Human Rights Quarterly* 13(2) (1991), 162.

41. Another aspect of the United Nations' involvement that galled the Chilean Government was the fact that since 1974 its case had been considered under a separate public agenda item entitled "The Situation of Human Rights in Chile." Only South Africa and Israel enjoyed this dubious distinction, and the Pinochet regime was angry at being singled out this way.

42. Bilateral sanctions were, in fact, imposed by the United States in 1975 and 1976 through amendments to the Foreign Assistance Act restricting military assistance, training, and sales.

43. See Chapters 3 and 4 for a description of these procedures.

44. Quoted in van Boven, " 'Political,' " 52.

45. *El Mercurio*, Mar. 28, 1981, cited in Munoz, "Chile's External Relations," 314.

46. Remmer, *Military Rule*, 160.

47. Ibid., 162–63.

48. Samuel and Valenzuela, Introduction, *Military Rule*, 10–11.

49. Tulchin and Varas, Introduction, *Dictatorship*, 3–4.

50. Carlos Portales, "The Transition to Democracy and US–Chilean Relations," in Tulchin and Varas, *Dictatorship*, 61.

51. Ibid., 61–62.

52. This time the voters rejected Pinochet's proposal to remain as president.

53. *UN Yearbook on Human Rights for 1988*, 71. The National Information Agency was the secret police.

54. Ibid., 72.

55. Ibid., 73

56. Reed Brody, Penny Parker, and David Weissbrodt, "Major Developments in 1990 at the UN Human Rights Commission," *Human Rights Quarterly* 12(4) (1990), 567 ff. Also see Commission Resolution 1990/78.

57. Portales, "The Transition," 66.

58. Alexander, *Tragedy*, 371.

7

Special Rapporteur on Iran

As in the case of Chile, human rights practices in Iran became the subject of sustained public consideration within the United Nations following the seizure of power by a radical regime. As with Chile, the United Nations decided to establish a country-specific mechanism to deal with human rights abuses. While there are, of course, important geographic, historical, political, and cultural differences between the two countries, there is a reason that the United Nations was to deal with them in similar fashion: while both Pinochet's Chile and fundamentalist Iran fought domestic Communists, neither country was on the front line of the Cold War in the sense of, for example, East Germany or Cuba. The East–West struggle was not the principal factor determining the way the United Nations dealt with the human rights situation in these countries, although, as pointed out in the previous chapter, the Soviet Union was able to use the Chilean case to some advantage. North–South issues likewise had little influence on the United Nations' treatment of Iran and Chile. While either or both of these sets of global issues shaped the international community's consideration of most matters that came before the United Nation during the 1970s and 1980s, neither predominated in these two cases. Yet member states of the United Nations came to care a great deal about what was happening to human rights in both Chile and Iran. One could say that their relative disentanglement from global geopolitical contests *permitted* the international community to take a stronger and more forthright approach to the *human rights* issues involved than would have been the case—and, indeed, was the case—when human rights in, say, the USSR or East Germany or Cuba were involved.

BACKGROUND: THE SHAH, THE MULLAHS, AND THE UNITED STATES

International concern about rights violations in Iran arose during the reign of the Shah and was beginning to reach major proportions when his government was replaced in February 1979 by the still more repressive regime of the Ayatollah Ruhollah Khomeini.[1]

Contemporary Islamic fundamentalism's campaign for a theocratic state traces its roots to a largely successful tobacco boycott organized by religious leaders in the late nineteenth century. Until Reza Shah, founder of the Pahlavi dynasty, seized power in the early 1920s, however, the clergy preferred, on the whole, to avoid active involvement in political life. Reza Shah's determination to create a modern secular state in Iran rekindled the clergy's political activism, and in Moslem schools, seminaries, and social and charitable institutions the mullahs began to instill a spirit of resistance among the people. Secularization, they charged, was threatening to turn Islamic influence into a merely cultural phenomenon, diluting its importance as a source of truth and value and weakening its role as a life-guiding philosophy. Some went so far as to charge that the Shah was trying to use the state to annihilate religion.[2]

Indeed, the Shah and his son Mohammed Reza Pahlavi did not hesitate to use violence against religious militants when they felt it was necessary. But over time, the doctrinal appeal of Islam grew stronger in the face of these assaults, and among the people there arose a powerful movement of resistance to what they saw as an attempt to take away their religion in return for something of lesser value. This movement, having grown through four decades, found in the 1960s a charismatic leader in Ayatollah Ruhollah Khomeini. The regime fought back even harder, exiling Khomeini and expanding the role of the secret police. But these measures were not enough; by the late 1970s popular fervor led to frequent protest demonstrations. When troops killed some demonstrators, a larger demonstration gathered for their funeral, and the troops killed even more, leading to more funeral demonstrations and still more killings.[3]

The Western world watched these events unfold but did not appear to understand what was happening. The United States in particular, seemed uncertain how to interpret what was going on in Iran and confused about how to react to it. The Shah had been a close ally of the United States for many years and by 1978 had become our number one customer for arms.[4] R. K. Ramazani says that the Carter Administration pursued a two-pronged policy based on contradictory premises. The prongs were support for the Shah and for political liberalization; but the Shah, he suggests, was not committed to genuine political liberalization; in the circumstances, that would mean sharing power with one or another opposition faction, something we should have known, after 37 years of working with him, that the Shah would never do. Moreover, the United States misread key elements of Iranian culture, believing incorrectly that such ideas as dialogue and compromise enjoyed broad support in Iranian society.[5] Gaddis Smith agrees with the view that the United States failed to read Iranian culture properly and notes that President Carter's effusive praise for the Shah in January 1978 came back to haunt him many times over. Smith faults the Carter administration for "lack of understanding of Iranian history and society, and especially of the political character of the Islamic clergy. It acted in a confused way in the face of a confusing situation."[6] Barry Rubin makes the same point, noting in addition that the Shah's regime and its enemies also had a distorted understanding of the United States and of our foreign policy.[7]

Throughout the autumn of 1978, the Shah vacillated between reform gestures and brute force, and his U.S. advisers gave divided counsel. Smith says that, even if the Carter administration had handled things better, the Shah's departure was inevitable, as was American identification with him. "President Carter inherited an impossible situation—and he and his advisers made the worst of it."[8]

In January 1979, the number of demonstrators killed by government troops in a single day reached 2,000; the next day a million people gathered in the main square of Teheran; two days later, 2 million gathered, and the Shah left the country. Two weeks later, Khomeini returned from exile to a tumultuous welcome.[9]

LIFE UNDER THE FUNDAMENTALISTS

Under the new regime, the victims changed, but the repression went on. In addition to officials of the Shah's government, members of non-Moslem minorities became targets of state violence. The severity and extent of abuses under the fundamentalist regime have been chronicled by many observers.[10] I will not recount them in detail here. Although the new regime and the constitution it adopted a few years later guaranteed religious liberty to Jews, Christians, and Zoroastrians, in fact all three groups were persecuted, and hundreds of thousands fled abroad to escape the terror. No group felt the fury of the new state as much as the Baha'is. The fundamentalists regarded Baha'is as heretics deserving of severe punishment. Baha'is were *not* guaranteed religious freedom in the new constitution. According to Khomeini, the "Baha'is are not a sect but a party which was previously supported by the British and now by the U.S. The Baha'is are also spies just like the Tudeh [the Communist Party]."[11]

The seizure of the American hostages in November 1979 touched off a power struggle within the government's ranks between moderates, led by elected President Bani-Sadr, and radical mullahs. By May 1980 the fundamentalists had won, and Iran's 180,000 mullahs successfully demanded purges of the government bureaucracy and the universities. The Prosecutor-General acknowledged in May that the regime held 1,500–1,700 political prisoners. What Barry Rubin calls "semi-official assassination teams" killed opposition figures in Paris and Washington.[12]

Shaul Bakshash estimates that the Khomeini regime killed 10,000 people during its first five years and caused a half million to go into exile. These figures do not seem excessive, in the light of information presented to international organizations by nongovernmental human rights and refugee assistance groups.[13] The Iranian Government acknowledged 4,400 executions during its first three and a half years in power.[14]

This writer can attest to the general accuracy of Bakshash's refugee estimate on the basis of his experience as an official of the Department of State's Bureau for Refugee Programs from 1986 to 1989; the number of refugees had increased shortly after the Islamic revolution and continued to grow through the 1980s. While most refugees waited (and in 1996 still wait) in neighboring countries for the chance to return home, many tens of thousands—particularly members of religious minorities—have sought permanent resettlement elsewhere. The United States alone admitted for permanent residence about 5,000 Iranian refugees a year through the 1980s. Most were members of the four persecuted religious minorities.

INITIAL UNITED NATIONS ACTION

At its annual meeting in the summer of 1981, the expert-level Subcommission on Prevention of Discrimination and Protection of Minorities, in which the writer participated as the accredited U.S. Government observer, heard graphic testimony on the persecution of members of the Bah'ai faith from British member Benjamin Whitaker, Ghanaian member Jonas Foli, Moroccan member Halima Warzazi, Zambian member L. C. Mubanga-Chipoya, and several others. My report to the Department of State notes that Whitaker said that "some 50 Baha'is have recently been executed in Iran because of their religion. The motive is clear from the fact that they were offered their lives in exchange for abandoning their religion." Foli said the Iranian Government was engaged in a "campaign of extermination against the Baha'is." Warzazi of Morocco said the wave of executions in Iran "violated basic tenets of Islam."[15] The Subcommission adopted a resolution expressing profound concern for the Baha'is, asked the Secretary-General to intercede on their behalf with the Iranian Government, and asked the Human Rights Commission to act on the matter when it met in February–March 1982.[16] At the same time, however, a working group of the Subcommission sent the regime a mixed message by declining to elevate complaints against Iran for further consideration under the confidential procedures established under Resolution 1503.[17]

In 1982, the Commission, after heated debate, adopted its first resolution on the human rights situation in Iran, voting 19 to 9 with 15 abstentions to condemn the practice of arbitrary and summary executions under way in that country and expressing particular concern for the plight of members of the Bah'ai faith.[18] But note that fewer than half of the 43 member states of the Commission were willing to take a strong stand on the matter at that time, even though the resolution contained no provision for follow-up action by a rapporteur or anyone else.

In the summer of 1982, Whitaker and other Subcommission members reported that the situation in Iran had worsened, citing the case of the secret execution of the poet Said Soltanpur, a member of the Executive Committee of the Iranian Writers' Association who had earlier been jailed by the Shah's regime but then became a target of the fundamentalists. Whitaker cited cases of execution of children and pregnant women, rape of women slated for execution, widespread torture, and sham trials with no defense lawyers. He named a lawyer who had recently been executed merely for having offered to defend an accused man. While the government had acknowledged 4,400 executions since their takeover, Whitaker said that "many more persons had been executed secretly or had died under torture. Many names of persons executed could not be published for fear of reprisals being taken against their families."[19]

THE UNITED NATIONS TRIES TO STEP UP THE PRESSURE

In the early 1980s there was a particularly strong wave of sympathy for Islamic countries in UN forums and in the world generally, due particularly to the plight and courageous struggle of the Afghan people against foreign (Soviet) invasion. Iran was sheltering about a million Afghan refugees. Pakistan, which was hosting over 3 million, was not willing to antagonize Iran in such circumstances. Similarly, Israel's 1982 invasion of Lebanon and bombing of Beirut had further raised the stock of the Islamic world in international forums. With the release in 1981 of the American hostages in Iran, the Reagan administration was less interested in joining a campaign against Iran than it might have been had the hostage situation not been resolved. (But the United States voted for the resolution at the Commission.) Moreover, with two Islamic countries (Iran and Iraq) at war, other Moslem states were reluctant to appear to be favoring one side by taking action on human rights issues.

When the Netherlands delegation proposed in 1983 that the Human Rights Commission take more meaningful action, the most that could be obtained was another resolution supporting the Baha'is and, this time, requesting the Secretary-General to intercede on their behalf, to use his good offices on behalf of religious liberty and tolerance in Iran, and to report to the Commission in 1984. The United States again voted in favor.[20] At least now the United Nations as an intergovernmental institution would be engaged, it was hoped, in confronting the regime on the issues and interceding on behalf of persecuted minorities and their right to practice their religion. Surprisingly, this time the Iranian delegate told the Commission that the Secretary-General's representative would be welcome to visit Iran.[21]

In the world of UN implementation mechanisms, asking the Secretary-General to undertake tasks of this nature is not generally considered as strong a step as appointing a special rapporteur, since the result often tends to be obscured amid the thousands of other activities performed by the Secretariat, and the report tends to have a bland, institutional character, lacking the higher public and diplomatic profile of a work issued in the name of a special rapporteur. These distinctions are not lost upon the member states of the Commission.

Although the Commission's decision thus called for less than the strongest available implementation mechanism, it still represented an escalation of UN attention to, and involvement in, Iran's human rights situation. Six months later, in August 1983, the Subcommission continued to spotlight the situation in an effort to build pressure on the regime and to push for more serious action by the United Nations.[22] However, at that session, in my presence the Iranian Government observer said that Iran had decided *not* to cooperate with the Secretary-General in the latter's efforts to carry out the Human Rights Commission resolution. In my report to the State Department, I commented that "the Government of Iran Observer's statement was fragmented and confusing, as he switched erratically from topic to topic. His 'reasoning' for the reported GOI decision to close the door to the Secretary-General was therefore unclear."[23] When I asked my British colleague, who sat next to me, what he thought the Iranian had meant, he said he was likewise perplexed by the general incoherence of his remarks; only the refusal to cooperate seemed clear.

In another switch a few months later, though, the Secretariat received word that Iran *would* receive a visit by the Secretary-General's representative. Then the regime once again inexplicably withdrew its consent.

It is difficult to explain these mercurial shifts in position. If one assumed that the Khomeini regime were behaving according to a rational actor model of foreign policy making, the changes would make no sense. But the regime was not following this model. The extremely ideological—even fanatic—character of the Islamic fundamentalist government meant that, at least during its first several years, the regime was not engaging in the more usual type of state calculation of interest in reaching decisions on the question of how far to cooperate with the United Nations on human rights issues. However, as John Esposito points out, there had been divisions within the ruling elite since the beginning; militants argued with pragmatic moderates over domestic and foreign policy issues such as land reform, nationalization, export of the revolution, and relations with the West.[24] As we know of no major event in 1983 that would account for the reversals in position, it is reasonable to ascribe them to the ebb and flow of these largely hidden factional conflicts.

Some of the more usual sources of information on a country were unavailable during this period. The United States had no embassy in Teheran, for instance. Foreign journalists were likewise impeded in their work or simply forbidden entry, and the domestic press was severely hindered. Writing of internal power struggles within the leadership that occurred in the 1984–85 period, David Minashri, former editor of a prestigious Teheran daily, wrote in 1990, "The dearth of reliable information makes it difficult for outsiders to assess accurately the particular ideologies of the various groupings, the personal affiliations of the contenders, and the measure of support they had."[25]

Minashri added that Prime Minister Rafsanjani had, however, admitted that the rift(s) were paralyzing the ruling Islamic Republican Party and obstructing the working of the executive and legislative branches.[26] These labyrinthine behind-the-scenes struggles may have caused some of the shifts in policy toward the United Nations, both then and later in the decade.

THE SPECIAL REPRESENTATIVE (RAPPORTEUR) ON IRAN

After receiving another gloomy report from the Secretary-General in 1984 on Iranian abuses and on the regime's noncooperation,[27] the Commission finally decided to establish a special representative (rapporteur) on Iran.[28] The division in the Commission was again apparent in the vote; the resolution was adopted by 21 to 6, with 15 abstentions. As in the case of the two earlier resolutions, those seeking a more assertive UN effort regarding Iranian human rights abuses were unable to muster majority affirmative support. The Commission had 43 member states at the time; Mauritania's one-person delegation was not present for the vote. Only one Moslem nation (Jordan) voted in favor of the resolution, the other six dividing equally between abstention and voting against. Further evidence of the prevailing nervousness was the statement by the Bangladesh delegate that he had intended to vote no instead of abstaining.[29]

The choice of the term ''representative'' rather than the more customary ''rapporteur'' had no significance insofar as the mandate of the new office was concerned. The representative's terms of reference were substantially the same as those of other special rapporteurs of the Commission, and I use the terms interchangeably when referring to Iran.

The first representative, Andres Aguilar (Venezuela), a former chairman of the UN Human Rights Commission as well as of the Inter-American Commission and a member of the UN Human Rights Committee (of the Covenant on Civil and Political Rights), was not permitted to visit Iran. Instead, he was forced to defend the legal status of the Universal Declaration and the two Covenants against Iranian claims that Islamic law took priority over any international standards. In his first report (1985) he said:

States of all political, economic, social, cultural and religious persuasions participated in the drafting of the Charter, the Universal Declaration and the Covenants . . . [which contain] norms distilled from the collective experience of the common heritage of the world's peoples represent[ing] universal standards of conduct for all peoples and all states.

Therefore . . . no State can claim to be allowed to disrespect basic, entrenched rights such as the right to life, freedom from torture, freedom of thought, conscience and religion, and the right to a fair trial which are provided for under the Universal Declaration and the Covenants . . . on the ground that departure from these standards might be permitted under national or religious law.

The Universal Declaration ... gives expression to the human rights principles of the Charter of the United Nations and its essential provisions such as those referred to above represent not only rules of international customary law but rules which also have the character of *jus cogens*.[30]

The Commission explicitly endorsed these conclusions in its 1985 resolution on Iran,[31] and the Subcommission added its own independent support for these views a few months later.[32] Three years later, the representative was finally able to report to the Commission that the Iranian Government had agreed that

some provisions of the Covenant on Civil and Political Rights [to which Iran was, and remained, a party], particularly those which might be considered as *jus cogens*, are compatible with Islamic law. This statement cleared the normative basis for the examination of the concrete allegations of violations of human rights submitted to the attention of the Iranian Government ... [a] working arrangement with respect to concrete cases might be worked out in order to overcome obstacles of a local character while ensuring compliance with international norms.[33]

Given the difficulties involved in tracing the domestic sources of shifts in Iranian policy, it is not easy to conclude why the regime finally accepted that at least some parts of international human rights law apply to Iran. By 1988, however, Iran had found that international human rights and humanitarian law could sometimes be useful; in its war with Iraq, Iran succeeded in bringing substantial international pressure to bear on the Iraqis for their use of poison gas. The United Nations was the forum for marshaling this pressure, and it was UN investigators who prodded the Iraqis and confirmed the violations of international humanitarian law in this regard.

Also, John Esposito points out that, in the ongoing back-and-forth struggle between hard-liners and pragmatic moderates in the Iranian ruling elite,

Between August 1988 and February 1989, it looked as if the pragmatists were in the ascendancy as relations with the West warmed, diplomatic and economic missions from the West increased, and Iran worked in the United Nations and through international delegations to shore up its image, particularly in the area of human rights.[34]

Another reason for Iran's concession on the legal issue was probably that, like most revolutionary-ideological states, it came to power determined to do away with traditional modes of conducting international relations and to do business in new, "revolutionary" ways. After almost a decade of this behavior, Iran, like most other states that had conducted similar experiments in nontraditional foreign policy and diplomacy, gradually decided to act more like a state within a community of states, since this seemed to offer better prospects for successful achievement of state goals.

But this process of accommodation to the state system was interrupted in early 1989 by the case of Salman Rushdie, a crisis in which ideology prevailed over traditional conceptions of state interest and over a desire to repair relations with the West. In response to the publication of Rushdie's book, *Satanic Verses*, the Ayatollah Khomeini called for the author's execution. The issue strengthened the hand of Khomeini and the hard-liners within the Iranian power structure and led to the forced resignation of Khomeini's designated successor, Ayatollah Montazeri, who had criticized the regime's human rights abuses, and of other moderates and pragmatists.[35] At the same time, the regime suffered a further decline in international prestige. As Fred Halliday put it, with reference to the Rushdie case:

The internal bases of the Islamic Republican Party, one of the sources of strength in one respect, have repeatedly harmed Iran on the international scene and limited its sphere of action. . . . Iranian leaders have repeatedly miscalculated about the actions of external forces . . . [in response to outbursts of fanaticism].[36]

Special Representative Aguilar did not confine his reports to the issue of the applicability of international law; he reported credible testimony from numerous nongovernmental witnesses concerning human rights abuses in Iran, including summary executions, torture, religious discrimination, and denial of fair trial. Still, he was forced to base his reports only on information he could obtain outside the country.

SECOND SPECIAL REPRESENTATIVE FINALLY ABLE TO VISIT IRAN

In 1988 Aguilar was succeeded by Reinaldo Galindo Pohl (El Salvador), who, unlike his predecessor, was able to visit Iran three times between January 1990 and December 1991. Even before Galindo Pohl's first visit, he regularly documented the sad record of summary executions, arbitrary arrests, torture, and unfair trials.[37]

To convey a sense of the difficulties facing the Commission and its special representative, it is worth mentioning that from 1988 through 1990 no delegation to the annual Commission session formally introduced the resolution on Iran because of fear of retaliation by Iranian agents abroad. The draft resolution had sponsors listed thereon, as required by ECOSOC rules, but no one took the floor as primary sponsor formally to introduce it and argue for its passage. The chair simply announced that it was the next item of business, opponents had their say, and then it was brought to a vote. The fundamentalist regime was waging a program of state-sponsored international terrorism that involved kidnappings, shootings, and other acts of violence abroad against its opponents, and the 1989 death sentence in absentia on Salman Rushdie was to be carried out by Iranian agents wherever Rushdie might be found. No delegation wished to incur the risk of sudden violent recrimination against themselves or their capitals or citizens.

Galindo Pohl's first visit to Iran took place just before the 1990 session of the Commission. He reported to the Commission that throngs of people had sought to speak with him in Iran and that he had received many detailed allegations of unlawful executions, torture, imprisonment beyond expiration of sentence, and unfair trials, including trials conducted without defense lawyers. He sought, however, to balance his report by describing the government's expressions of concern about terrorism and by ruling out, absent specific proof to the contrary, allegations that political prisoners had been executed under false charges of drug trafficking.[38]

Some observers reportedly felt that the attempt to achieve a balanced report was part of a deal to obtain permission for a second visit.[39] Another noted scholar/participant in international human rights work, Tom Farer, went further in his criticism, heaping scorn on the whole enterprise:

Two successive Special Rapporteurs have enjoyed absolutely no cooperation from the Iranian government. The first brief report went no further than to find that allegations against Iran could not be dismissed as groundless. . . . While a Special Rapporteur's conclusions should not be and often are not predictable, the energy with which he or she carries out the Commission's assignment usually is. In other words, the failure of a Special Rapporteur is fairly imputable to the Commission.[40]

Farer's comment about lack of cooperation must be read in light of the fact that he was writing before the first Galindo Pohl visit to Iran. His criticism of Aguilar's reports seems overdrawn, however. As noted earlier, Aguilar confronted the Iranian government on the core issue of whether it could exempt itself from the accepted international law of human rights, and he seems to have made headway on this point. Also, Aguilar's reports to the Commission did not shrink from recounting reports of major human rights violations.[41]

The Commission did not create a special rapporteur on Iran as an empty gesture to appease public opinion that it was doing something. The intent was quite different. But Farer's comment and the observation that Galindo Pohl may have pulled punches in order to assure a second visit raise important questions about what one can expect from a country-specific rapporteur.

In his February 1991 report, following his second visit, Galindo Pohl again recounted detailed reports of serious violations in the same categories as the previous year. But he was also able to note signs of progress: the government's replies to many allegations, a favorable outcome in a number of cases submitted on humanitarian grounds, periodic clemency decrees, a decree requiring a defense lawyer to be present at all stages in criminal proceedings, and permission to the International Committee of the Red Cross (ICRC) to visit prisons and all prisoners.[42]

In its 1991 resolution extending the rapporteur's mandate for another year—adopted by consensus, thanks to the spirit of cooperation then obtaining between the rapporteur and the Iranian Government—the Commission welcomed Iran's cooperation, again called upon the government to halt abuses, noted the invitation to ICRC to visit prisons, and endorsed various recommendations by the rapporteur.

In December 1991, Galindo Pohl made a third visit to Iran and reported thereon to the Commission in January 1992. This time, however, he said that Iran had made no further progress toward improved compliance with international human rights instruments, although ICRC prison visits were about to begin.

The Commission, sensing a trend toward deterioration in the human rights situation, extended his office for another year and called for an interim report to the General Assembly in the autumn of 1992.[43] Unfortunately, by the time of his report to the Assembly, matters had indeed gone from bad to worse, including the expulsion of the ICRC. In its resolution, the Assembly said that "Iran has discontinued its cooperation with the Special Representative," that it had not granted permission for another visit or replied to the latest batch of allegations submitted to it, and that it had not given adequate follow-up to many of the recommendations in his previous reports. The Assembly appealed to the government to resume cooperation with the special representative and to comply with international human rights obligations.[44]

The previous year, when things seemed to be getting better both in Iran and in terms of Iranian cooperation, the Commission had adopted its resolution on Iran by consensus. In 1992, with deterioration setting in on both counts, the Commission had to return to the earlier practice of taking a recorded vote (22 to 12, with 15 abstentions) to adopt its resolution extending the rapporteur's mandate.[45] At the Assembly, the margin was greater, probably because the resolution was framed in milder terms: 86 to 16, with 38 abstentions. The 16 negative votes were cast by Asian Communist states, by some Moslem states, and by Cuba. But most Moslem states either abstained or voted in favor.[46]

For reasons discussed earlier, it is not easy to determine the causes for the erratic shifts in Iranian government policy toward cooperation with UN human rights agents. In addition to whatever combination of behind-the-scenes domestic power struggles and ideological considerations contributed to the temporary re-hardening of position in late 1991–92, the aftermath of the Persian Gulf War probably also played a role. It seems clear that, for their part, neither the United Nations nor the special representative did anything new to offend the regime in what concerns the latter's work.

It is more interesting for our purposes to consider probable reasons why they decided to cooperate in 1990 and early 1991. These appear to have included the determination of at least a substantial plurality of the Commission, as well as of the expert-level Subcommission, to persevere in efforts to deal assertively with abuses in Iran on behalf of the international community. Not being discouraged by initial failure is a key to any successful initiative in UN human rights forums. Second, the personality of the rapporteur is important; even more crucial is the kind of approach he or she takes toward the specific mandate and toward the target state. In the case of Iran, perseverance by the rapporteur was needed in the face of considerable opposition by the government. Moreover, the experience of the first few years showed that it was necessary in this case to change the incumbent for progress to occur.

This is not to say, of course, that perseverance by the Human Rights Commission and a more skillful approach by the rapporteur were the *primary* factors in Iranian decision making on whether to cooperate with the United Nations on human rights. The cooperative spirit displayed in 1990–91 may have owed something to a desire to offset some of the unusually strong negative international reaction to the Rushdie affair. After all, the pragmatists in the power structure had been gaining the upper hand since 1988, and although they suffered a setback because of the Rushdie case, the Foreign Ministry at least remained in the hands of the pragmatic Ali Adbar Velayati, and the moderate Hashemi Rafsanjani became President after the death of Ayatollah Khomeini. What we can say is that the Human Rights Commission's action and the rapporteur's specific approach were probably important contributing factors to the decision to lessen, for a while, the scale of repression and to cooperate, for a while, with the United Nations.

SOME ELEMENTS OF EFFECTIVENESS OF COUNTRY-SPECIFIC MECHANISMS

The Commission does not expect or want its representative to charge off like Don Quixote, raging publicly with every gallop against the evils and evildoers he or she is assigned to combat and then unleashing an incandescent denunciation at the next annual meeting. Such an approach would almost certainly preclude the possibility of an on-site visit or return visit, destroy the rapporteur's potential ability to play a good-offices role with the regime in working to lessen abuses, and, if an on-site visit has occurred, increase the danger to individuals with whom the rapporteur spoke on the first trip. Nor does the Commission want its representative to serve as a tame press agent for an abusive regime. Both approaches would properly be called failure.

The Commission wants its agent to represent the community of states *and* the body of international human rights law, vigorously and pragmatically, to the authorities of a sovereign state that is violating human rights. The aim is to bring to bear a structured international presence and influence on that government to cease violations and to restore respect for human rights. This is, of course, also the aim of the thematic mechanisms, but the concentrated focus of country-specific mechanisms heightens the need for a carefully balanced approach. The country-specific rapporteur is prima facie always operating in a more highly politicized atmosphere. How well a rapporteur tailors strategy and tactics to the specific features of the target state will help significantly in determining how successful he or she will be in achieving the goals set forth in the mandate. Not all rapporteurs have given this requirement sufficient attention.

A rapporteur has behind him or her the backing of political bodies of the organized community of states—always the UN Human Rights Commission and the UN Economic and Social Council and, by reference, the General Assembly.[47] In some cases, including the representative on Iran, the General Assembly explicitly endorses a rapporteur's mandate, although this is not a prerequisite.

When individual governments press another government to cooperate with a UN agent, such bilateral pressure enhances the effectiveness of the multilateral mechanism. To serve the cause of human rights effectively, a minimum of cooperation on the part of the target state is needed. On-the-spot fact-finding can scarcely occur without a visa, for example, unless one is prepared to effect clandestine entry into the country. For credible fact-finding, access to victims and witnesses is required; to influence a state to halt violations and to restore respect for rights, access to decision makers is likewise necessary.

Onetime access is not enough and may even be counterproductive. Victims, witnesses, and their foes alike should have assurance that the rapporteur will be back for another visit and perhaps others after that. The International Committee of the Red Cross long ago established the principle that follow-up visits to places of detention must be guaranteed in advance of the first visit. This obviously protects the detainees against reprisals and provides an opportunity to determine whether recommendations for needed improvements in prison conditions have been carried out. The principle of follow-up visits to the country and its people is fundamental to the success of the Red Cross enterprise, and it is just as important to the United Nations. It is therefore not surprising that Galindo Pohl *may have* exercised restraint in writing his first report on human rights in Iran. But he *did*, as noted, provide an honest account of serious abuses, not a whitewash. He was able, apparently, to influence the regime to reduce some abuses for a while. For the particular beneficiaries of that action, the exercise was certainly worth it. For the United Nations, the experience underscored once again the importance of carefully balancing public criticism with good-offices diplomacy both in developing the mandates of human rights agents and in carrying them out.

NOTES

1. One of the standard accounts of the Pahlavi Dynasty's efforts to suppress the rise of Islamic fundamentalism in Iran is Hamed Algar, "Religious Forces in Twentieth Century Iran," in P. Avery, G. Hambly, and C. Melville, eds., *The Cambridge History of Iran*, Vol. 7 (Cambridge: Cambridge University Press, 1991), 732–65.

2. Haleh Afshar, "The Iranian Theocracy," in H. Afshar, ed., *Iran: A Revolution in Turmoil* (London: Macmillan, 1985), 222–23. See also Algar, "Religious Forces," 757–65.

3. Algar, "Religious Forces," 760–64.

4. R. K. Ramazani, *The United States and Iran: The Patterns of Influence* (New York: Praeger, 1982), 137–38.

5. Ibid., 139–40.

6. Gaddis Smith, *Morality, Reason, and Power: American Diplomacy in the Carter Years* (New York: Hill and Wang, 1988), 185–87.

7. Barry Rubin, *Paved with Good Intentions: The American Experience and Iran* (New York: Oxford University Press, 1980), xi.

8. Smith, *Morality*, 188–89.

9. David Minashri, *Iran: A Decade of War and Revolution* (New York: Holmes and Meier, 1990), Ch. 1. See also Algar, "Religious Forces," 760–64.

10. For example, Amnesty International, *Iran* (London: Amnesty International, 1987); British Parliamentary Human Rights Group, *The Abuse of Human Rights in Iran* (London: Macmillan, 1986).

11. The quotation is from Cheryl Benard and Zalmay Khalizad, *The Government of God: Iran's Islamic Republic* (New York: Columbia University Press, 1984), 133. For further discussion of persecution of religious minorities, see Martin Wright, ed., *Iran: The Khomeini Revolution* (Harlow, Essex: Longmans, 1989), 25, 27, 32.

12. Rubin, *Paved with Good Intentions*, 332–34.

13. Shaul Bakshash, *The Reign of the Ayatollahs: Iran and the Islamic Revolution* (New York: Basic Books, 1984), 4. Bakshash also cites Amnesty International as his source for a figure of nearly 3,000 people killed by the regime during and after a failed 1981–82 uprising by the Moslem Mojahadin (219). Thus, not all of Khomeini's victims were non-Moslems.

14. Summary Record of the Aug. 24, 1982, afternoon meeting of the subcommission, E/CN.4/Sub.2/1982/SR.13, para. 45.

15. U.S. Mission Geneva telegram 8571, Aug. 25, 1981.

16. Subcommission resolution 8 (XXXIV), Sept. 3, 1981.

17. Although the working group's deliberations and decisions are supposed to be strictly confidential, unidentified sources leaked this information to the *International Herald Tribune*, which published it on September 30, 1982, about two weeks after the end of the annual subcommission session.

18. U.S. Mission Geneva telegrams 2062, Feb. 19, 1982, and 3170, Mar. 15, 1982. Commission resolution 1982/27, Mar. 11, 1982.

19. Summary Record of the Aug. 24, 1982, afternoon meeting of the Subcommission, E/CN.4/Sub.2/1982/SR.13, paras. 39–45.

20. Commission resolution 1983/34 of Mar. 8, 1983.

21. U.S. Mission Geneva telegram 3133, Mar. 25, 1983.

22. Subcommission resolution 1983/14, Sept. 5, 1983.

23. U.S. Mission Geneva telegram 7762, Aug. 23, 1983.

24. John L. Esposito, *The Iranian Revolution: Its Global Impact* (Miami: Florida International University Press, 1990), 36.

25. Minashri, *Iran*, 350–52.

26. Ibid.

27. E/CN.4/1984/28.

28. Commission resolution 1984/54.

29. Report of the Human Rights Commission, E/CN.4/1984/77, paras. 336–43.

30. E/CN.4/1985/17. The term *Jus cogens* refers to legal rules of a peremptory nature, from which no derogation is permissible.

31. Commission Resolution 1985/39.

32. Subcommission Resolution 1985/17.

33. E/CN.4/1988/24.

34. Esposito, *The Iranian Revolution*, 37.

35. Ibid.

36. Fred Halliday, Introduction, in A. Ehteshami and M. Varasteh, eds., *Iran and the International Community* (London: Routledge, 1991), 5–6. For more details on religious aspects of the Rushdie case, see, in the same book, Ian Hampshire-Monk, "Salman Rushdie, the Ayatollah, and the Limits of Toleration," 162–72.

37. For instance, E/CN.4/1989/26. Also, the Commission's special rapporteur on summary or arbitrary executions—a thematic institution—reported that thousands of persons had been executed without trial or after summary proceedings in Iran. See E/CN.4/1989/25.

38. E/CN.4/1990/24.

39. This view was reported by Reed Brody, Penny Parker, and David Weissbrodt in "Major Developments at the UN Commission on Human Rights in 1990," *Human Rights Quarterly* 12(4) (1991), 559–90.

40. Tom J. Farer, "Less than a Roar, More than a Whimper," in Adam Roberts and Benedict Kingsbury, *United Nations, Divided World: The UN's Role in International Relations* (New York: Oxford University Press, 1988), 138.

41. But is the "failure of a Special Rapporteur . . . fairly imputable to the Commission," as Farer charges? I do not think so. First, as Farer does not make clear what he means by the "failure of a Special Rapporteur," it is difficult to make sense of the rest of the charge. If he means that the rapporteur did not even try to bring about change for the better, such negligence would be fairly imputable to the rapporteur. If he means that the rapporteur erred by warming up to the target government to the point of covering up its abuses, this, too, would be the rapporteur's responsibility. What Farer seems to be suggesting is that the rapporteur receives his mandate from the Commission along with a collective wink that he is not expected to carry it out too vigorously, so as not to upset higher-order interests of member states. But there is no evidence for this sort of conspiracy, and it did not occur at the Commission during the four years I participated as a U.S. delegate (1981–84, inclusive) or the two preceding years when I shared responsibility for Commission affairs in the Department of State's Bureau for Human Rights.

42. E/CN.4/1991/91.

43. Commission resolution 1992/67.

44. Assembly resolution 47/146.

45. Commission resolution 1992/67. By this time the membership of the Commission had been expanded to 53 states. Three states did not vote on the resolution. Once again, however, it proved impossible to obtain an absolute majority affirmative vote for a resolution on Iran in the Commission.

46. Assembly resolution 47/146.

47. The Council ratifies Commission decisions to establish new mechanisms and approves their funding. If new funding is required, a new rapporteur or other implementation mechanism cannot start operating until ECOSOC ratifies the resolution. Ratification takes place routinely at the spring ECOSOC session, shortly after the Commission session ends. Implementation need not await General Assembly concurrence.

8

Factors Influencing the Effectiveness of UN Human Rights Institutions

This study began with the questions, How does the international community, through UN human rights institutions, seek to influence states to observe accepted human rights standards? Which types of UN human rights institutions have worked well, and which have not, and why? What factors contribute to, or impede, their effectiveness? In this chapter I comment further on these matters and draw some conclusions in the light of the case studies and the theoretical, historical, legal, and institutional analyses discussed earlier. Also, because the post of UN High Commissioner for Human Rights includes many of the kinds of authorities and functions previously assigned only to thematic and country-specific implementation mechanisms, I include an account of the long-term effort to create this post—an effort in which I played a role for several years in the 1980s—and brief commentary on the potential scope of activity of the office.

OVERVIEW

As the preceding chapters point out, the international community of states has conferred specific authority on designated UN human rights institutions to hold states accountable for their conduct regarding internationally accepted human rights standards and has authorized these institutions to act on the community's behalf as agents to implement these standards. The case studies demonstrate how this system has contributed to influencing some states to reduce human rights abuses under certain circumstances.

The General Assembly and the Economic and Social Council have legislative authority under the Charter to establish implementation mechanisms for purposes that come within their purview, including human rights. I have argued that UN human rights mechanisms based on the Charter are more effective than treaty-based institutions, mainly because the former act as agents of a *political* body of the community of states. The treaty-based mechanisms set up under the Covenants on Civil and Political Rights and on Economic, Social and Cultural Rights and other conventions are useful additions to the United Nations' set of tools to promote human rights, but they have less impact on state practice than Charter-based institutions. Charter-based mechanisms constitute an element in the external policy environment of factors that a state takes into account in its domestic and foreign policy making. The case studies illustrate that their impact is further strengthened if states of importance to a target state take bilateral policy initiatives for human rights purposes, as well as actively support action by UN human rights agencies. Their effectiveness is also enhanced by the sustained commitment of the community of states to a particular mechanism, as expressed in periodic reaffirmation of its mandate.

Among Charter-based institutions, thematic and country-specific mechanisms have different structural and procedural advantages and disadvantages, but they are, in general, equally effective. Which of the two will have greater impact in a case depends on the specific circumstances and issues to be addressed. As the case studies show, a state's readiness to cooperate with a UN human rights institution is greater when the state faces pressure from both a thematic and a country-specific mechanism. The case studies also highlight the importance of on-site visits, including follow-up visits, by UN human rights agents both for fact-finding and for energetic UN diplomatic efforts to promote concrete improvement in human rights practices. Similarly important is an effort by UN agents and policy-making bodies to balance public criticism and/or praise with diplomatic efforts. Finally, the personality and energy of the individual chosen to carry out a UN human rights mission contribute in important ways to the degree of success or failure of the mission.

Charter-based approaches depend on the notion that states are members of an international community to which they are politically, ethically, and, in some sense, also legally accountable for their conduct toward their own citizens, and they are designed to enhance a climate in which this sense of accountability is more acceptable to states. The aim is to bring to bear a structured international presence and influence on a government to cease violations and to restore respect for human rights. Most of the time, the international community relies on psychological means, principally persuasion in its many positive and negative, public and private forms. To say that these have been the methods of choice does not mean, of course, that they are always or even almost always successful. What it suggests is that discussion of a human rights system can focus on different ways the community has sought to structure these psychological tools and procedures in order to maximize their influence on state behavior.

Member states of the United Nations came but slowly to the view that it is legitimate to employ multilateral persuasion on behalf of the community vis-à-vis sovereign states in human rights matters. At first it could not be exercised at all, then only in secret and at specified times (in the Resolution 1503 procedures), then, slowly, gradually, in public, and finally on a broad, year-round basis through the thematic and country-specific mechanisms and now also through the office of the High Commissioner for Human Rights. These institutions have gradually strengthened the concept and practice of state accountability to the international community for human rights practices.

THE RECORD

In four selected cases—the thematic issues of enforced disappearances and of official religious discrimination and the country-specific abuses in Chile and Iran—the United Nations decided to address specific problems by designating Charter-based agents to represent the community of states to involved governments on a continuing, year-round basis. The goal was to *persuade* the states concerned to abandon conduct that diverged from community standards. The approach included ethical and legal elements as well as diplomatic appeals to the target states to act in a way that made it easier for other states to conduct normal international dealings with them, and thereby to avoid actions that could lead to, or prolong, their political isolation.

As illustrated in the cases of Chile, Iran, and Argentina, states extended some degree of cooperation with UN human rights agents, at least for a time. The state's desire to avoid or reverse political isolation increased gradually over the first three or four years of its rule, so that the need for renewed "full political acceptance" gained increasing weight in their foreign policy calculations. Economic difficulties began to affect these states in about the fourth or fifth year of the government's tenure, problems that were exacerbated by the state's then-advanced stage of political isolation.

Also, while these governments had, early on, defeated their most militant internal opponents and intimidated their other domestic foes, they were aware that their hold on power was hardly solid. Ruling by active intimidation is not a normal thing and cannot be continued indefinitely; most governments aim at some sort of institutionalization and at developing a climate of at least passive acceptance on the part of their populations. These regimes decided that improvement in their international standing would be useful for these purposes.

Thus, the decision to respond positively, even to a limited extent, to external human rights pressure took a few years. This is another reason why it is important for international institutions to sustain their efforts over time.

CREATION OF THE POST OF HIGH COMMISSIONER FOR HUMAN RIGHTS

Charter-based procedures were taken a major step further in December 1993 with the establishment by the General Assembly, by consensus, of the post of UN High Commissioner for Human Rights.[1] The first incumbent, Jose Ayala Lasso of Ecuador, took office in April 1994. (He resigned the office in March

1997 to accept the post of Foreign Minister of Ecuador. His successor is Mary Robinson, former President of Ireland.)

As the text of the General Assembly resolution makes clear, the High Commissioner has the authority to employ all of the techniques and methods of fact-finding, good offices, negotiation, advisory services, conciliation, and public pressure available to the various thematic and country-specific mechanisms developed earlier. In addition, the High Commissioner has direct authority over the resources of the UN Human Rights Center. In 1996, the Center employed about 70 professional and 35 supporting staff, mostly based in Geneva, and had an annual regular budget of $22 million, supplemented by about $14 million in voluntary funds. The voluntary portion of the budget is quite obviously subject to great fluctuation from year to year. In addition to the regular staff at Geneva and a small liaison office in New York, the High Commissioner has been able to deploy several hundred temporary employees in field missions in such troubled areas as Cambodia, Rwanda, Burundi, Bosnia, Haiti, and El Salvador. Finally, the High Commissioner is given specific authority to coordinate human rights protection, promotion, education, and information activities throughout the UN system and to "adapt [and] strengthen" UN human rights machinery "with a view to improving its efficiency and effectiveness."[2]

Establishment of the High Commissioner's office represents a new high point in decades of development of UN human rights implementation activities. The concentration of diplomatic, operational, budgetary, personnel, program, and systemwide coordinating authority in a single, high-ranking, international official symbolizes a commitment by states to further strengthen the practice of state accountability to the international community in the human rights field. The resolution makes clear that the General Assembly intended that the High Commissioner stand at the apex of the United Nations human rights system, under the authority only of the Secretary-General and of the Assembly itself.

Other evidence of greater institutionalization of the human rights system lies in the fact that in the late 1970s and early 1980s, the special rapporteur posts and the Working Group on Disappearances were created for only one year, and their existence had to be renewed annually; by the late 1980s and early 1990s this had grown to two-year and then three-year terms. The High Commissioner's *office* is permanent; the Commissioner has a four-year term, renewable once.

Apart from this organic link to the development of the UN human rights system, the struggle to establish the High Commissioner post has a long and interesting history of its own. Uruguay introduced the first such proposal in 1952; nothing came of it. Costa Rica revived it in 1965, but again it languished.[3]

On both occasions the initiative was strongly opposed by the USSR on the grounds that it would give authority to a supranational office in matters that, it asserted, are exclusively subject to domestic jurisdiction. I believe that the real reason was that it feared that a High Commissioner, as an advocate of the values expressed in the Universal Declaration, would focus much of his or her attention on abuses in Communist states. The Soviets naturally opposed creating what they saw as a new anti-Soviet pressure point. Worse, such a pressure point would speak and act in the name of the whole community of states and could thereby help frustrate Soviet efforts to project their power and influence in the Third World.

In addition to Soviet opposition, these early initiatives suffered from a lack of enthusiasm among some of the states that might be expected to champion them. As of the time of the 1965 proposal, no human rights implementation machinery of any kind existed, and while some Western and Latin American countries thought that a High Commissioner was just the right way to fill this gap, others wanted to study alternative options before making up their minds.

In 1977 the United States, Costa Rica, and Sweden relaunched the initiative at the General Assembly, this time almost succeeding. By 1977, the earliest forms of UN implementation structures were in existence: since 1970, the Resolution 1503 procedures had involved the Human Rights Commission and its expert Subcommission in confidential debates on alleged violations, and in 1977 the Human Rights Committee of the Covenant on Civil and Political Rights had begun its work of examining the reports of state parties.

The Soviets now claimed that these two mechanisms were sufficient and that to go further would trespass to an unacceptable degree on state sovereignty. By 1977, the majority of UN members were recently independent ex-colonies. The Soviets were able to play effectively on these countries' sensitivities concerning their colonial past to portray the High Commissioner proposal as a neocolonialist Trojan Horse. They found willing allies among the leaders of the Non-Aligned Movement: India, Algeria, Yugoslavia, and, of course, Cuba. These factors, plus a poorly organized lobbying effort by pro-High Commissioner forces, led sponsors to withdraw the resolution, to prevent its being laden with hostile amendments that would have made it unacceptable to the original sponsors.[4]

Italy joined Costa Rica, Senegal, and others to try again in the early 1980s. At that time I became personally involved in this matter in the course of my service at the U.S. Mission to the United Nations in Geneva from 1980 to 1984. I became convinced that establishment of the post was essential to give the United Nations the capacity to act swiftly and effectively. Debating human rights abuses six months or a year after they had occurred was simply an inadequate response by the international community. In a January 1981 telegram to the Department of State outlining U.S. interests, objectives, and strategies for the upcoming annual session of the Human Rights Commission, I wrote, on behalf of the U.S. Mission:

The session provides an opportunity to achieve significant advances in the multilateralization of efforts to implement universal human rights standards. Success in this institution-building effort would assure more even-handed and less-politicized treatment of human rights issues in the UN. . . . Establishment of the post of High Commissioner would bring greater impartiality, coordination, and year-round continuity to UN human rights activities. We believe the terms of reference for a High Commissioner should strike a balance between independence and power of initiative to engage in direct contacts, on the one hand, and periodic policy supervision of activities by an "intergovernmental oversight committee" (which could be the Human Rights Commission itself). . . . A balanced approach of the type just described could command sufficient support.[5]

My confidence, shared by my colleagues at the Mission, was borne out. But not for 12 more years! The struggle to establish the High Commissioner illustrated the truth of a remark by Jerome Shestack, U.S. representative to the Commission during the Carter administration, as he took leave of his duties in December 1980: "The campaign for human rights is not a race for the short-winded."

At its 1981 session, the Commission took no substantive action on the High Commissioner, merely adopting a brief decision to consider the idea the following year, and its backers were not sure what to do next. That summer, the expert-level Subcommission reinvigorated the effort by spontaneously issuing an enthusiastic appeal to the Commission to take steps toward creating the post.[6] I thereupon developed a comprehensive proposal to this end, submitted it to the Department of State in December 1981,[7] and received verbal encouragement and authorization to circulate it among the Geneva missions of the ten Western member states of the Commission.

Most of the missions liked it, although three or four thought it was too ambitious. As I have mentioned, lukewarmness among some Western delegations had impeded progress on this project in the past. At the 1982 Commission session, however, all Western delegations were convinced of the merits of creating a post of High Commissioner. This time the Western internal debate turned mainly on another point: in light of the project's earlier history, ensuring passage would require giving it very high priority—which would, in turn, demand expenditure of a great deal of political capital as well as time and energy, not only in Geneva but through supporting demarches in New York and in national capitals as well. This would reduce the relative amount of these diplomatic resources available to support other Western objectives; in February 1982 these resources were almost fully absorbed by the United States–led effort to pass a resolution condemning human rights abuses in Poland, where two months earlier martial law had been imposed in an attempt to crush the Solidarity movement.

There is always a feeling among some delegations to international conferences that long-range institutional improvements can wait until next year or the year after that and that one should focus instead on the crisis of the moment at the expense of strengthening the institution's ability to deal with crises. While there may have been some justification for this attitude in 1982 because of the Polish crisis, it hardly explains why the Commission did little more to advance matters in 1983 and 1984.

Despite the priority of the Polish issue at the 1982 session, Italy and Costa Rica—both of which actively supported the effort on Poland—were able to push successfully for a resolution requesting the Subcommission to prepare comprehensive terms of reference for the High Commissioner post (i.e., a job description). That summer, the Subcommission carried out this task and forwarded the draft terms of reference to the Commission.[8]

At the Commission session in 1983, I drafted resolutions, based on the Subcommission proposals, that would have established the office of High Commissioner and defined its mandate. I advocated these texts first within the Western group and then in other regional groups. As in the past, within the Western group I encountered strong support among some delegations and opposition or indifference among others. In addition to the usual argument that we should really spend our valuable time on the headline issues of the day, I encountered a defeatist attitude on the part of some Western delegates.

This defeatism was a curious phenomenon. Outside the Western group, there was strong and growing support for a High Commissioner, especially among Latin American and African delegations; Costa Rica and Senegal led in their respective regions, and I joined them in lobbying efforts. Oddly, some of the Western delegates who were reluctant to take an initiative were trapped by their own fears of defeat and perceptions of nonsupport, both of which were based on much earlier experiences, and they did not even bother to take a current reading of sentiment in other regional groups.[9] Of course, the Soviet bloc, including Cuba, was opposed. India, Yugoslavia, and Pakistan also fought the High Commissioner.

Nevertheless, in 1983 pro-High Commissioner forces again succeeded in passing (by a vote of 24 to 11, with 7 abstentions) a very positive resolution that significantly carried forward the drafting process, praising the Subcommission's first draft and asking it to improve it in certain ways and resubmit a revised version for possible final adoption at the 1984 Commission session.[10] The Subcommission did so that August, approving its recommendation by the overwhelming majority of 16 to 3, with 3 abstentions; the tally would have been 18 in favor had the chair, a longtime supporter, not recused herself from voting on any resolutions and had another strong supporter been present for the vote. Also, the Subcommission defeated the Yugoslav member's motion to defer the matter for further study. As I said in my reporting cable, "[B]y the overwhelming rejection of this [Yugoslav] proposal, the Subcommission has expressed its view that it has fully carried out the Commission's mandate, no further studies are needed, and it is now up to the Commission to act."[11]

But the Commission did not act. At the 1984 session, I worked intensively with other Western delegations and with Latin American and African delegations to produce a resolution that I am convinced could have won majority support.[12] This text was in the form of a substantive resolution approving establishment of the post and its terms of reference and forwarding these decisions to the Economic and Social Council for confirmation and referral to the General Assembly for final approval. Although Western delegations agreed on a draft text in consultation with leading Latin American and African supporters, some Westerners again raised the same old fears of defeat, still unwilling to look at the changed situation in other regional groups. Others, however, wished to push the matter forward. The delay in resolving this tactical issue, in fact, determined the outcome of the substantive project. The text was formally introduced in the full Commission by Costa Rica, Colombia, and Peru only on the next-to-last day of the session and was not brought to a vote because hostile amendments introduced by Cuba and the German Democratic Republic confused many delegations already weary from the weeks of struggle over the dozens of other contentious issues on the agenda and entangled this project in the last-minute rush of other business. Once again, the Commission decided that the proposal was too important to be decided.[13]

The Commission promised to take up the resolution the following year; however, such pledges depend on the presence next year of someone to remind the delegates of what they promised and to stimulate and encourage them to reinitiate action. But my tour of duty was over, my successor took little interest in the project, Italy's term on the Commission expired, and faintheartedness inhibited fresh initiative in the Western caucus. Non-Western sponsors hesitated to move without encouragement from the West, and the proposal lay fallow for the next several years.[14]

I should point out that the Department of State consistently supported the concept of a High Commissioner, and the U.S. delegation voted for the various positive procedural resolutions that came to an actual vote at the Commission. There were times during 1981–84 when I had to work hard to keep the Department and especially the Reagan administration political leadership of the U.S. delegation even minimally committed to the project. While this made my job more difficult in advocating the measure with other delegations, I went forward as forthrightly and vigorously as circumstances allowed, believing that in the long run something like this was crucial to enable the UN human rights effort to reach its potential.[15]

In June 1993, the Clinton administration decided to give the project high priority at the World Conference on Human Rights in Vienna. An intensive, United States–led lobbying effort finally succeeded in gaining a consensus for establishing the post, and that momentum carried forward to the General Assembly, which in December of that year adopted a consensus resolution actually creating the post. The text of the resolution[16] bears a remarkable resemblance to the 1984 draft. Success came in 1993, not in 1983 or 1984, because of a number of factors:

- the end of the Cold War removed the obstacle of Soviet intransigence; while this obstacle could have been overcome earlier by majority vote, its removal now made it thinkable to try to achieve consensus;

- the passage of an additional decade allowed the colonial era to fade further into the past, and the prospect of new human rights machinery began to appear less threatening to ex-colonial states;

• the High Commissioner's terms of reference include an explicit mandate to promote a people's right to development in addition to traditional individual rights; and

• energetic support by the United States lifted this topic from "one among many" to the number one priority issue at the World Conference and, a few months later, at the General Assembly. Official U.S. support, under the leadership of Secretary of State Warren Christopher and Assistant Secretary for Human Rights John Shattuck, was enhanced by the personal intercession of former President Jimmy Carter.

SEARCHING FOR SIGNS OF EFFECTIVENESS

When I began this study, I expected to find that thematic mechanisms are significantly more effective than country-specific procedures because their structure spreads their political character over a much wider field than one country, thereby permitting human rights considerations to stay in focus without distraction. But I discovered a more complex reality.

For instance, as there were few reports of disappearances in Chile after 1979, where country-specific mechanisms had been in existence for four years, it is difficult to argue that the establishment in 1980 of a universal thematic mechanism for disappearances (the working group) was more effective than the previous country-specific effort. However, I believe that the international community's decision to establish a thematic mechanism added credibility and moral force to the country-specific procedure already in existence, because it demonstrated to the Chilean Government that the community of states truly meant to do something about the problem *as a human rights problem* and not merely as a weapon with which to attack the Chilean regime. While the evidence is suggestive rather than conclusive, it strengthens the inference that this action by the United Nations made the government more willing to cooperate with the country rapporteur, even to the extent of permitting him to visit Chile three times.

In the case of Iran, where disappearances and religious persecution had drawn the attention of the respective thematic rapporteurs as well as the geographic rapporteur, the record is similarly resistant to attempts to assign significantly more credit for improvement or deterioration to one or the other type of Charter-based mechanism. During the first eight years of the work of the successive rapporteurs on Iran—which overlapped with the Working Group on Disappearances and, since 1986, with the rapporteur on religious discrimination—the Iranian Government alternately cooperated with, and rejected, all of these mechanisms, repeating this sequence at least three times.

But in the case of Iran, as of Chile, if the documentary evidence points in the direction of either type of mechanism as being more influential, one would have to acknowledge that the geographic rapporteur seems to have had more impact. In both cases, the country rapporteur was at least able to make three on-site visits (versus none by thematic agents), and, for a time, they appeared to be making headway on some actual human rights problems. After Galindo

Pohl's 1991 visit to Iran, for instance, he was able to note signs of progress that corresponded to some of the chief findings and recommendations of his previous report: the government had replied to many allegations, there had been a favorable outcome in a number of cases submitted by the rapporteur on humanitarian grounds, there had been periodic clemency decrees and a decree requiring a defense lawyer to be present at all stages in criminal proceedings, and permission had been granted to the International Committee of the Red Cross to visit prisons and all prisoners.

ADVANTAGES OF THE THEMATIC APPROACH

What, then, are the advantages of thematic mechanisms? First, the urgent-action procedure, pioneered by Amnesty International but first brought into the UN system in the thematic procedures (and later adopted by country rapporteurs), has saved lives. As B. G. Ramcharan put it, "[p]rotection is afforded to some individuals and this is always worthwhile, for a life saved . . . is justification in and of itself."[17]

Other commentators claim more for the thematic approach. For instance, in 1989 Reed Brody and David Weissbrodt said: "Together, the theme mechanisms do the most important concrete work of the Commission in protecting rights in specific cases by saving lives, stopping torture, resolving disappearances, etc. Nevertheless, the theme procedures are still evolving and being improved."[18]

In their 1989 book, A. H. Robertson and J. G. Merrills concur:

Both [types] are concerned with the collecting of information . . . as a means of keeping questions of human rights on the international agenda and enabling pressure to be put on governments to change their practices. Since the aim is to change governmental behavior, the country type . . . with its sharper focus, may seem superior. . . . [t]his is not so, and the thematic approach has several advantages.[19]

Robertson and Merrills said these advantages are (1) greater geographic scope, (2) ability to investigate abuses in countries enjoying political popularity in the United Nations, and (3) the conviction that certain issues—such as mass exoduses, slavery, and the rights of indigenous peoples—must, by their nature, be considered on a global basis. Even issues such as torture or summary executions, they said, "[which] can be exposed by a country-oriented investigation . . . can be illuminated by the thematic approach."[20]

Also, thematic procedures demonstrate the determination of the international community systematically to address a particular abuse on a *global* basis with a view to reducing it, rather like the World Health Organization's campaign to eradicate smallpox. While it is, of course, not possible to vaccinate the heart against committing the atrocities of enforced disappearance, religious oppression, summary execution, torture, and other antihuman abuses, it is at least possible to institutionalize persuasive powers against these evils on behalf of the community at large. This has a valuable pedagogical effect as well; it educates people about the abuse being dealt with, and it teaches something about the priorities of the organized international community.

It is easier to *create* thematic mechanisms, because here the politically explosive atmosphere generated by debate over establishing a country-specific procedure is absent. When one of the latter is being established, the target state behaves as if it is on trial, protesting that it is the victim of political motivation, cultural prejudice, and the like. Regional bonding sometimes plays a role; as Theo van Boven has pointed out, initiatives to create new country-specific procedures are often impeded by regional-bloc voting behavior.[21]

But, as I noted earlier, to recount the structural advantages of thematic mechanisms is not to claim that they are always superior in practice. In the two country studies, the available evidence points in the opposite direction. We do not know whether or not this would have been the result with disappearances in Argentina, because no country-specific institution was established in this case. Instead, we know that the thematic mechanism proved effective, at least in a significant minority of cases where a disappearance had just taken place or was still recent.

TWO PROCEDURES ARE BETTER THAN ONE

Theo van Boven, who has served as Director of the UN Human Rights Center and at other times as a member of the expert Subcommission and as Netherlands representative to the Commission, wrote in an essay published in 1992:

[When we review the work of country-specific mechanisms,] a mixed picture presents itself. Either there is no cooperation at all (South Africa), or a gradual evolution from non-cooperation to some cooperation (Afghanistan, Iran), or a cooperation under certain conditions and during certain periods (Chile), or limited cooperation (El Salvador). . . . But . . . the thematic procedures . . . have only occasionally benefited from the cooperation of governments. In many instances the response on the part of governments is absent or dilatory and not meaningful. There are, nevertheless, growing assumptions and expectations [expressed in General Assembly resolutions] that governments should cooperate.[22]

In my view, it is in *combination* that the two approaches have greater impact. Chile and Iran have had to deal with both types, and their decisions to cooperate for a time with the United Nations and to improve, for a while, domestic human rights performance appear to have coincided with the coming into being of a second type of mechanism. In Chile, the thematic structure came after the geographic; in Iran, two of the thematics were already in existence when the Commission appointed a country-focused special representative. In both cases, the government was faced with steadily increasing multilateral pressure, expanding into additional forms. As it gained momentum, this process contributed to the growing diplomatic isolation of the two states. This, in turn, raised the level of discomfort of the state concerned and increased the psychological and political price it had to pay if it chose to continue its conduct.

Although UN rapporteurs and the Human Rights Commission cannot force a change in conduct by a state, they can praise or blame, publicly and privately, and thereby potentially affect other interests of that state. As I said earlier, states deal with each other in a multiplicity of bilateral and multilateral activities and structured relationships. If a government becomes a pariah because of human rights abuses, it is likely to find its foul reputation becoming entwined with other aspects of its bilateral and multilateral relationships.

Thus, when UN activity is on the increase, for example, by adding a country rapporteur to a thematic rapporteur, or vice versa, a government is more likely to extend some degree of cooperation with the United Nations.

Why did not Chile and Iran decide to cooperate with the thematic mechanisms instead of the country rapporteurs and thereby obtain a measure of "cover" by being grouped with other countries? I think it is because a country rapporteur can do more to raise a state's reputation for human rights observance, since he or she is writing only about that country and is comparing it both with international standards and with past performance by that state. A state that is currently *improving* its human rights performance is more likely to cooperate with a country-specific rapporteur than with a thematic mechanism because in the former's public report the government's positive measures stand out in higher relief, and thus it gets more international "credit" for its efforts to improve.

When there is no country rapporteur, but there is growing criticism within the United Nations of a state's practices, a government may choose to cooperate with the thematic mechanism as a way to blunt criticism, tell its side of the story, avoid creation of a country-specific mechanism, and perhaps even gain credit for trying to improve. Colombia invited the Working Group on Disappearances and the Rapporteur on Summary Executions to visit the country; the visits took place in 1988 and 1989, respectively, and honest, fully documented public reports were presented to the Commission.[23] In neither case, however, did the Commission take any subsequent action directed at Colombia. I attribute this outcome to the fact that the Colombian Government extended such full cooperation before and during the visits and because it was able to convince UN investigators that it was making a serious effort to control and halt abuses. In 1996 Colombia even agreed to permit the UN Human Rights Center to open a field office.

THE FACTOR OF PERSONALITY

To create receptivity to a request to make an on-site visit, to have assurance that the state will allow genuine fact-finding and dialogue to occur during the visit and afterward and will grant a return visit, a UN rapporteur must be able to convince the state that the mission is not being undertaken with a subversive

purpose and that any resulting report will be honest without being unduly condemnatory. These comments apply to geographic as well as to thematic mechanisms and, of course, to the High Commissioner.

Here one enters the zone of the personality and style of the individual tasked
with carrying out the human rights mandate. It is not easy to develop an approach that will win sufficient cooperation to enable genuine fact-finding to
occur and to provide a realistic opportunity to work for a lessening of abuses.

The intelligence, good judgment, eloquence, and determination of Lord Colville helped the Working Group on Disappearances maintain unity among its
multiregional membership and to make significant progress in its work. Judge
Abdoulaye Dieye (Senegal), the first rapporteur on Chile, who had a distinguished record in other UN human rights activities, crossed swords publicly
with the Pinochet regime, received little cooperation, and was not permitted to
make on-site visits; while it is not certain that the regime would have cooperated
with any UN representative in the early 1980s, the tenor of Dieye's approach
may have influenced Chile to be intransigent. His successor, Rajsoomar Lallah
of Mauritius, adopted a lower profile and was able to make three on-site visits
later in the decade. Somewhat the same pattern presented itself in Iran, where
the more combative stance of rapporteur Andres Aguilar (Venezuela) was followed by the moderately lower profile of Reinaldo Galindo Pohl (El Salvador),
who, unlike his predecessor, was able to make three on-site visits.

Of course, a government's decision is based on factors additional to the personality and style of the UN agent. But when a state sees the decision whether
or not to cooperate with the United Nations as closely balanced, considerations
of personality can make the difference. An individual seen as biased, filled with
antipathy toward one's country, or simply abrasive is unlikely to receive *any*
cooperation, let alone an invitation to visit. The personal qualities that contribute
most to a UN human rights representative's success are objectivity, a sense of
balance and fairness, a clear commitment to human rights for their own sake
and not for narrow political or geopolitical reasons, steady determination, energy, and a style that is neither abrasive nor overly passive.

We see signs of passivity, for instance, in the work of the special rapporteur
on the elimination of religious discrimination, whose reports show relatively
little effort to engage in urgent-action procedures, to make on-site visits, or
actively to press governments beyond writing to them once or twice a year.
Instead, he seemed to get bogged down in the issue of whether or not the United
Nations should proceed to adopt a convention on the subject. In this case, too,
implementation was affected by the style and approach of the rapporteur.

POLITICAL AND ETHICAL ELEMENTS OF PERSUASION

The intensified activity of UN human rights institutions since the mid-1970s
has introduced a distinct political-cost element into the scales of national policy

making. Governments recognize the potential effect of their own position on attitudes of governments and parliaments, and they weigh whether more is to be gained or lost by, for example, accepting a proposed visit by a UN rapporteur. Some specialists, however, see the glass half-empty, or perhaps even emptier; Jack Donnelly, for instance, after reviewing some of the initiatives taken by the United Nations in the human rights field since 1990 and acknowledging that "lives are being saved in ways that just a few years ago would not have seemed possible to most observers," sees "no evidence to suggest that the international community is willing to undertake major new initiatives to deal with direct violations of internationally recognized human rights by governments in control of their states."[24] In fairness to Donnelly, it should be noted that he was writing before the Vienna World Conference on Human Rights (summer 1993) and its surprising consensus recommendation to establish the post of High Commissioner for Human Rights and the even more surprising consensus decision by the General Assembly in December to establish the post.

Agreeing to cooperate with a UN human rights agent did not mean that Pinochet or the mullahs or the Argentine junta acknowledged that what they had been doing was objectively wrong in terms of universal standards. That sort of admission is typically made only by a successor government, if at all. But I think they did come to realize that the good name of their state, not only of their government, was at stake and that this was a genuine political cost.

Appeals to a government to halt human rights abuses can originate from other governments, from international nongovernmental organizations, and from authorized agents of the community of states. There are qualitative differences in the nature and impact of these appeals, however, and these are worth noting.

A government can appeal to its fellow sovereign on the basis of interest: "If you want to do business as usual with my government, you will need to forswear this abuse." Or it can appeal on the basis of traditional friendship and cultural links. A state seeking to persuade another state through bilateral channels to halt human rights abuses can combine ethical appeals with elements of material interest (trade, aid, credit, arms sales, military training, alliances, and the like). But it is very difficult to frame a *bilateral* appeal on *ethical* grounds without appearing to be engaging in a form of cultural imperialism, unless that appeal is itself based on commonly accepted standards. Even such an appeal, however, is seen as more legitimate if it is initiated by an agent who has a specific international mandate to apply these standards; it is almost always more effective to be able to say that one is supporting a community initiative rather than one's own.

Appeals from an international nongovernmental organization to a government are *usually* based on ethical grounds, but their impact is limited by the fact that these organizations represent the views of only their members. If their membership is large, and if they have access to the media and to means of rapid, worldwide communication, they may nevertheless influence state conduct. The record of Amnesty International provides the best example of this. Nongovernmental organizations also sometimes exercise significant influence on intergovernmental bodies to take initiatives by providing well-substantiated evidence.

An appeal by an international agent, such as a special rapporteur, has no direct relationship with positive or negative material incentives but has sufficient moral authority that a government may weigh whether or not refusal to cooperate with the agent might lead indirectly to material repercussions in the policies of states of importance to it. A target state is aware that the agent will report at intervals to the body of states, that his or her reports will provide material for criticism or praise by that body, and that such praise or criticism can have further impact on national attitudes and policies of states important to it.

Negative economic incentives, in the form of denial of loans by multilateral banks and trade and financial restrictions, have not yet been fully utilized by the United Nations explicitly for human rights purposes except in the cases of South Africa, Rhodesia, and, most recently, Haiti. The same is true of arms embargoes. On the positive side, the United Nations is still in the early stages of developing programs of positive material incentives to states to improve human rights performance. These small, but growing, programs—totaling about $14 million a year in 1996—are managed by the Human Rights Center under the direction of the High Commissioner. They are becoming increasingly well integrated with the thematic and country-specific mechanisms, thereby reinforcing the impact of ethical and political persuasion.[25]

CONCLUSION

A Charter-based UN human rights institution's authority as a designated agent of the whole community of states gives it a form of effectiveness that enables it sometimes to provide practical help to real human beings, particularly when action is taken promptly, vigorously, and prudently. The methods of persuasion have not helped all victims, nor have they produced by themselves dramatic changes in a state's behavior. In combination with bilateral pressure, domestic political forces, and internal and external economic factors, however, they have become important factors influencing state conduct.

The techniques employed have been developed to a high degree of sophistication through decades of experimentation. Thematic and country-specific mechanisms are the community's agents for carrying out the Charter obligations to ''promote and encourage universal respect for human rights and fundamental freedoms for all.'' As an integral part of the growing constellation of international institutions in the political universe within which states function and interact, these mechanisms constitute an increasingly influential deterrent to human rights abuse by states. To this constellation has now been added the High Commissioner for Human Rights, who is building on the experience of thematic and country-specific mechanisms to further improve the United Nations' ability to carry out the Charter mandate to make human rights more secure in the world.

Factors Influencing UN Human Rights Institutions   131

NOTES

1. General Assembly Resolution 48/141, reproduced as Appendix H.

2. Ibid.

3. The early history of the proposal can be consulted in the analytical and technical study by the Secretary-General for the Commission, E/CN.4/AC.21/L.1, Dec. 30, 1966.

4. This account comes from a conversation in 1981 in Geneva with B. G. Ramcharan, then Special Assistant to the Director of the Division (later, Center) of Human Rights, who was present at the 1977 General Assembly debate.

5. U.S. Mission Geneva telegram 108, Jan. 6, 1981.

6. U.S. Mission Geneva telegram 9068, Sept. 11, 1981. The Subcommission vote was 15 to 2, with 5 abstentions.

7. U.S. Mission Geneva telegram 12615, Dec. 24, 1981.

8. U.S. Mission Geneva telegram 9432, Sept. 21, 1982. Also, Mission Geneva telegram 9832, Sept. 30, 1982.

9. U.S. Mission Geneva telegram 2594, Mar. 15, 1982.

10. U.S. Mission Geneva telegrams 2594, Mar. 15, 1982, and 3133, Mar. 25, 1983.

11. U.S. Mission Geneva telegram 8505, Sept. 15, 1983.

12. U.S. Mission Geneva telegram 78, Jan. 6, 1984.

13. E.CN.4/1984/L.23, reproduced as Appendix G.

14. This case illustrates how a change of personnel can affect the fate of a substantive initiative. For instance, at my first Commission session in 1981, a British delegate, Richard Edis, was the principal Western advocate of prompt action to establish the High Commissioner; in 1984, the principal opponent of a High Commissioner was his successor, Richard Fursland. In the meantime, pro-High Commissioner support outside the Western group had increased notably. In 1981–83, delegates from Canada, Ireland, and the Netherlands were lukewarm toward the initiative, but by 1984 their successors were enthusiastic advocates. Greece, previously a leader of the lukewarm, was no longer a member state of the Commission.

15. After the 1982 Subcommission session, for example, I reported to the Department of State (U.S. Mission Geneva telegram 9832, Sept. 30):

If the project is approved . . . it will significantly improve the way the UN does business on human rights issues by adding a capacity for prompt action in urgent situations, particularly through vigorous quiet diplomacy . . . We urge the Department to give it high priority in our pre-Commission consultations with Western and selected Third World colleagues.

This high priority was not forthcoming. On this issue I was left largely to my own devices in a pre-Commission lobbying effort limited mainly to other diplomatic missions in Geneva. Once the Commission session opened, I also lobbied visiting delegates, of course.

16. General Assembly Resolution 48/141, Appendix H.

17. B. G. Ramcharan, *The Concept and Present Status of the International Protection of Human Rights* (Netherlands: Nijhoff, 1989), 193.

18. Reed Brody and David Weissbrodt, ''Major Developments at the 1989 Session of the UN Commission on Human Rights,'' *Human Rights Quarterly* 11(4) (1989), 602.

19. A. H. Robertson and J. G. Merrills, *Human Rights in the World*, 3d ed. (Manchester: Manchester University Press, 1989), 88–89.

20. Ibid.

21. Ibid., 44, 59.

22. Theo van Boven, " 'Political' and 'Legal' Control Mechanisms," in A. Eide and B. Hagtvet, eds., *Human Rights in Perspective* (Oxford: Blackwell, 1992), 48–49. B. G. Ramcharan makes the same point in "Strategies for the International Protection of Human Rights in the 1990s," *Human Rights Quarterly* 13(4) (1991), 156.

23. E/CN.4/1989/18/Add. 1, and E/CN.4/1990/94.

24. Jack Donnelly, *International Human Rights* (Boulder, CO: Westview Press, 1993), 145.

25. For a good overview of these programs, see *Advisory Services and Technical Cooperation in the Field of Human Rights (Human Rights Fact Sheet No. 3, rev. 1* (Geneva: United Nations Center for Human Rights, 1996). The World Conference on Human Rights called for much closer integration of the United Nations' economic development and human rights work (*Vienna Declaration and Programme of Action* [A/ CONF.157/23]). The High Commissioner has since taken a number of initiatives to improve coordination between the United Nations' human rights and development activities, as recounted in his 1996 report to the Human Rights Commission, E/CN.4/1996/ 103, and to the General Assembly, A/51/36.

Appendixes

Appendix A: The Universal Declaration of Human Rights (1948)

PREAMBLE

Whereas recognition of the inherent dignity and of the equal and inalienable rights of all members of the human family is the foundation of freedom, justice and peace in the world,

Whereas disregard and contempt for human rights have resulted in barbarous acts which have outraged the conscience of mankind, and the advent of a world in which human beings shall enjoy freedom of speech and belief and freedom from fear and want has been proclaimed as the highest aspiration of the common people,

Whereas it is essential, if man is not to be compelled to have recourse, as a last resort, to rebellion against tyranny and oppression, that human rights should be protected by the rule of law,

Whereas it is essential to promote the development of friendly relations between nations,

Whereas the peoples of the United Nations have in the Charter reaffirmed their faith in fundamental human rights, in the dignity and worth of the human person and in the equal rights of men and women and have determined to promote social progress and better standards of life in larger freedom,

Whereas Member States have pledged themselves to achieve, in co-operation with the United Nations, the promotion of universal respect for and observance of human rights and fundamental freedoms,

Whereas a common understanding of these rights and freedoms is of the greatest importance for the full realization of this pledge,

Now, therefore,

The General Assembly

Proclaims this Universal Declaration of Human Rights as a common standard of achievement for all peoples and all nations, to the end that every individual and every organ of society, keeping this Declaration constantly in mind, shall strive by teaching and education to promote respect for these rights and freedoms and by progressive measures, national and international, to secure their universal and effective recognition and observance, both among the peoples of Member States themselves and among the peoples of territories under their jurisdiction.

Article 1

All human beings are born free and equal in dignity and rights. They are endowed with reason and conscience and should act towards one another in a spirit of brotherhood.

Article 2

Everyone is entitled to all the rights and freedoms set forth in this Declaration, without distinction of any kind, such as race, colour, sex, language, religion, political or other opinion, national or social origin, property, birth or other status.

Furthermore, no distinction shall be made on the basis of the political, jurisdictional or international status of the country or territory to which a person belongs, whether it be independent, trust, non-self-governing or under any other limitation of sovereignty.

Article 3

Everyone has the right to life, liberty and security of person.

Article 4

No one shall be held in slavery or servitude; slavery and the slave trade shall be prohibited in all their forms.

Article 5

No one shall be subjected to torture or to cruel, inhuman or degrading treatment or punishment.

Article 6

Everyone has the right to recognition everywhere as a person before the law.

Article 7

All are equal before the law and are entitled without any discrimination to equal protection of the law. All are entitled to equal protection against any discrimination in violation of this Declaration and against any incitement to such discrimination.

Article 8

Everyone has the right to an effective remedy by the competent national tribunals for acts violating the fundamental rights granted him by the constitution or by law.

Article 9

No one shall be subjected to arbitrary arrest, detention or exile.

Article 10

Everyone is entitled in full equality to a fair and public hearing by an independent and impartial tribunal, in the determination of his rights and obligations and of any criminal charge against him.

Article 11

1. Everyone charged with a penal offence has the right to be presumed innocent until proved guilty according to law in a public trial at which he has had all the guarantees necessary for his defence.

2. No one shall be held guilty of any penal offence on account of any act or omission which did not constitute a penal offence, under national or international law, at the time when it was committed. Nor shall a heavier penalty be imposed than the one that was applicable at the time the penal offence was committed.

Article 12

No one shall be subjected to arbitrary interference with his privacy, family, home or correspondence, nor to attacks upon his honour and reputation. Everyone has the right to the protection of the law against such interference or attacks.

Article 13

1. Everyone has the right to freedom of movement and residence within the borders of each State.

2. Everyone has the right to leave any country, including his own, and to return to his country.

Article 14

1. Everyone has the right to seek and to enjoy in other countries asylum from persecution.

2. This right may not be invoked in the case of prosecutions genuinely arising from non-political crimes or from acts contrary to the purposes and principles of the United Nations.

Article 15

1. Everyone has the right to a nationality.
2. No one shall be arbitrarily deprived of his nationality nor denied the right to change his nationality.

Article 16

1. Men and women of full age, without any limitation due to race, nationality or religion, have the right to marry and to found a family. They are entitled to equal rights as to marriage, during marriage and at its dissolution.
2. Marriage shall be entered into only with the free and full consent of the intending spouses.
3. The family is the natural and fundamental group unit of society and is entitled to protection by society and the State.

Article 17

1. Everyone has the right to own property alone as well as in association with others.
2. No one shall be arbitrarily deprived of his property.

Article 18

Everyone has the right to freedom of thought, conscience and religion; this right includes freedom to change his religion or belief, and freedom, either alone or in community with others and in public or private, to manifest his religion or belief in teaching, practice, worship and observance.

Article 19

Everyone has the right to freedom of opinion and expression; this right includes freedom to hold opinions without interference and to seek, receive and impart information and ideas through any media and regardless of frontiers.

Article 20

1. Everyone has the right to freedom of peaceful assembly and association.
2. No one may be compelled to belong to an association.

Article 21

1. Everyone has the right to take part in the government of his country, directly or through freely chosen representatives.
2. Everyone has the right of equal access to public service in his country.
3. The will of the people shall be the basis of the authority of government; this will

shall be expressed in periodic and genuine elections which shall be by universal and equal suffrage and shall be held by secret vote or by equivalent free voting procedures.

Article 22

Everyone, as a member of society, has the right to social security and is entitled to realization, through national effort and international co-operation and in accordance with the organization and resources of each State, of the economic, social and cultural rights indispensable for his dignity and the free development of his personality.

Article 23

1. Everyone has the right to work, to free choice of employment, to just and favourable conditions of work and to protection against unemployment.

2. Everyone, without any discrimination, has the right to equal pay for equal work.

3. Everyone who works has the right to just and favourable remuneration ensuring for himself and his family an existence worthy of human dignity, and supplemented, if necessary, by other means of social protection.

4. Everyone has the right to form and to join trade unions for the protection of his interests.

Article 24

Everyone has the right to rest and leisure, including reasonable limitation of working hours and periodic holidays with pay.

Article 25

1. Everyone has the right to a standard of living adequate for the health and well-being of himself and of his family, including food, clothing, housing and medical care and necessary social services, and the right to security in the event of unemployment, sickness, disability, widowhood, old age or other lack of livelihood in circumstances beyond his control.

2. Motherhood and childhood are entitled to special care and assistance. All children, whether born in or out of wedlock, shall enjoy the same social protection.

Article 26

1. Everyone has the right to education. Education shall be free, at least in the elementary and fundamental stages. Elementary education shall be compulsory. Technical and professional education shall be made generally available and higher education shall be equally accessible to all on the basis of merit.

2. Education shall be directed to the full development of the human personality and to the strengthening of respect for human rights and fundamental freedoms. It shall promote understanding, tolerance and friendship among all nations, racial or religious groups, and shall further the activities of the United Nations for the maintenance of peace.

3. Parents have a prior right to choose the kind of education that shall be given to their children.

Article 27

1. Everyone has the right freely to participate in the cultural life of the community, to enjoy the arts and to share in scientific advancement and its benefits.
2. Everyone has the right to the protection of the moral and material interests resulting from any scientific, literary or artistic production of which he is the author.

Article 28

Everyone is entitled to a social and international order in which the rights and freedoms set forth in this Declaration can be fully realized.

Article 29

1. Everyone has duties to the community in which alone the free and full development of his personality is possible.
2. In the exercise of his rights and freedoms, everyone shall be subject only to such limitations as are determined by law solely for the purpose of securing due recognition and respect for the rights and freedoms of others and of meeting the just requirements of morality, public order and the general welfare in a democratic society.
3. These rights and freedoms may in no case be exercised contrary to the purposes and principles of United Nations.

Article 30

Nothing in the Declaration may be interpreted as implying for any State, group or person any right to engage in any activity or to perform any act aimed at the destruction of any of the rights and freedoms set forth herein.

Appendix B: General Assembly Resolution 33/173 on Disappeared Persons (1978)

The General Assembly,

Recalling the provisions of the Universal Declaration of Human Rights,[1] in particular articles 3, 5, 9, 10 and 11 concerning, *inter alia*, the right to life, liberty and security of person, freedom from torture, freedom from arbitrary arrest and detention, and the right to a fair and public trial, and the provisions of articles 6, 7, 9 and 10 of the International Covenant on Civil and Political Rights,[2] which define and establish safeguards for certain of these rights,

Deeply concerned by reports from various parts of the world relating to enforced or involuntary disappearances of persons as a result of excesses on the part of law enforcement or security authorities or similar organizations, often while such persons are subject to detention or imprisonment, as well as of unlawful actions or widespread violence,

Concerned also at reports of difficulties in obtaining reliable information from competent authorities as to the circumstances of such persons, including reports of the persistent refusal of such authorities or organizations to acknowledge that they hold such persons in their custody or otherwise to account for them,

Mindful of the danger to the life, liberty and physical security of such persons arising from the persistent failure of these authorities or organizations to acknowledge that such persons are held in custody or otherwise to account for them,

Deeply moved by the anguish and sorrow which such circumstances cause to the relatives of disappeared persons, especially to spouses, children and parents.

1. *Calls upon* Governments:

(a) In the event of reports of enforced or involuntary disappearances, to devote appropriate resources to searching for such persons and to undertake speedy and impartial investigations;

(b) To ensure that law enforcement and security authorities or organizations are fully

1. Resolution 217 A (III).
2. Resolution 2200 A (XXI), annex.

accountable, especially in law, in the discharge of their duties, such accountability to include legal responsibility for unjustifiable excesses which might lead to enforced or involuntary disappearances and to other violations of human rights;

(c) To ensure that the human rights of all persons, including those subjected to any form of detention and imprisonment, are fully respected;

(d) To co-operate with other Governments, relevant United Nations organs, specialized agencies, intergovernmental organizations and humanitarian bodies in a common effort to search for, locate or account for such persons in the event of reports of enforced or involuntary disappearances;

2. *Requests* the Commission on Human Rights to consider the question of disappeared persons with a view to making appropriate recommendations;

3. *Urges* the Secretary-General to continue to use his good offices in cases of enforced or involuntary disappearances of persons, drawing, as appropriate, upon the relevant experience of the International Committee of the Red Cross and of other humanitarian organizations;

4. *Requests* the Secretary-General to draw the concerns expressed in the present resolution to the attention of all Governments, regional and interregional organizations and specialized agencies for the purpose of conveying on an urgent basis the need for disinterested humanitarian action to respond to the situation of persons who have disappeared.

Appendix C: Commission on Human Rights Resolution 20 (XXXVI) on Disappeared Persons (1980)

The Commission on Human Rights.

Bearing in mind General Assembly resolution 33/173 of 20 December 1978, which requested the Commission on Human Rights to consider the question of missing or disappeared persons with a view to making appropriate recommendations,

Taking into account resolution 1979/38 of 10 May 1979 of the Economic and Social Council, which requested the Commission to consider the question as a matter of priority, and resolution 5 B (XXXII) of the Sub-Commission on Prevention of Discrimination and Protection of Minorities,

Convinced of the need to take appropriate action, in consultation with the Governments concerned, to promote the implementation of the provisions of General Assembly resolution 33/173 and other United Nations resolutions relevant to the plight of missing and disappeared persons,

1. *Decides* to establish for a period of one year a working group consisting of five of its members, to serve as experts in their individual capacities, to examine questions relevant to enforced or involuntary disappearances of persons;

2. *Requests* the Chairman of the Commission to appoint the members of the group;

3. *Decides* that the working group, in carrying out its mandate, shall seek and receive information from Governments, intergovernmental organizations, humanitarian organizations and other reliable sources;

4. *Requests* the Secretary-General to appeal to all Governments to co-operate with and assist the working group in the performance of its tasks and to furnish all information required;

5. *Further requests* the Secretary-General to provide the working group with all necessary assistance, in particular staff and resources they require in order to perform their functions in an effective and expeditious manner;

6. *Invites* the working group, in establishing its working methods, to bear in mind the

Adopted at the 1563rd meeting on February 29, 1980, without a vote.

need to be able to respond effectively to information that comes before it and to carry out its work with discretion;

7. *Requests* the working group to submit to the Commission at its thirty-seventh session a report on its activities, together with its conclusions and recommendations;

8. *Further requests* the Sub-Commission on Prevention of Discrimination and Protection of Minorities to continue studying the most effective means for eliminating enforced or involuntary disappearances of persons, with a view to making general recommendations to the Commission at its thirty-seventh session;

9. *Decides* to consider this question again at its thirty-seventh session under a subitem entitled "Question of Missing and Disappeared Persons."

Appendix D: Human Rights Commission Resolution 1986/20 on the Elimination of Religious Discrimination and Intolerance

The Commission on Human Rights,

Recalling the Declaration on the Elimination of All Forms of Intolerance and of Discrimination Based or Belief on Religion or which was proclaimed without a vote by the General Assembly in its resolution 36/55 of 25 November 1981,

Bearing in mind that the General Assembly has, most recently in resolution 40/109 of 13 December 1985, repeatedly requested the Commission on Human Rights to continue its consideration of measures to implement the Declaration,

Seriously concerned by frequent, reliable reports from all parts of the world which reveal that, because of governmental actions, universal implementation of the Declaration has not yet been achieved,

Determined to promote full implementation of the existing guarantees under the relevant international instruments of the right to freedom of thought, conscience and religion, including the freedom of everyone to have a religion or whatever belief of his choice without fear of intolerance or discrimination,

Recognizing the value of constructive dialogue on the complex and serious questions of intolerance and of discrimination based on religion or belief, and that the problem of such intolerance and discrimination requires sensitivity in its resolution,

Recognizing the valuable nature of the study undertaken by Mrs. Odio Benito, the Special Rapporteur of the Sub-Commission on Prevention of Discrimination and Protection of Minorities, on the root causes and current dimensions of the general problems of intolerance and of discrimination on the grounds of religion or belief, including recommended educational and other specific measures to combat these problems,

Convinced also of the need to deal urgently with questions of intolerance and of discrimination based on religion or belief by promoting implementation of the Declaration,

1. *Expresses its deep concern* about reports of incidents and governmental actions in

Adopted at the 50th meeting on March 10, 1986, by a roll-call vote of 26 to 5, with 12 abstentions.

all parts of the world which are inconsistent with the provisions of the Declaration on the Elimination of All Forms of Intolerance and of Discrimination Based on Religion or Belief;

2. *Decides* therefore to appoint for one year a special rapporteur to examine such incidents and actions and to recommend remedial measures, including, as appropriate, the promotion of a dialogue between communities of religion or belief and their Governments;

3. *Requests* the Chairman of the Commission, after consultations within the Bureau, to appoint an individual of recognized international standing as special rapporteur;

4. *Decides further* that the Special Rapporteur in carrying out his mandate shall seek credible and reliable information from Governments, as well as specialized agencies, intergovernmental organizations and non-governmental organizations, including communities of religion or belief;

5. *Requests* the Secretary-General to appeal to all Governments to co-operate with and assist the Special Rapporteur in the performance of his duties and to furnish all information requested;

6. *Further requests* the Secretary-General to provide all necessary assistance to the Special Rapporteur;

7. *Invites* the Special Rapporteur, in carrying out his mandate, to bear in mind the need to be able to respond effectively to credible and reliable information that comes before him and to carry out his work with discretion and independence;

8. *Requests* the Special Rapporteur to submit a report to the Commission at its forty-third session on his activities regarding questions involving implementation of the Declaration, including the occurrence and extent of incidents and actions inconsistent with the provisions of the Declaration, together with his conclusions and recommendations;

9. *Decides* to consider the question again at its forty-third session under the agenda item "Implementation of the Declaration on the Elimination of All Forms of Intolerance and of Discrimination Based on Religion or Belief."

Appendix E: Human Rights Commission Resolution 1984/63[1] on Human Rights in Chile

The Commission on Human Rights,

Aware of its responsibility to promote and encourage respect for human rights and fundamental freedoms for all and resolved to remain vigilant with regard to violations of human rights wherever they occur,

Emphasizing the obligation of all Governments to respect and protect human rights and to fulfil the responsibilities they have assumed under various international instruments,

Recalling its resolution 11 (XXXV) of 6 March 1979, in which it decided to appoint a Special Rapporteur on the situation of human rights in Chile, and its resolution 1983/38 of 8 March 1983, in which it decided to extend the mandate of the Special Rapporteur for one more year, as well as General Assembly resolutions 33/173 of 20 December 1978 on disappeared persons and 38/102 of 16 December 1983, in which the Assembly decided, *inter alia*, to invite the Commission on Human Rights to extend the mandate of the Special Rapporteur,

Once again expressing its grave concern at the general persistence of the serious situation of human rights in Chile, which, as established by the Special Rapporteur, has not only not improved, but has worsened, while the repeated appeals of the General Assembly and the Commission on Human Rights for the re-establishment of human rights and fundamental freedoms have been ignored by the Chilean authorities, which continue to refuse to co-operate with the Commission on Human Rights and its Special Rapporteur,

Taking note of the developments which, according to the Special Rapporteur, frustrated the *"apertura política"* announced by the Chilean authorities in August 1983, and thus disappointed certain hopes raised by this announcement,

1. *Commends* the Special Rapporteur for his report[2] on the situation of human rights in Chile, prepared in accordance with its resolution 1983/38,

---

1. Adopted at the 62d meeting on March 15, 1984, by a roll-call vote of 31 to 5, with 6 abstentions.

2. A/38/385 and Add. 1 and E/CN.4/1984/7.

2. *Expresses its profound distress* at the persistence of and increase in serious and systematic violations of human rights in Chile, as described in the reports of the Special Rapporteur, and, in particular, at the violent suppression of popular protests in the face of the refusal to restore the democratic order and human rights and fundamental freedoms on the part of the authorities, which have in fact committed further serious and flagrant violations of human rights, with mass arrests and numerous deaths;

3. *Alarmed* by the fact that the repressive activities of the police and security agencies and, in particular, the National Information Agency (Centro Nacional de Investigaciones) have gone unpunished, as pointed out in the reports of the Special Rapporteur;

4. *Reiterates once again its dismay* at the disruption in Chile of the traditional democratic legal order and its institutions, particularly through the maintenance of emergency legislation, the institutionalization of states of emergency, the extension of military jurisdiction and the existence of a constitution which does not reflect the will of the people freely expressed and whose provisions not only fail to guarantee human rights and fundamental freedoms, but suppress, suspend or limit their enjoyment and exercise;

5. *Once again views with concern* the ineffectiveness of the remedies of habeas corpus or *amparo* and of protection, owing to the fact that the judiciary does not exercise its powers of investigation, monitoring and supervision in this respect and performs its functions under severe restrictions;

6. *Once again calls on* the Chilean authorities to restore and respect human rights in accordance with the obligations they have assumed under various international instruments and, in particular, to put an end to the regime of exception and the practice of declaring states of emergency, under which serious and continuing violations of human rights are committed, and to re-establish the principle of legality, democratic institutions and the effective enjoyment and exercise of civil and political rights and fundamental freedoms;

7. *Once more urges* the Chilean authorities to investigate and clarify the fate of persons who were arrested for political reasons and who later disappeared, to inform their families of the results of such investigation and to bring to trial and punish those responsible for their disappearance;

8. *Once again draws the attention* of the Chilean authorities to the need to put an end to intimidation and persecution, as well as to arbitrary or illegal arrests and imprisonment in secret places, and to respect the right of persons to life and physical integrity by halting the practice of torture and other forms of cruel, inhuman or degrading treatment which have, in some cases, resulted in unexplained deaths;

9. *Once again urges* the Chilean authorities to respect the right of Chilean nationals to live in and freely enter and leave their country, without restrictions or conditions of any kind, and to cease the practices of ''relegation'' (assignment to forced residence) and forced exile;

10. *Renews its appeal* to the Chilean authorities to restore the full enjoyment and exercise of trade union rights, in particular the right to organize trade unions, the right to collective bargaining and the right to strike;

11. *Once more urges* the Chilean authorities to respect and, where necessary, restore economic, social and cultural rights and, in particular, the rights intended to preserve the cultural identity and improve the social status of indigenous populations;

12. *Once again exhorts* the Chilean authorities to co-operate with the Special Rapporteur and to submit their comments on his report to the Commission on Human Rights at its forty-first session;

13. *Decides* to extend the mandate of the Special Rapporteur for a year and to request him to report on the situation of human rights in Chile to the General Assembly at its thirty-ninth session and to the Commission on Human Rights at its forty-first session;

14. *Recommends* to the Economic and Social Council that it make appropriate arrangements to ensure that the necessary financial resources and sufficient staff are provided to implement this resolution;

15. *Decides* to consider at its forty-first session, as a matter of high priority, the question of human rights in Chile.

Appendix F: Human Rights Commission Resolution 1984/54[1] on Human Rights in Iran

The Commission on Human Rights,

Guided by the principles embodied in the Charter of the United Nations, the Universal Declaration of Human Rights and the International Covenants on Human Rights,

Reaffirming that all Member States have an obligation to promote and protect human rights and fundamental freedoms and to fulfil the obligations they have undertaken under the various international instruments in this field,

Recalling its resolutions 1982/27 of 11 March 1982 and 1983/34 of 8 March 1983, in which, *inter alia*, the Commission expressed concern about the human rights situation in the Islamic Republic of Iran,

Taking into account the information on the human rights situation in the Islamic Republic of Iran contained in the report of the Secretary-General,[2]

Regretting the refusal of the Government of the Islamic Republic of Iran to receive the mission arranged by the Secretary-General in agreement with the Government,

Encouraging the Government of the Islamic Republic of Iran to co-operate with the Commission on Human Rights in the future,

Mindful of resolution 1983/14 of 5 September 1983 of the Sub-Commission on Prevention of Discrimination and Protection of Minorities,

1. *Expresses its deep concern* at the continuing serious violations of human rights and fundamental freedoms in the Islamic Republic of Iran as reflected in the report of the Secretary-General, and particularly at the evidence of summary and arbitrary executions, torture, detention without trial, religious intolerance and persecution, in particular of the Baha'is, and the lack of an independent judiciary and other recognized safeguards for a fair trial;

2. *Urges once more* the Government of the Islamic Republic of Iran, as a State party

1. Adopted at the fifty-eighth meeting, on March 14, 1984, by a roll-call vote of 21 to 6, with 15 abstentions.
2. E/CN.4/1984/28.

to the International Covenant on Civil and Political Rights, to respect and ensure to all individuals within its territory and subject to its jurisdiction the rights recognized in that Covenant;

3. *Expresses its appreciation* to the Secretary-General for the efforts deployed by him in the framework of his ongoing direct contacts[3] with the Government of the Islamic Republic of Iran;

4. *Requests* the Chairman to appoint, after consultation within the Bureau, a special representative of the Commission whose mandate will be to establish contacts with the Government of the Islamic Republic of Iran and to make a thorough study of the human rights situation in that country based on such information as he may deem relevant, including comments and materials provided by the Government, containing conclusions and appropriate suggestions, to be presented to the Commission at its forty-first session;

5. *Requests* the Government of the Islamic Republic of Iran to extend its co-operation to the Special Representative of the Commission;

6. *Requests* the Secretary-General to give all necessary assistance to the Special Representative of the Commission;

7. *Decides* to continue its consideration of the situation of human rights and fundamental freedoms in the Islamic Republic of Iran at its forty-first session.

3. See E/CN.4/1984/32.

Appendix G: Human Rights Commission Draft Resolution E.CN.4/1984/L.23 on Establishing the Post of UN High Commissioner for Human Rights

FURTHER PROMOTION AND ENCOURAGEMENT OF HUMAN RIGHTS AND FUNDAMENTAL FREEDOMS, INCLUDING THE QUESTION OF THE PROGRAMME AND METHODS OF WORK OF THE COMMISSION; ALTERNATIVE APPROACHES AND WAYS AND MEANS WITHIN THE UNITED NATIONS SYSTEM FOR IMPROVING THE EFFECTIVE ENJOYMENT OF HUMAN RIGHTS AND FUNDAMENTAL FREEDOMS

Costa Rica: Draft Resolution

The Commission on Human Rights,

Bearing in mind its resolution 1983/49 of 10 March 1983 as well as resolution 1983/36 of 6 September 1983 of the Sub-Commission on Prevention of Discrimination and Protection of Minorities,

Recommends the following draft resolution to the Economic and Social Council for adoption:

The Economic and Social Council,

Conscious that Member States have pledged themselves to achieve, in co-operation with the United Nations, the promotion of universal respect for and observance of human rights and fundamental freedoms for all without distinction as to race, sex, language or religion,

Reaffirming that the Universal Declaration of Human Rights is a common standard of achievement for all peoples and all nations,

Noting that the entry into force of the International Covenant on Economic, Social and Cultural Rights and the International Covenant on Civil and Political Rights constitutes a great achievement by the international community towards the establishment of effective means of promoting respect for and observance of human rights and fundamental freedoms,

Concerned, however, by the existing disparity between established principles and standards and their implementation,

Believing that the international promotion and encouragement of human rights and fundamental freedoms may be enhanced through further improvement of the existing machinery set up by the Organization, in order to meet the need for more continuous and timely action and for facilitating the co-operative fulfilment by Member States of their commitments to human rights under the Charter of the United Nations,

Considering that the approach to the future work within the United Nations system in the field of human rights should take due account of the experiences and the general situation of, as well as the efforts made by, the developing countries to implement human rights and fundamental freedoms,

1. *Suggests* to the General Assembly that it establish a post of United Nations High Commissioner for Human Rights;

2. *Declares* that the work of the High Commissioner should be humanitarian in character, guided solely by an impartial concern for the promotion and protection of human rights and fundamental freedoms;

3. *Considers* that the High Commissioner should possess the degree of personal independence, prestige and integrity required for the discreet and impartial performance of his humanitarian functions;

4. *Suggests* that the High Commissioner should be elected by the General Assembly on the nomination of the Secretary-General for a five-year term, which may not be renewed more than once. The Secretary-General shall endeavour not to nominate two successive High Commissioners from the same regional group, giving due and equal consideration to qualified individuals from all regions of the world;

5. *Suggests also* that the following administrative arrangements concerning the High Commissioner be adopted:

(a) The High Commissioner and the Secretary-General shall make appropriate arrangements for liaison and consultation on matters of mutual interest;

(b) The Secretary-General shall provide the High Commissioner with all necessary facilities within budgetary limitations;

(c) The expenses of the High Commissioner shall be financed under the budget of the United Nations;

(d) The emoluments of the High Commissioner shall be equivalent to those of an Under-Secretary-General of the United Nations;

(e) The staff of the High Commissioner, which shall be limited in size, shall be appointed by the High Commissioner within the limits of the budgetary appropriations. They shall be responsible to the High Commissioner in the exercise of their functions. Their conditions of employment shall be those provided under the Staff Regulations adopted by the General Assembly and the Staff Rules promulgated thereunder by the Secretary-General;

(f) The administration of the office of the High Commissioner shall be subject to the Financial Regulations of the United Nations and to the Financial Rules promulgated thereunder by the Secretary-General;

(g) Transactions relating to the High Commissioner's funds shall be subject to audit by the United Nations Board of Auditors;

6. *Suggests* that the High Commissioner should have the functions and responsibilities set out in the annex to the present resolution;

7. *Calls upon* Governments, specialized agencies, regional intergovernmental organi-

zations, non-governmental organizations and the Secretary-General to co-operate with the High Commissioner in the fulfillment of his responsibilities.

ANNEX

Functions and Responsibilities of the United Nations High Commissioner for Human Rights

The United Nations High Commissioner for Human Rights shall:

(a) Carry out specific mandates and tasks assigned by the General Assembly, the Economic and Social Council, and the Commission on Human Rights;

(b) Consult as appropriate with other elements of the United Nations system, including the Secretary-General and the Centre for Human Rights, and appropriate specialized agencies, which may have or share responsibilities for promoting or safeguarding specific human rights for the purpose of exchanging information and of collaborating with them in developing and implementing appropriate co-ordinated action;

(c) Initiate direct contacts with Governments, whenever such action appears necessary or desirable, to safeguard or assist in restoring respect for human rights, bearing in mind the following principles:

(i) Such contacts shall be prompt, confidential and exclusively humanitarian in purpose;

(ii) In undertaking such action, the High Commissioner shall pay particular attention to urgent situations;

(iii) Direct contacts shall have the specific purpose of ascertaining the facts and, when appropriate in the light of the facts, of assisting the parties concerned with a view to ensuring full respect for the human rights of individuals or groups on whose behalf the contacts were undertaken;

(iv) Such assistance may include, *inter alia*, technical advice on measures which could be taken to promote the effective observance of human rights, offers to conciliate or mediate in situations and provision of information on the availability of appropriate assistance from other elements of the United Nations system, including the Centre for Human Rights and the specialized agencies;

(d) Report annually to the General Assembly, the Economic and Social Council and the Commission on Human Rights on his or her activities. These reports should constitute a separate item on the agenda of these bodies. Such reports might, with the consent of the Government concerned, include a summary of the results of the High Commissioner's direct contacts with the Government. With the consent of the Government concerned, the Commissioner might also announce the results of such direct contacts at other times during the year;

(e) Promote and protect the observance of human rights and fundamental freedoms for all, as defined in the Universal Declaration of Human Rights, without distinction as to race, colour, sex, language, religion, political or other opinion, national or social origin, property, birth or other status;

(f) Give special attention to the importance of ensuring the effective enjoyment by all of their civil and political rights and their economic, social and cultural rights and such other rights as are recognized by the Charter of the United Nations and by the General Assembly, bearing in mind that all human rights and fundamental freedoms are indivisible and interdependent;

(g) Accord priority to such massive violations of human rights as *apartheid*, racism and racial discrimination, colonial domination, foreign occupation and alien subjugation;

(h) Consider as situations of special concern those resulting from aggression and threats against national sovereignty, the denial of the fundamental and inalienable rights of peoples to self-determination and the refusal to recognize the right of every nation to the exercise of full sovereignty over its wealth and resources.

Appendix H: General Assembly Resolution 48/141 Establishing the Post of UN High Commissioner for Human Rights (1993)

The General Assembly,

Reaffirming its commitment to the purposes and principles of the Charter of the United Nations,

Emphasizing the responsibilities of all States, in conformity with the Charter, to promote and encourage respect for all human rights and fundamental freedoms for all, without distinction as to race, sex, language or religion,

Emphasizing the need to observe the Universal Declaration of Human Rights[1] and for the full implementation of the human rights instruments, including the International Covenant on Civil and Political Rights,[2] the International Covenant on Economic, Social and Cultural Rights,[3] as well as the Declaration on the Right to Development,[4]

Reaffirming that the right to development is a universal and inalienable right which is a fundamental part of the rights of the human person,

Considering that the promotion and the protection of all human rights is one of the priorities of the international community,

Recalling that one of the purposes of the United Nations enshrined in the Charter is to achieve international cooperation in promoting and encouraging respect for human rights,

Reaffirming the commitment made under Article 56 of the Charter to take joint and separate action in cooperation with the United Nations for the achievement of the purposes set forth in Article 55 of the Charter,

Emphasizing the need for the promotion and protection of all human rights to be guided by the principles of impartiality, objectivity and non-selectivity, in the spirit of constructive international dialogue and cooperation,

1. Resolution 217 A (III).
2. See resolution 2200 A (XXI), annex.
3. Ibid.
4. Resolution 41/128, annex.

Aware that all human rights are universal, indivisible, interdependent and interrelated and that as such they should be given the same emphasis,

Affirming its commitment to the Vienna Declaration and Programme of Action,[5] adopted by the World Conference on Human Rights, held at Vienna from 14 to 25 June 1993,

Convinced that the World Conference on Human Rights made an important contribution to the cause of human rights and that its recommendations should be implemented through effective action by all States, the competent organs of the United Nations and the specialized agencies, in cooperation with non-governmental organizations,

Acknowledging the importance of strengthening the provision of advisory services and technical assistance by the Centre for Human Rights of the Secretariat and other relevant programmes and bodies of the United Nations system for the purpose of the promotion and protection of all human rights,

Determined to adapt, strengthen and streamline the existing mechanisms to promote and protect all human rights and fundamental freedoms while avoiding unnecessary duplication,

Recognizing that the activities of the United Nations in the field of human rights should be rationalized and enhanced in order to strengthen the United Nations machinery in this field and to further the objectives of universal respect for observance of international human rights standards,

Reaffirming that the General Assembly, the Economic and Social Council and the Commission on Human Rights are the responsible organs for decision-and policy-making for the promotion and protection of all human rights,

Reaffirming the necessity for a continued adaptation of the United Nations human rights machinery to the current and future needs in the promotion and protection of human rights and the need to improve its coordination, efficiency and effectiveness, as reflected in the Vienna Declaration and Programme of Action and within the framework of a balanced and sustainable development for all people,

Having considered the recommendation contained in paragraph 18 of section II of the Vienna Declaration and Programme of Action,

1. *Decides* to create the post of the High Commissioner for Human Rights;

2. *Decides* that the High Commissioner for Human Rights shall:

(a) Be a person of high moral standing and personal integrity and shall possess expertise, including in the field of human rights, and the general knowledge and understanding of diverse cultures necessary for impartial, objective, non-selective and effective performance of the duties of the High Commissioner;

(b) Be appointed by the Secretary-General of the United Nations and approved by the General Assembly, with due regard to geographical rotation, and have a fixed term of four years with a possibility of one renewal for another fixed term of four years;

(c) Be of the rank of Under-Secretary-General;

3. *Decides* that the High Commissioner for Human Rights shall:

(a) Function within the framework of the Charter of the United Nations, the Universal Declaration of Human Rights, other international instruments of human rights and international law, including the obligations, within this framework, to respect the sovereignty, territorial integrity and domestic jurisdiction of States and to promote the universal respect for and observance of all human rights, in the recognition that, in the

5. A/CONF.157/24 (Part I), chap. III.

framework of the purposes and principles of the Charter, the promotion and protection of all human rights is a legitimate concern of the international community;

(b) Be guided by the recognition that all human rights—civil, cultural, economic, political and social—are universal, indivisible, interdependent and interrelated and that, while the significance of national and regional particularities and various historical, cultural and religious backgrounds must be borne in mind, it is the duty of States, regardless of their political, economic and cultural systems, to promote and protect all human rights and fundamental freedoms;

(c) Recognize the importance of promoting a balanced and sustainable development for all people and of ensuring realization of the right to development, as established in the Declaration on the Right to Development;

4. *Decides* that the High Commissioner for Human Rights shall be the United Nations official with principal responsibility for United Nations human rights activities under the direction and authority of the Secretary-General; within the framework of the overall competence, authority and decisions of the General Assembly, the Economic and Social Council and the Commission on Human Rights, the High Commissioner's responsibilities shall be:

(a) To promote and protect the effective enjoyment by all of all civil, cultural, economic, political and social rights;

(b) To carry out the tasks assigned to him/her by the competent bodies of the United Nations system in the field of human rights and to make recommendations to them with a view to improving the promotion and protection of all human rights;

(c) To promote and protect the realization of the right to development and to enhance support from relevant bodies of the United Nations system for this purpose;

(d) To provide, through the Centre for Human Rights of the Secretariat and other appropriate institutions, advisory services and technical and financial assistance, at the request of the State concerned and, where appropriate, the regional human rights organizations, with a view to supporting actions and programmes in the field of human rights;

(e) To coordinate relevant United Nations education and public information programmes in the field of human rights;

(f) To play an active role in removing the current obstacles and in meeting the challenges to the full realization of all human rights and in preventing the continuation of human rights violations throughout the world, as reflected in the Vienna Declaration and Programme of Action;

(g) To engage in a dialogue with all Governments in the implementation of his/her mandate with a view to securing respect for all human rights;

(h) To enhance international cooperation for the promotion and protection of all human rights;

(i) To coordinate the human rights promotion and protection activities throughout the United Nations system;

(j) To rationalize, adapt, strengthen and streamline the United Nations machinery in the field of human rights with a view to improving its efficiency and effectiveness;

(k) To carry out overall supervision of the Centre for Human Rights;

5. *Requests* the High Commissioner for Human Rights to report annually on his/her activities, in accordance with his/her mandate, to the Commission on Human Rights and, through the Economic and Social Council, to the General Assembly;

6. *Decides* that the Office of the High Commissioner for Human Rights shall be located at Geneva and shall have a liaison office in New York;

7. *Requests* the Secretary-General to provide appropriate staff and resources, within the existing and future regular budgets of the United Nations, to enable the High Commissioner to fulfill his/her mandate, without diverting resources from the development programmes and activities of the United Nations;

8. *Also requests* the Secretary-General to report to the General Assembly at its forty-ninth session on the implementation of the present resolution.

85th plenary meeting
20 December 1993

Selected Bibliography

UN DOCUMENTS

The UN Charter
The Universal Declaration of Human Rights
The International Covenant on Civil and Political Rights
The International Covenant on Economic, Social and Cultural Rights
Resolutions of the General Assembly, the Economic and Social Council, the Commission
    on Human Rights, and the Subcommission on Prevention of Discrimination and
    Protection of Minorities
Reports of UN Human Rights Commission implementation agents:
    UN Working Group on Enforced Disappearances
    UN Special Rapporteur on Elimination of Religious Discrimination
    UN Special Rapporteur on Chile
    UN Special Representative on Iran
United Nations. *Human Rights: A Compilation of International Instruments* (ST/HR/1
    Rev. 4, 1992). New York: United Nations, 1992.
———. *Yearbook for 1991*. New York: United Nations, 1992.
———. *Yearbook for 1992*. New York: United Nations, 1993.
———. *Yearbook on Human Rights for 1988*. New York: United Nations, 1992.

DOCUMENTS OF THE WORLD CONFERENCE ON HUMAN RIGHTS (VIENNA, 1993)

Vienna Declaration and Programme of Action (A/CONF.157/23).
Final Report of the NGO-Forum, "All Human Rights for All," held in Vienna, June
    10–12, 1993 (A/CONF.157.7).
Alston, Philip. "The Importance of the Interplay between Economic, Social and Cultural
    Rights and Civil and Political Rights." In *Human Rights at the Dawn of the 21st*

Century (hereafter *HR/COE*), report of an interregional meeting organized by the Council of Europe (A/CONF.157/PC/66/Add.1).

American Society for International Law (A/CONF.157/PC/79).

Amnesty International. "Facing up to the Failures: Proposals for Improving the Protection of Human Rights by the United Nations" (A/CONF.157/PC/Add.1).

Comments by specialized agencies on the World Conference on Human Rights (A/CONF.157/PC/61/Add.18).

Conference on Security and Cooperation in Europe/Office for Democratic Institutions and Human Rights (A/CONF.157/PC/62/Add.10).

Fall, Ibrahima, Assistant Secretary-General for Human Rights. Closing Statement by the Secretary-General of the World Conference on Human Rights, Vienna, June 25, 1993.

Mattarollo, Rodolfo. "The Role and Functioning of International Machinery." *HR/COE*.

Martin, Ian. "The Promotion of Human Rights and Prevention of Human Rights Violations." *HR/COE*.

Pocar, Fausto. "Enhancing the Universal Application of Human Rights Standards and Instruments." Study commissioned by the UN Center for Human Rights (A/CONF.157/PC/60/Add.4).

Tiruchelvam, Neelan. "Development and the Protection of Human Rights." *HR/COE*.

DOCUMENTS OF U.S. DEPARTMENT OF STATE

The Department of State documents cited in this study were written by the author, primarily during the period 1978–86. Classified documents were obtained under the Freedom of Information Act.

BOOKS

Afshar, Haleh. *Iran: A Revolution in Turmoil*. London: Macmillan, 1985.

Alexander, Robert J. *The Tragedy of Chile*. Westport, CT: Greenwood Press, 1978.

Amnesty International. *Iran*. London: Amnesty International, 1987.

Andersen, Martin Edwin. *Dossier Secreto: Argentina's Desaparecidos and the Myth of the "Dirty War."* Boulder, CO: Westview Press, 1993.

Arriagada, Genaro. *Pinochet: The Politics of Power*. Trans. Nancy Morris, with Vincent Ercolano and Kristen A. Whitney. Boston: Unwin Hyman, 1988.

Avery, Peter, Hambly, Gavin, and Melville, Charles, eds. *The Cambridge History of Iran*. Vol. 7. Cambridge: Cambridge University Press, 1991.

Bakshash, Shaul. *The Reign of the Ayatollahs: Iran and the Islamic Revolution*. New York: Basic Books, 1984.

Benard, Cheryl, and Khalizad, Zalmay. *The Government of God: Iran's Islamic Republic*. New York: Columbia University Press, 1984.

Bernstein, Richard. *New Constellation: The Ethical/Postethical Horizons of Modernity/Postmodernity*. Cambridge: MIT Press, 1992.

Bethell, Leslie, ed. *Argentina since Independence*. Cambridge: Cambridge University Press, 1993.

Bouvard, Marguerite Guzman. *Revolutionizing Motherhood: The Mothers of the Plaza de Mayo*. Wilmington, DE: SR Books, 1994.

British Parliamentary Human Rights Group. *The Abuse of Human Rights in Iran*. London: Macmillan, 1986.

Brown, Peter G., and Shue, Henry, eds. *Boundaries: National Autonomy and Its Limits*. Totowa, NJ: Rowman and Littlefield, 1981.

Cassese, Antonio. *Human Rights in a Changing World*. Philadelphia: Temple University Press, 1990.

Cranston, Maurice. *What Are Human Rights?* New York: Basic Books, 1963.

Crawford, James, ed. *The Rights of Peoples*. New York: Oxford University Press, 1988.

Deutsch, Sandra McGee, and Dolkart, Ronald H., eds. *The Argentine Right: Its History and Intellectual Origins, 1910 to the Present*. Wilmington, DE: SR Books, 1993.

Donnelly, Jack. *Universal Human Rights in Theory and Practice*. Ithaca, NY: Cornell University Press, 1989.

————. *International Human Rights*. Boulder, CO: Westview Press, 1993.

Ehteshami, Anoushiravan, and Varasteh, Mansour, eds. *Iran and the International Community*. London: Routledge, 1991.

Eide, Asbjorn, and Hagtvet, Bernt, eds. *Human Rights in Perspective: A Global Assessment*. Oxford: Blackwell, 1992.

Esposito, John L., ed. *The Iranian Revolution: Its Global Impact*. Miami: Florida International University Press, 1990.

Falk, Richard A. *The Promise of World Order: Essays in Normative International Relations*. Philadelphia: Temple University Press, 1987.

Falk, Richard A., Kim, Samuel S., and Mendlovitz, Saul H., eds. *The United Nations and a Just World Order*. Boulder, CO: Westview Press, 1991.

Falk, Richard A., and Mendlovitz, Saul, eds. *The Strategy of World Order*. Vol. 2. New York: World Law Fund, 1966.

Farer, Tom J., ed. *Toward a Humanitarian Diplomacy: A Primer for Policy*. New York: New York University Press, 1980.

Faundez, Julio. *Marxism and Democracy in Chile: From 1932 to the Fall of Allende*. New Haven, CT: Yale University Press, 1988.

Forsythe, David P. *Human Rights and World Politics*. 2d ed. Lincoln: University of Nebraska Press, 1989.

————. *The Internationalization of Human Rights*. Lexington, MA: Lexington Books, 1991.

————. *Human Rights and Peace: International and National Dimensions*. Lincoln: University of Nebraska Press, 1993.

————, ed. *Human Rights and Development*. New York: St. Martin's Press, 1989.

Glendon, Mary Ann. *Rights Talk*. New York: Free Press, 1991.

Government of Argentina. *Observaciones y Comentarios Criticos del Gobierno Argentino al Informe de la CIDH sobre la Situacion de los Derechos Humanos en Argentina*. Buenos Aires: Circulo Militar, 1980.

Guest, Iain. *Behind the Disappearances: Argentina's Dirty War against Human Rights and the United Nations*. Philadelphia: University of Pennsylvania Press, 1990.

Haas, Ernst B. *Human Rights and International Action: The Case of Freedom of Association*. Stanford, CA: Stanford University Press, 1970.

Heller, Agnes. *Can Modernity Survive?* Berkeley: University of California Press, 1990.

Henkin, Louis. *The Age of Rights*. New York: Columbia University Press, 1990.

————, ed. *The International Bill of Rights*. New York: Columbia University Press, 1981.

Hodges, Donald C. *Argentina, 1943–47: The National Revolution and Resistance*. Rev. and enlarged ed. Albuquerque: University of New Mexico Press, 1988.

Human Rights Research and Education Center, University of Ottawa. *Canadian Human Rights Yearbook 1989–90*. Ottawa: University of Ottawa Press, 1990.

Kaufman, Edy. *Crisis in Allende's Chile: New Perspectives*. New York: Praeger, 1988.

Krasner, Stephen, ed. *International Regimes*. Ithaca, NY: Cornell University Press, 1983.

Maritain, Jacques. *Man and the State*. Chicago: University Chicago Press, 1951.

Meron, Theodor. *Human Rights and Humanitarian Norms as Customary Law*. New York: Oxford University Press, 1989.

Minashri, David. *Iran: A Decade of War and Revolution*. New York: Holmes and Meier, 1990.

Newsom, David D., ed. *The Diplomacy of Human Rights*. Lanham, MD: Institute for the Study of Diplomacy (Georgetown University)/University Press of America, 1986.

Nolan, Cathal J. *Principled Diplomacy: Security and Rights in U.S. Foreign Policy*. Westport, CT: Greenwood Press, 1993.

Nunn, Frederick M. *The Military in Chilean History: Essays on Civil-Military Relations, 1810–1973*. Albuquerque: University of New Mexico Press, 1976.

Peralta-Ramos, Monica, and Waisman, Carlos, eds. *From Military Rule to Liberal Democracy in Argentina*. Boulder, CO: Westview Press, 1987.

Poneman, Daniel. *Argentina: Democracy on Trial*. New York: Paragon House, 1987.

Ramazani, R. K. *The United States and Iran: The Patterns of Influence*. New York: Praeger, 1982.

Ramcharan, B. G. *Humanitarian Good Offices in International Law: The Good Offices of the UN Secretary General in the Field of Human Rights*. Boston: Nijhoff, 1983.

———. *The Concept and Present Status of the International Protection of Human Rights: Forty Years after the Declaration*. Dordrecht, Netherlands: Nijhoff, 1989.

Remmer, Karen L. *Military Rule in Latin America*. Boston: Unwin Hyman, 1989.

Roberts, Adam, and Kingsbury, Benedict. *United Nations, Divided World: The UN's Role in International Relations*. New York: Oxford University Press, 1988.

Robertson, A. H., and Merrills, J. G. *Human Rights in the World*. 3d ed. Manchester: Manchester University Press, 1989.

Rock, David. *Argentina 1516–1982: From Spanish Colonization to the Falklands War*. Berkeley: University of California Press, 1985.

Roxborough, Ian, O'Brien, Philip, and Roddick, Jackie. *Chile: The State and Revolution*. London: Macmillan, 1977.

Rubin, Barry. *Paved with Good Intentions: The American Experience and Iran*. New York: Oxford University Press, 1980.

Schachter, Oscar, and Joyner, Christopher, eds. *United Nations Legal Order*. 2 vols. Cambridge: Cambridge University Press, with the American Society of International Law, 1995.

Scully, Timothy. *Reappraising the Role of the Center: The Case of the Chilean Party System*. Notre Dame, IN: Helen Kellogg Institute for International Studies, 1990.

Shepherd, George W., and Nanda, Ved, eds. *Human Rights and Third World Development*. Westport, CT: Greenwood Press, 1985.

Shue, Henry. *Basic Rights: Subsistence, Affluence, and U.S. Foreign Policy*. Princeton, NJ: Princeton University Press, 1980.

Smith, Gaddis. *Morality, Reason, and Power: American Diplomacy in the Carter Years*. New York: Hill and Wang, 1988.

Talmon, J. L. *The Origins of Totalitarian Democracy*. New York: Praeger, 1960.

Timerman, Jacobo. *Prisoner without a Name, Cell without a Number*. Trans. Toby Talbot. New York: Alfred A. Knopf, 1981.

Tulchin, Joseph S. *Argentina and the United States: A Conflicted Relationship*. Boston: Twayne, 1990.

Tulchin, Joseph S., and Varas, Augusto, eds. *From Dictatorship to Democracy: Rebuilding Political Consensus in Chile*. Boulder, CO: Lynne Rienner, 1991.

United Nations Association of the USA. *A Successor Vision: The United Nations of Tomorrow*. New York: UNA/USA, 1987.

Valenzuela, Julio Samuel, and Valenzuela, Arturo, eds. *Military Rule in Chile: Dictatorship and Opposition*. Baltimore: Johns Hopkins University Press, 1986.

van Boven, Theo. *People Matter*. Amsterdam: Meulenhoff, 1982.

Vincent, R. J. *Human Rights and International Relations*. Cambridge: Royal Institute of International Affairs/Cambridge University Press, 1986.

Weil, Simone. *The Need for Roots: Prelude to a Declaration of Duties toward Mankind*. New York: G. P. Putnam's Sons, 1952.

Whelan, James R. *Out of the Ashes: Life, Death and Transfiguration of Democracy in Chile, 1833–1988*. Washington, DC: Regnery Gateway, 1989.

Wright, Martin, ed. *Iran: The Khomeini Revolution*. Harlow, Essex: Longmans, 1989.

SERIAL

Carey, John, ed. *Unofficial Reports concerning Legal Matters in the United Nations*. New York: Walker and Co. Especially issues from December 1989–.

ARTICLES

Brody, Reed, Parker, Penny, and Weissbrodt, David. "Major Developments in 1990 at the UN Human Rights Commission." *Human Rights Quarterly* 12(14) (1990), 559–90.

Brody, Reed, and Weissbrodt, David. "Major Developments at the 1989 Session of the UN Commission on Human Rights." *Human Rights Quarterly* 11(4) (1989), 586–611.

Burgers, Jan Herman. "The Road to San Francisco: The Revival of the Human Rights Idea in the 20th Century." *Human Rights Quarterly* 14(4) (1992), 447–77.

Crawford, Neta C. "Changing International Norms: An Argument about Arguments." Paper prepared for the Thomas J. Watson, Jr. Institute for International Studies, Brown University, 1994.

Crossette, Barbara. "After 50 Years, the United Nations Must Redefine Itself for a New World." *New York Times*, Sept. 18, 1994.

Forsythe, David P. Review essay on Vernon Van Dyke's "Human Rights, the United States, and the World Community." *Human Rights Quarterly* 14(4) (1992), 502–9.

———. "The UN and Human Rights at Fifty: An Incremental but Incomplete Revolution." *Global Governance* 1 (1995), 297–318.

Garrett, Stephen A. "Ethics, Duty, and the Tricky Business of Intervening in International Affairs." *Chronicle of Higher Education*, June 8, 1994, B1–3.

"Hot Air: Human Rights." *The Economist*, June 26, 1993.

Lyons, Richard D. "A Renewed Sense of Mission Is Rousing the UN." *New York Times*, Sept. 18, 1994.

Mason, Paul E., and Marsteller, Thomas F. "U.N. Mediation: More Effective Options." *SAIS Review* 5(2) (1985), 271–84.

Metzger, Jennifer, and Piasecki, Edmund. *The Forgotten U.N.: An Inside Look at the 45th General Assembly.* United Nations Association of the USA, 1991.

Nickel, James W. "How Human Rights Generate Duties to Protect and Provide." *Human Rights Quarterly* 14(1) (1993), 77–86.

"1992 Session of the Commission on Human Rights." *UN Chronicle*, June 1992.

"1993 Session of the Commission on Human Rights." *UN Chronicle*, June 1993.

Parker, Penny, and Weissbrodt, David. "Major Developments at the UN Commission on Human Rights in 1991." *Human Rights Quarterly* 13(4) (1992), 573–613.

Pion-Berlin, David, and Lopez, George. "Of Victims and Executioners: Argentine State Terror, 1975–79." *International Studies Quarterly* (35) (Mar. 1991).

Pitts, J. W., and Weissbrodt, David. "Major Developments at the UN Commission on Human Rights in 1992." *Human Rights Quarterly* 15(1) (1993), 122–96.

Ramcharan, B. G. "Strategies for the International Protection of Human Rights in the 1990s." *Human Rights Quarterly* 13(2) (1991), 155–69.

Rorty, Richard. "Universality and Truth." Draft paper, June 14, 1993.

Ruggie, John Gerard. "Human Rights and the Future International Community." *Daedalus* 112(4) (1983), 93–110.

———. "Multilateralism: The Anatomy of an Institution." *International Organization* 46(3) (1992), 561–98.

Sikkink, Kathryn. "Human Rights, Principled Issue–Networks, and Sovereignty in Latin America." *International Organization* 47(3) (1993), 411–41.

———. "Ideas and Foreign Policy: The State of the Study." Memo for the APSA Roundtable on Ideas and Foreign Policy, APSA Convention, 1993.

Symposium on Implementation of the International Covenant on Economic, Social and Cultural Rights. *Human Rights Quarterly* 9(2) (1987), 121–285.

UN Department of Public Information. "Voluntary Contributions Finance United Nations Trust Funds in Support of Human Rights." *Objective: Justice* 19(2) (1987), 3–13.

van Boven, Theo. "Advances and Obstacles in Building Understanding and Respect between People of Diverse Religions and Beliefs." *Human Rights Quarterly* 13(4) (1991), 437–52.

Index